The Desert King

The Desert King

The Life of Ibn Saud

David Howarth

Q

QUARTET BOOKS

LONDON   MELBOURNE   NEW YORK

Published by Quartet Books Limited 1980
A member of the Namara Group
27 Goodge Street, London W1P 1FD

First published in Great Britain by William Collins & Son
Ltd, 1965

Copyright © 1965, 1980 by David Howarth

ISBN 0 7043 3308 2

Printed and bound in Great Britain by
Hazell Watson & Viney Ltd,
Aylesbury, Bucks

CONTENTS

PROLOGUE

I wrote this book in 1964, but after reading it again I cannot
find much to change for this new edition. It seems to me an even
more remarkable story now than it did then. Then, Saudi
Arabia was a country in transition, and its future was impossible
to foresee. Now, it is firmly established, and so rich and powerful that it can change the policies of the whole western world.
Yet it was created out of nothing, within the twentieth century,
by a single man: Abdul-Aziz ibn Saud.

Ibn Saud grew up as a penniless prince when the desert of
Arabia was lawless and torn by tribal feuds. In twenty-two years
he united it, by his own skill as a hand-to-hand fighter with
sword and musket on camel and horseback, and by the force
and charm of his own personality. For another twenty years he
ruled it in poverty, saved from bankruptcy only by occasional
gifts of a few thousand pounds from the British government.

The kingdom he founded was strictly puritan. Its people lived
as they had at the time of Abraham. Their material possessions
were nothing but a desert, one third of the size of the United
States; as education, the learned men among them knew the
Koran by heart, and the history of Islam, but very little more;
spiritually, they had dignity, piety of their own kind, and an
extreme but capricious sense of honour.

In 1938, oil was discovered underneath their sands, and suddenly a deluge of wealth in thousands of millions of dollars and
golden sovereigns was poured upon ibn Saud. In the last ten
years of his reign, through no effort or intention of his own, he
was probably the richest man in the world, with perhaps the
exception of his neighbour the Sheik of Kuwait, who ruled a
country only seventy miles square; and he died an unhappy
man, because he had never wanted so much money, and did not
understand it or have any idea what to do with it, and was
afraid it would corrupt his family and destroy the religious
principles on which he had founded his kingdom.

For a while it did. Many of his numerous sons and grandsons
became a laughing-stock throughout the world for ludicrous extravagance, easy victims of every rogue they met. In that period,
untold millions were squandered on useless projects and sense-
less escapades. But it passed. It will always be a defiance of logic
that so much of the wealth of the world should belong to people
who merely happened to live as nomads on the barren sand and
rock that hid the oil. But the old austerity of the desert lies deep
in the Saudi character, and now it begins to seem that they have
survived the onslaught of unimaginable riches with as much
success as anyone else might have shown.

Ibn Saud did nothing to find the oil, but he did a great deal to preserve his people's character. Some people have compared him with King Solomon for his power and ruthlessness, his rough justice and simple wisdom, his methods of war, and the extraordinary number of his wives. Perhaps that comparison is too fanciful, and probably he would not have liked it, but certainly his personality and deeds had an early Biblical air. Yet his conquests only began in 1901.

PART ONE

THE PRINCE

CHAPTER ONE

CAPTURE OF A CAPITAL

In the autumn of 1901, a column of forty men, mounted on camels, left the town of Kuwait on the shore of the Persian Gulf and rode westwards into the desert of Arabia. By day, a green standard was carried at their head, and by night a lantern on a staff; and they were led by a man of twenty-one, conspicuously tall, and already a veteran of desert raids and wars: Abdul-Aziz ibn Abdul-Rhaman al Faisal al Saud, the son of a royal house in exile.

In retrospect, their journey seems forlorn. The desert had always been perilous, and at that time, for them, it was much more perilous than ever. Vast tracts of it had been the domain of the House of Saud, but the young man's father had lost his throne through murder and trickery and battle; and for the past eleven years the desert had fallen under the sovereignty of a rival dynasty, the House of Rashid, the implacable enemies of the Saudis. Recently, the ex-ruler himself, together with the ruler of Kuwait, had organised an expedition into the desert of ten thousand men; and it had ended in ignominious defeat, and had only proved that the nomads of the desert had lost their old allegiance to the Saudis and were willing to fight to the death for the Rashidis. So there was no place in the seven hundred miles of desert before those forty men where they could hope to find comfort or safety, and any man they met could be reckoned as an enemy.

Yet they started, in the recollection of those who completed the journey, with eager anticipation. They themselves were Arabs of the desert or the desert towns, Bedouin by heritage; their ideals of sport were either hunting the animals of the desert, with hawks or saluki dogs, or raiding other clans, with rifles and swords on camel-back. But since the fall of the House of Saud, they had been confined in the sordid coastal towns of Kuwait and Bahrain. Town life had irked them; the quick-triggered freedom of desert life enchanted them.

The men of the column expected no more than a winter's raiding, certainly exciting and probably profitable within the limits of the chivalry of the desert; but their leader had wider plans, dreams so ambitious, and so youthfully romantic, and so unlikely to be fulfilled, that he did not tell anyone what was in his mind. He intended, with the help of his forty

11

men, to recapture his father's kingdom. Nobody but himself would have thought he had the slightest chance of succeeding; but he did succeed. The band of raiders grew to the largest peaceful kingdom which had ever been established in Arabia in the last thousand years.

The meagre expedition, in the mind of its leader, had an even higher aim than worldly power; it was also a crusade. The heads of the House of Saud had not only been rulers of an area of desert; they had also been the leaders, the Imams, of a strictly puritan sect of the Moslem world: the Wahhabis. This sect was founded by a holy man of the eighteenth century whose name was Mahomed ibn Abdul-Wahhab. He disapproved of the superstitions and luxurious living which had overgrown the Moslem creed since it was first proclaimed by Mahomed in the seventh century of the Christian era. He preached a return to the simplicity of the early religion, which had been founded entirely on the Koran (which Moslems believe to be the word of God revealed to Mahomed) and on the sayings and manner of life of the Prophet himself. For many years, ibn Abdul-Wahhab's reforms attracted nobody, and he led the life of a wandering scholar, but at length, about 1750, he won the support of the Saudi ruler of his time. With worldly and religious power combined, the Saudi domain, which had been no more than a petty sheikdom, expanded until its raiding parties covered the whole of Arabia, and its doctrines were imposed on everyone it conquered. By Moslem precept, soldiers who fell in holy battle were promised immediate entry into Paradise; and it has been said, perhaps by the enemies of Wahhabism, that each Wahhabi soldier was given a written order from his leader to the keeper of the gates of heaven to let him in.

In this bleak and stubborn creed young ibn Saud, the leader of the expedition of 1901, had had his training. It was a creed which suited the austerity of desert life, and he hoped to carry it back to the desert where it had been founded. The green standard which his column followed was the symbol of Wahhabism; and Wahhabism had never changed or compromised. The House of Saud did not allow smoking or drinking, or dressing in silken robes, or any of the other luxuries known to the Arabs, and it did not allow anything which suggested the worship of saints or shrines or idols, or of Mahomed. In accordance with the Koran, it did allow its adherents to have four wives – though few could afford so many – with the provision that they must treat them all with equal consideration; and it allowed instantaneous divorce. Ibn Saud was brought up to believe that the answers to all life's problems could be found in the Koran and nowhere else; and he had also been taught that it was

12

a holy deed to wage war on all infidels and heretics. The principal enemies of his experience were heretics, Moslems who were not Wahhabis. He had probably never met a Christian or a Jew. Arabia was still surrounded by other Moslem lands, and cut off from Christendom and Jewry; very few explorers from Western Europe had ever adventured beyond its outer coasts, and most of those few had depended for their lives on disguising themselves as Moslems. But foremost among the heretics on whom he hoped to wage a holy war were the minions of ibn Rashid who had seized his father's throne.

The journey began with several of the enjoyable raids his followers had expected. They were travelling light, carrying nothing but their rifles and daggers and swords and ammunition, and dates and flour and water. The men and their camels had been chosen carefully. So they were able to descend on camps of nomads and the caravans of merchants, to seize camels with impunity and carry off whatever could be carried; and by night, between their raids, they were able to range the desert over distances which only the hardest riders could have travelled.

This kind of sport was almost all that the men of the expedition would have asked of life, and ibn Saud himself was not too ambitious to enjoy it. But he can only have thought of it then as an early step in fulfilling his deeper secret hope: the hope of reviving the ancient loyalty of the tribesmen and lighting a flame of revolt which would spread through the desert and the desert towns. It had never been difficult to rouse the desert Arabs to fight, either through the hope of heaven or of plunder, or simply for love of fighting; and ibn Saud may well have expected to rouse them again by a series of raids so audacious and successful that news of them would travel, spreading both fear and admiration, and offering the people of the desert the choice of joining him or suffering at his hands.

But if this was his hope, it failed. From Kuwait, he first rode west and south, into the area which had been his father's, and the first of his raids were against the very tribe which had rallied to ibn Rashid and helped to defeat his father's expedition. In these Bedouin raids, it was not the custom for very much blood to be drawn. Usually, the attack was so sudden that the camp or the caravan had no time to do anything but surrender; but if it put up a defence which promised to be hard to overcome, the raiders drew off and searched for other victims. Ibn Saud and his men were able to keep themselves well provided by capturing all the necessities of life, and it was said in later years that they captured a chest of gold; but very few of the Bedouin joined his

13

column, and ibn Rashid sent major forces to try to hunt him down.

He therefore turned eastwards again, into the coastal area called the Hasa, which was then under Turkish rule; but the Turks turned out their regular troops against him. Between the Turks in the east and hostile Bedouin of ibn Rashid in the west, he was forced to ride farther south, until he came to the edge of the fearful desert within the desert which is known as Rub al Khali, which means the Empty Quarter: an enormous tract of utterly barren sandhills where few Bedouin can travel, and camels can find no pasture; where there were no more caravans and no more camps to raid.

At one time in his forced march to the south, the followers of ibn Saud had increased to four hundred men, including the slaves whom the richer Bedouin had brought with them. But as he approached the Empty Quarter, with its promise of hard living and an end to booty, the force began to melt away again until he was left with no more than when he started. Somewhere on the verges of that melancholy land, he had to admit his failure and contemplate other plans; and his thoughts began to turn to the desert town of Riyadh.

Riyadh had been his father's capital, and there ibn Saud had been born and had lived till he was ten, and taken part as a child in ghastly scenes of carnage. It was one of the least accessible capitals of the world; nearly a thousand miles from the civilised cities of the Mediterranean shore, 250 miles from the nearest barren sea-coast, protected against intrusion from the outer world by the desert which no vehicle could cross, and protected also by Wahhabi fanaticism and the predatory habits of the Bedouin. In 1901, it was a town of more than five thousand but less than ten thousand people, of mud-brick houses cramped together, a dilapidated rambling palace, a fort and several mosques, surrounded by crumbling mud-brick walls and dependent on its own oasis. In its plan and construction it was like Jericho, and the other walled cities of early Biblical times; and apart from the change in religion, the lives which its people led had hardly changed in the thousands of years since the fall of Jericho.

Only eight, or possibly nine, Europeans had ever seen this forbidding and mysterious place, so far as anyone knows. Explorers had been in that part of the desert in 1793 and 1829; and in 1862, the English Jesuit traveller William Palgrave reached the town, disguised as a Syrian doctor, in the course of a mission, the purpose of which is unknown, for the Emperor Napoleon III. According to his own story, he practised medicine successfully for a few weeks in the town; but he indiscreetly refused to give his supply of strychnine to the Saudi heir-apparent who wanted it to poison his
14

brother; and consequently he had to leave the place hurriedly, to avoid being poisoned himself.

On his escape from Arabia, Palgrave reported that another European explorer, disguised as a dervish, had been to Riyadh seven years before him, but had been escorted politely out of the town and executed when the Saudis discovered he was not a dervish at all. But Palgrave suppressed the name of this pioneer, and now both his name, and Palgrave's reason for hiding it, are forgotten.

Three years after Palgrave's visit, in 1865, a British officer, Colonel Lewis Pelly, paid an official visit to Riyadh on behalf of the Government of India, taking with him a lieutenant and a doctor of the Royal Navy, an interpreter and a Portuguese cook. He intended to negotiate with the Saudi ruler for his help in suppressing piracy and slave-trading in the Persian Gulf, and he was granted an audience; but he found that the ruler was very old and blind, and the enmity of the ruler's sons was so evident that he left the town and returned to the coast after staying there only three days. A few months later, the ruler died and his sons began a long and murderous quarrel for the throne. The kingdom began to disintegrate in civil war, and it was over forty years before another European ventured into it. It was during this period that the coastal province of the Hasa was taken by the Turks. Tribes deserted to rival kingdoms, or to barbaric independence. By the time when ibn Saud was born, in 1880, the kingdom was in chaos and Riyadh itself reduced to anarchy, terrorised by spies and counter-spies of the rival factions and by bloodthirsty fights through the markets and alleys in which the losers were hanged from the battlements.

This state of civil war made the kingdom an easy victim for ibn Rashid, whose own domains adjoined it on the north. In the years between 1880 and 1890, he captured Riyadh and beat the reigning Saudi several times; but even in war, the Arab princes were often guided by the Bedouin concept of chivalry. In Bedouin raids, the raiders might shoot to kill if it was necessary; but even when they succeeded, the surviving victims recognised the game as fair, and did not resent their defeat much more than a losing football team in the western world. Either the victors or the victims might ask the other, soon afterwards, for the hospitality which was never refused in the desert to people who came in peace; and both would enjoy it without much fear that a fair defeat might be avenged by trickery. So ibn Rashid, each time he defeated the Saudis in battle, put one or other of them back in power at Riyadh, sometimes alone and sometimes with a governor from among his own men to keep them in order.

But pride, and the foolishness engendered by years of an-

archy, impelled the Saudis again and again into battles with
ibn Rashid which they always lost; and at length ibn Rashid's
fury at their intemperance drove him to break the bonds of
chivalry. He ordered his governor to get rid of the Saudi
family once and for all. The governor invited all the men
of Saud to hear a message of greeting from his master on a
feast-day; but the Saudis were forewarned, and while they
were sipping coffee and exchanging polite conversation with
the governor, on a signal, they butchered the governor's re-
tainers and tied up the governor himself and threw him down
a well to die. Ibn Saud, at the age of ten, took part in this
holocaust. Such was his childhood training.

But this was the end of the rule of the House of Saud. Ibn
Rashid, in vengeance, laid siege to Riyadh, cut down its groves
of palms and poisoned its wells. The townspeople, driven by
thirst and hunger, threatened to turn against the Saudis; and
finally the father of ibn Saud, with his wives and a few of his
slaves and retrainers, carrying his children in the saddle-bags
of his camels, fled from the town by night, to wander discredited in the desert until he was given sanctuary by the
independent ruler of Kuwait.

When ibn Saud led his weary disheartened band to the
edge of the Empty Quarter, his family had been outlaws in
Riyadh since he left it in such sordid circumstances. In the
intervening eleven years, ibn Rashid had died, but his son,
who is usually known by the same family name, had kept
the people of the Saudi domain under strict control. The
fire which ibn Saud had hoped to light in their hearts had not
kindled; their spirits were damped by fear of their present
ruler. Those whom ibn Saud had met in conversation, rather
than battle, had made it clear that he would never win a
following unless he had already been proved to be a leader.
Mere raids were not enough; and his raids so far, rather
than rouse the Bedouin, had only roused ibn Rashid to re-
prisals against anyone he suspected of harbouring the raiders.
Two courses were left: to go back to his father at Kuwait,
defeated, or else to gamble the kingdom and his life in a
single master-stroke which would ring through the desert.
There was only one possible place for a stroke which could
be dramatic enough, and that was Riyadh.

Ever since the fall of the House of Saud, ibn Rashid had
kept a ruthless governor and a garrison in Riyadh, and now
that ibn Rashid knew that ibn Saud was on the warpath,
it was likely that the garrison would be alert and reinforced;
so ibn Saud decided to wait hidden, alone with his forty men
in the desert, avoiding meetings with other Bedouin, until he
was sure that ibn Rashid would think he was dead.

That decision may have had a religious motive, in addition to being a matter of Bedouin tactics. The month of Ramadan was approaching, when pious Moslems fast between dawn and sunset from the day of one new moon till the day of the next. By custom, travellers are excused the fast, provided they observe it later on; but ibn Saud's Wahhabi principles, at that stage of his career, would not have let him make use of that dispensation. Yet, on the other hand, not even the Bedouin could lead an active life of hard riding in the desert while they were fasting; and besides, an attack on a town during Ramadan was foolish, because many citizens who fasted all day stayed up all night.

The wait was a harder test of his leadership than the raiding. From the traditional moment before each dawn when a black and a white thread of cotton could be distinguished, until the sun was below the horizon again, his men had nothing to eat or drink, and nothing to shelter them, and worst of all they had nothing whatever to do; and even at night, when the strictest of Moslems can make up for the day's distresses, they had no women and no comfort and no more than a mere starvation ration. At the end of Ramadan, by argument and persuasion and threats, and by putting the men on oath to follow him to whatever death he chose, ibn Saud still had the survivors of the faithful forty with him; but perhaps nobody ever searched the sky more eagerly for the first sight of the new moon. As soon as it was seen, he gave the orders to saddle the camels and march.

Riyadh was more than a hundred miles away. Released from the dangerous boredom of the Empty Quarter, they rode out on a raid which became in later years a legend in modern Arabian folk-lore, and a story which ibn Saud was often asked to tell. On the way, they watered their camels at a deep natural well called Ain Hit, which was the scene of another but totally different drama of Arabian history thirty-five years afterwards. While the end of Ramadan was still being celebrated by more peaceful people, they approached the town by night and couched the camels in a distant part of the oasis. Ibn Saud left a few of the men with the camels, and led the rest of them on foot through the groves and gardens, silently in the darkness. When they came within sight of the walls he halted, and chose six men to come with him; and he told the others to wait till midday, and then, if they had heard no news of him, to escape if they could and take the camels and ride to Kuwait, because by then he would either be victorious or dead.

Ibn Rashid had neglected the walls of Riyadh, and ibn Saud and his six companions scrambled over them, using a palm trunk as a scaling-ladder, and entered the sleeping town without alarm. They were surprised to make their way in so

17

easily, and ibn Saud had not thought what to do next; he believed his cause was God's and that God would guide him. But he led his men into the alleys he remembered from his youth. They were hushed and empty. In the centre of the town the Rashids had built a fortress, and opposite the fortress gate, across a square, they had fortified a house where the governor, whose name was Ajlan, kept his women. Both of these strongholds were locked and barred, but next to the women's house there was another, which belonged to a seller of cattle called Juwaisir. Ibn Saud knocked on his door, and after a while a girl's voice answered: "Who are you?" And he remembered that Juwaisir had two daughters.

"I am sent by the Amir Ajlan," he said through the closed door. "He wants to buy two cows. I have to see your father."

The girl said: "You should be ashamed, son of a woman accursed. Does anyone knock on a woman's door at this time of night unless he is whoring? Go away."

"Be quiet," ibn Saud said. "In the morning I shall tell the Amir and he will rip your father open."

This gruesome and plausible threat was heard by Juwaisir, and he hastily opened the door: and ibn Saud seized him and scared him into silence. The daughters recognised the son of their exiled ruler and began to cry out a greeting, but he bundled them into the house and told his men to shut them in a cellar. In the moment of confusion Juwaisir escaped and ran away.

By then, the raiders had made a simple plan: to go up to the flat roof of Juwaisir's house and jump to the roof of Ajlan's and force an entrance there. But the gap was too wide. Instead, they jumped to another house, where they found a man in bed with his wife, and tied them both up in their bedclothes, and gagged the wife, and threatened them both with death if they made a sound. Then they waited, to see if Juwaisir had given the alarm. But the town remained silent. Ibn Saud sent two of his men to bring in the rest who were hiding in the palm groves.

Ajlan's house was a storey higher than the others. They climbed on each other's shoulders, and forced the roof door open and crept through the house seizing the slaves of the household one by one, until they came to the bedroom which seemed to be Ajlan's. Ibn Saud went in with his rifle; another man followed with a candle. There were two mounds in the bed, and he peered at them – but neither was Ajlan, one was his wife and the other was her sister. He unloaded his gun and prodded them, and they jumped up screaming. "Enough," he said. "I am Abdul-Aziz."

Ajlan's wife was a Riyadh woman and knew him. "What do you want?" she asked in terror.

"I want your husband, shameless woman, you who have taken a Rashid."

"I am no shameless woman," she said. "I only took a Rashid when you left us. What brings you here?"

"I have come to look for your man to kill him," he said.

"You may kill ibn Rashid and all his people," she said, "but I could not wish you to kill my husband. And how can you deal with him? He sleeps in the fortress, with eighty men, and if he discovers you, you will never have the power to save your souls and escape from the country."

Ibn Saud asked her when Ajlan would leave the fortress. "He will not come out until after sunrise," she said. The raiders locked her up with her sister and the slaves, and broke a hole in the soft mud wall and brought the rest of the party in from the house next door; and then they settled down to rest, and ate some dates and drank the governor's coffee, and slept and prayed and wondered what they should do. They had come too far to retreat.

During that vigil while they waited for the dawn, their only thought was to lure the governor into the house and kill him there, and with that in their minds they asked the women which of them usually opened the door to him in the morning; and they chose one of the men who was small enough and dressed him in the woman's clothes and left him to let Ajlan in when he knocked.

The others went up to a room above, where there was an opening from which the gate of the fortress could be seen across the square. It was a heavy studded wooden door with a very small postern in it, only two feet high, so designed that a man could only go through it head first, exposing his neck to the sword of the keeper inside.

After the call to prayer from the mosques of the town, when the raiders hidden within the house performed their own devotions, and as the morning light refilled the square, the gate was opened, and servants began to bring out the governor's horses. The sight of the open gate was too much for ibn Saud. He jumped to his feet and ran downstairs, determined to rush it, shouting to some of his musketmen to cover him from the window. But while he was going down, Ajlan himself emerged with a dozen men, and the gate was closed behind him.

The fight was merciless. Ibn Saud flung open the door of the women's house and charged across the square. Ajlan and his followers turned at the sound, and seeing him the followers ran for the fortress gate and bolted through the postern one by one. When ibn Saud reached it, Ajlan was left alone. He had drawn his sword; ibn Saud had nothing but his rifle. Ajlan made at him, sword raised to strike. Ibn Saud

19

covered his face with his arm and fired his rifle point-blank, single handed, and heard the sword clatter on the ground and knew he had wounded Ajlan. Ajlan plunged at the postern, ibn Saud caught his legs, and his own men pulled his arms; and Ajlan gave ibn Saud such a kick in the stomach that he started to faint and let him go. For a half second then the history of Arabia hung on the postern gate. Before the defenders could slam it shut, a cousin of ibn Saud named Abdullah ibn Jiluwi thrust himself into the hole and wriggled through. In the narrow gateway within, the defenders were too confused to decapitate him as he came, and he laid about him with his sword. Others followed and threw the main gate open, and the rest of the horde of ibn Saud swarmed in and started a bloodthirsty fight, outnumbered two to one, through the courtyards and towers of the fortress. They slaughtered half the defenders. Some fell or were thrown from the battlements. Ibn Jiluwi cut Ajlan down and killed him. Thirty or forty surrendered and were locked in their own dungeons; and before the morning ended, ibn Saud sent his men through the town to proclaim that God's will had been done, and the House of Saud was master again in Riyadh.

CHAPTER TWO

BEDOUIN AT WAR

That hour of bloody entertainment won far more than a town for ibn Saud: it instantly won the nucleus of a kingdom. The news of it spread as fast as men on camelback could travel, and it was discussed with relish and admiration and amusement. Such a feat of arms and impudence appealed exactly to the macabre humour of the Bedouin. Ibn Rashid had suffered an ignominious reverse, and people who live under tyranny are always happy to see their tyrants made ridiculous; so the Bedouin gladly acknowledged that the House of Saud, after twenty-five years of ineffectiveness, had fathered a leader again. The sheiks of the desert began to come in to Riyadh, to welcome ibn Saud and swear their new allegiance. Perhaps in their pleasure at his deed they preferred to forget that the Saudis had once been as tyrannous as any Arab ruler, and were likely to be as tyrannous again.

Surveying his new dominion from Riyadh, ibn Saud could not have said where it ended. Fixed frontiers had never counted for anything in Arabia. The desert land itself was hardly of any value; outside the towns, a kingdom only existed in the loyalty of the nomads who wandered across the desert, and it extended as far as its subjects drove their herds. All that could have been said of the nascent kingdom of Saudi Arabia was that it was land-locked and surrounded by enemies. Ibn Rashid, to the north of it, was merely the most belligerent of many.

In the west, the Sherif of Mecca ruled the wide strip of the Red Sea coast called the Hejaz. A hundred years before, the Wahhabis in their puritan devotion had invaded the Hejaz, and captured the holy cities of Mecca and Medina, and demolished the shrines which they thought were idolatrous; but they had been driven out again by Egyptian troops under Turkish orders, and now the country was firmly held against them. The people who lived near the coast were more sophisticated than the wild men of the bare interior – or at least, they thought they were. Once a year, tens of thousands of pilgrims from every Moslem country thronged up the road from the sea to the city of Mecca, bringing with them not only the fees which enabled the people of Mecca to live in comfort, but also some cosmopolitan interests and knowledge of the world: that is, of the Moslem world. So, both for financial and religious reasons, the ruler and people of the Hejaz were jealous of their custody of the holy places, and they still regarded Wahhabis with fear and distaste.

In the east, the previous kingdom of the Saudis had had a wide outlet to the shore of the Persian Gulf, extending all the way from Kuwait to the mainland opposite Bahrain; but that part of the country, the Hasa, was held by the Turks, as ibn Saud already had reason to know. They valued it and were most unlikely to let it go, because they could levy duty on goods which came through it from India and the East; silks, and rice and coffee and sugar, and rifles and ammunition. North of the Hasa, the Saudis had their only friends in the tiny independent sheikdom of Kuwait, which was no more than a seaport town with a few square miles of barren desert round it; and south of the Hasa, on the part of the Gulf which was known to Europeans as the Pirate Coast, there were other minor skeikdoms, warlike out of proportion to their size, and resentful of interference.

In the south, the influence of the House of Saud, and of the whole of humanity, was lost in the Empty Quarter. Beyond it were other lands, the Hadramaut, and Muscat, and the Yemen, and the British port of Aden; but these were another world which was scarcely known by the people of Central Arabia, for only the bravest traveller or the most primitive Bedouin succeeded in crossing the Empty Quarter alive. It was a natural boundary, as final as the sea.

Behind this ring of enemies, two alien powers influenced Arabia: the Turkish Empire and the British Empire. The Turks were long past the peak of their power in Europe, which had taken them to the gates of Vienna in the seventeenth century; but their dominion still extended through Mesopotamia to the Persian Gulf and through Palestine to a frontier with Egypt. The Hasa was not their only property in Arabia: the Sherif of Mecca was under their control, the Yemen was theirs, and ibn Rashid was an ally in their pay, so that ibn Saud was almost surrounded by them. And apart from their political and military power, they exercised religious power through most of the Moslem world, because the Sultan of Turkey, in the eyes of most Moslems, was also the Caliph, the true successor of the Prophet. Ibn Saud could have no doubt of what the Turks would think of his new régime when they heard about it. As a fighter, he had affronted their ally ibn Rashid; as a ruler, he was claiming independence; and as a Wahhabi, he denied the authority of the Caliph.

The influence of the British Empire was more subtle, and less openly hostile. Arabia had always been too poor a country to interest the British as a colony; the principal selfish interest they had in it was the protection of their route to the

22

riches of India and the East. But the building of empire, and the keeping of the Pax Britannica, and the protection of underdogs against their natural enemies, were habits of mind in the British of the nineteenth century, and their activities in Arabia extended beyond mere blatant self-interest. Ever since the eighteenth century, the Royal Navy had ruled the waters of the Persian Gulf, to suppress the lawlessness at sea which had given the Pirate Coast its name and reputation, and to try to stop the shipment of slaves from East Africa. In these good causes, Britain had made treaties with the sheiks of the coast of the Gulf as early as 1820: and having imposed some degree of truce between them, they changed the old name: the Pirate Coast became the Trucial Coast. The treaties were still observed; but towards the end of the nineteenth century, other European powers had started to take an interest in the Gulf. The Germans had made an ambitious plan for a Berlin-to-Baghdad railway, with a terminus on the sea-coast near Kuwait; and the Russians and French had tried to gain concessions for building coaling depots for their fleets. Foreseeing rivalry, the British had made their treaties closer; and by the end of the century, all the rulers of the Arabian coast of the Gulf, except the Turks in the Hasa, had undertaken not to cede any part of their territories to anyone but the British Government, and the British, in return, had guaranteed the rulers against aggression. These treaties had been made with European powers in mind as possible aggressors, but ibn Saud knew that they could be applied to him, and that if he were ever tempted to attack his smaller neighbours in the east, they could turn to the British for help. On the other hand, he could be sure that the British would leave him alone, so long as he left their protégés alone.

But in the first few turbulent days of excitement and jubilation at Riyadh, the thoughts of ibn Saud can hardly have ranged so far ahead or so far afield. He was only twenty-one; the events of the moment were all-absorbing and delightful; and it would have been hard to imagine that what he was doing in Riyadh might solemnly be discussed in London or Constantinople. Each day, new sheiks rode in, attended and armed, the heads of tribes and families large and small, to be received with sober Wahhabi hospitality, and to pay ibn Saud their tributes and offer their followers' strength to his command. His youth was no bar to their submission. It was not unusual for Arab boys to take their place in battle when Europeans would still have thought them children; the Egyptian army of ten thousand men which beat the Wahhabis after their invasion of the Hejaz was commanded by a boy of sixteen. But to have won a kingdom single-handed when he was still so young had made ibn Saud a hero among the heroes of the desert, and exposed him at once to the dangers of flattery. To value the homage of older seasoned fighters, without being dazzled by it, was the first test of his character as a ruler.

But two of the first of his actions suggest that he kept his head; one of them showed common sense, and the other wisdom. He set everybody rebuilding the dilapidated city wall, to prepare for the counter-attack which was certain to come; and he sent for the whole of his family from Kuwait, his father and mother and brothers and sisters, and his own wife and two sons. Perhaps he was lonely without them; but perhaps he had also reckoned, rightly, that nothing else he could do would give the people of Riyadh so much assurance. It changed the town from a Bedouin camp of war to a home, and gave his régime an air of permanence. When his father arrived, the welcome of the people was renewed; but he publicly abdicated in favour of ibn Saud, presenting him with an historic sword which had belonged to ibn Abdul-Wahhab himself and had then been handed down through generations of the family of Saud as a symbol of majesty.

Ibn Saud did not linger long in Riyadh. Perhaps even there he felt confined, as he had in Kuwait, and perhaps he already had enough sense of tactics to see that the proper place to defend the town was outside it; for, if all his forces were stationed inside the walls, the place might fall to a siege as it had before; but if he were at large in the desert he would be free to relieve a siege or to choose a time and a place for a battle with ibn Rashid. So when the walls were repaired and his family had taken up their quarters in the palace, he left his father to command the town and rode into the desert again, no longer as a secret raider, but as a sheik of sheiks. He travelled south, into the valleys and oases and the small walled towns which lay between Riyadh and the Empty Quarter. In that district, the rule of ibn Rashid had been weaker than in the north, and there he intended to raise and train and organise an army.

Nearly fifty years later, when ibn Saud was old and very rich, he said that the years he spent in the desert, living the frugal life of the Bedouin, were the happiest he remembered. Exalted people sometimes like to surprise their public by affecting simple tastes, but this reminiscence of ibn Saud was probably sincere. All his life, his religion was austere, and physical austerity attracted him strongly too, until riches and the pomp expected of kings made life too complicated. Austerity was not inconsistent, in the Arab world, with the remarkable marital prowess for which he was later distinguished. Heart and soul, he was a Bedouin himself, and all his life the Bedouin were the only people he really understood and felt at home with, just as the desert was the only country he ever saw.

The Bedouin were unique. Bedouin simply means desert people. They believed they could trace their lineage back to Ishmael the son of Abraham; and like the mud-brick cities scattered so sparsely through the desert, they had scarcely changed since the Children of Israel made their exodus from Egypt. Within the twentieth century, they still maintained the primitive war-torn society of the books of Moses, and some of them are maintaining it to-day.

They were herdsmen, breeding camels and horses and sheep; and the whole of their lives, except when they were fighting, was spent in a search for pasture, which sprang up after the unpredictable showers of rain and withered quickly, and might not be found in the same place again for many years. Most of them were desperately poor, and lived very near to starvation; and since they had hardly enough water to drink, they were often extremely dirty. They could never get rich by successful herding; successful raiding was their only road to prosperity. In tribal affairs, they owed a kind of loyalty to their sheiks, whom they chose from among themselves for their courage or wealth or wisdom, or their reputation for good luck, or sometimes because they were the sons of sheiks; but they did not always accept their sheik's decisions. In personal matters, they had no respect for any human authority or law. Every Bedouin thought himself the equal of all other Bedouin, and the superior of other sorts of men, and he did what was right in his own eyes, or what was expedient. Even the Prophet Mahomed despaired of reducing them to order in the seventh century, and in the twentieth century they were still as unruly as ever.

Yet they were guided by a peculiar sense of honour. They loved robbery on a grand scale, but despised petty thieving. They set a very low value on human life, but usually were not deliberately cruel. If one of them was murdered, his family by law and custom could claim the life of the murderer or a heavy price in camels, so murder was rare. Robbing caravans which crossed their land was claimed to be a right, as good as the right which civilised countries claimed of charging customs dues or levying tolls on turnpikes; but if an appropriate sheik appointed a man to protect a caravan, they would let it pass. If one of them undertook to look after a traveller, he would defend him with his life, or expect to live in disgrace among his fellow Bedouin. Through scores of centuries, they had learned to live on a meagre diet without any physical comfort, but whenever they had a chance they enjoyed a tremendous feast of rice and mutton; and by necessity, the same alternation of feast and fasting distinguished

25

their sexual life. At the time when ibn Saud set out to lead them, a negligible number could read or write, but some of the Arab tradition of poetry and philosophy had come down to them through the ages by word of mouth, and in their camps at night there were stories and recitations, sometimes heroic and romantic, and sometimes funny, and often lewd.

Above all, they were proud of themselves and their desert skill. Their pride gave them an air of nobility, enhanced by their flowing robes and the splendour of their camels, and not entirely nullified by dirtiness, and this air, and their sense of honour, and the ultimate simplicity of their lives, evoked an intense romantic admiration among the few ascetic explorers who learned to trust them and be trusted by them.

These men were to be the material of ibn Saud's army, War in the desert was not like any other kind of conflict which man has invented. It also had never changed, or only changed in one particular, since Biblical times. The army ibn Saud began to raise was mounted and organised like the hosts of Midianites and Amalekites and the children of the east whom Gideon fought. The only innovation was the rifle. The Bedouin, and the Wahhabis in particular, disliked the inventions of infidels, but they never had any doubt about the usefulness of rifles. They became connoisseurs of rifles, as they already were of camels and of swords and lances, although the firearms they owned were obsolete long before they were bartered in the desert. But ammunition was scarce and expensive, and too heavy to be carried on camels in large enough quantities for anything which resembled a modern battle.

Generalship in a tribal army was mostly a matter of catching the enemy by surprise, which was never easy. It was impossible to hide an army in the desert. When it moved, it had to move from well to well, and for months after it had passed, the tracks and droppings of its camels could be seen. Consequently, for most of the period of any Bedouin war, the opposing armies marched and counter-marched and never met. This was an exciting game for the commanders and their scouts and trackers, but dull and unprofitable for the troops, and the second responsibility of successful generalship was to provide enough excitement; for Bedouin troops went home as soon as they grew bored or came to believe that they might be on the losing side – a common-sense convention which would make any war tolerable.

Once battle was joined, it was every man for himself, and the commanders had very little influence on the outcome, except through the fighting spirit they had already instilled in their troops. Armies charged one another on camels or Arab mares, and each man shouted his personal war-cry:

26

"Son of –" naming his father or a war-like ancestor, or "Brother of –" naming his favourite sister, for the thought that he was chivalrously defending his sister's chastity was a source of courage, although it was seldom true. There were clouds of dust and a splendidly martial noise, and when the charges met, men shot at each other from the saddle at point-blank range, until they ran out of ammunition or of time to reload their cumbersome weapons, and then they drew their swords. As they charged, they covered the lower parts of their faces with their headcloths, to keep the dust out of their lungs and also to disguise themselves, for to kill a man even in battle might have started a family feud if the killer were recognised. There was no kind of uniform dress, and consequently, as soon as the momentum of a charge was lost and both armies were milling around in all directions, nobody could tell who was who or distinguish friends from enemies. With luck, the enemy turned and fled, but if the armies were evenly matched the confusion was soon impossible to disentangle, and both sides had to retreat and re-organise. The fights which followed the charges were therefore short, and more exciting than dangerous. Far fewer men were hurt than the noise and dust and powder-smoke suggested.

Perhaps while ibn Saud rode south, in the long hot hours of sameness which were characteristic of a camel journey, or when he lay down to sleep on the sand at night, he counted his assets and qualities and wondered how he could use them best to rally the Bedouin in his call and induce them to fight this kind of battle for him. His advantages were mostly intangible. First, he had his noble heritage, symbolised by the sword of ibn Abdul-Wahhab; but that was a wasting asset. The reputation of the House of Saud had sunk low, and only his deed at Riyadh had revived it; and the excitement of Riyadh would soon be forgotten unless he could follow it by other rousing deeds.

Next, he had his own physical distinction, and that was worth more. Most of the Bedouin were small, but he was six feet three and lean and muscular, and he could out-run or out-ride or out-shoot almost anyone else in the desert. He towered above his companions; nobody could ever neglect his presence. He was not merely handsome; his dark stern eyes and strongly-jutting nose, and his black hair and sparse beard and full lips with their suggestion, contradicting the eyes, of amorous sensuality, made him the very type of Arab masculinity; and he was certainly aware of this quality and used it.

One may suppose he was less aware of his charm if only because the essence of charm is unawareness. There is no-

27

body still alive who can describe his charm as a young man, but when he was older there was nobody, Arab or foreigner, who met him and came away from his presence unaffected by it. Most of the men who suffered drastic punishment at his hands devoted themselves to him when their crimes were expiated; most of his enemies were those who had never met him. His rages were terrible, and his smile was totally disarming. One American, high in the world of oil and accustomed to think of himself as unimpressionable, compared him in old age to an ancient god: just and compassionate, but capable of ruthless anger; full of human foibles, yet larger than human. One can only imagine this strength of personality combined with the qualities of youth and virility, and one can only measure his youthful charm by its results: it united the most discordant people in the world, the Bedouin.

Of material benefit he had very little to offer his recruits. He could feed them, but he could not pay them; the treasury of Saud was almost empty. He might have promised them plunder, but that was not his to promise. Victory was in the hands of God; and besides, to promise plunder was hardly necessary. Kings and religious leaders waged wars for dynasties and creeds, but the Bedouin were only too apt to regard the holiest of wars as nothing but super-raids. Commanders of victorious Bedouin armies usually found that their armies vanished in the moment of victory, hastening off to their distant homes with the booty they had won; and consequently, victories in the desert were seldom decisive. The Bedouin would certainly judge for themselves, without any invitation, whether ibn Saud was likely to lead them to profitable battles.

Nevertheless, the last of his assets was probably the strongest: his own conviction that God was on his side and that the Moslem world still needed to be purified by Wahhabism. Religions have always been the strongest incentives to war, stronger even than patriotism. The technique of warmakers changes, and ibn Saud's technique was hundreds of years behind the times, but the moral aims they profess do not change so much. In that respect, he might be compared with the Prophet himself, or with the Christian Crusaders of the twelfth and thirteenth centuries, or with the British who, thirteen years after his sudden blow at Riyadh, when the first world war began, believed yet again in the holiness of their cause. Certainly ibn Saud drew men to follow him in battle by his faith, and infected them with fervent intolerant zeal.

But while the assets he could claim were insubstantial, they were enough. As he rode on, the Bedouin gathered, until he was followed from well to well by several thousand riders, each with his camel and sword and gun, informally organised

28

and held together by nothing but the power of his will; some of them hoping for plunder and some for spiritual glory; most of them probably secretly hoping for both.

CHAPTER THREE

BATTLES AND MARRIAGES

Ibn Rashid was slow to seek revenge. At the moment of the fall of Riyadh, he was three hundred miles away, on the edge of Kuwait, preoccupied with plans for ousting the ruler of Kuwait and capturing the seaport for himself.

Bedouin armies could move as quickly as any other armies of that era, when they were ready to move; but they were always very slow in making ready. Their commanders needed intelligence of their enemies, like other more sophisticated generals; but they had never invented the primitive systems of signalling, by smoke or fire or semaphore, which were used in the western world before the electric telegraph. Even the simplest of messages had to be carried, and intelligence had to be gathered by spies and scouting parties at the archaic speed of a mounted man. By the time that ibn Rashid had learned of the death of his governor, and had been informed that ibn Saud had ridden south, and prepared to withdraw his army from Kuwait and make it ready for a punitive expedition, the summer had begun; and in summer, nobody could move an army through the desert. There was not enough water.

In consequence, ibn Saud had been the undisputed ruler of Riyadh for seven months before he heard, from his own spies in the desert to the north, that ibn Rashid's hosts were advancing on him. By then, he was ready to defend what he had won, if it can ever be said that an army commander is ready for defence; and he waited, concealing whatever doubts he may have felt. Ibn Rashid's forces were larger than his own, and seasoned in war, but he could not avoid a battle. He was encamped in a large oasis near the walls of a village called Dilam when riders brought him the news that ibn Rashid was passing Riyadh, fifty miles away, and had not attacked it. The first encounter was imminent: the first in a desultory war which lasted twenty years.

That battle was far from typical. Ibn Saud elected to wait among the palms, and behind the embrasures of the village wall, rather than sally out to meet his enemy in the desert. Ibn Rashid dismounted his men and advanced across the sand towards the oasis, which was silent. Ibn Saud had ordered his men to lie quiet until the attackers were easily in range, and then to open fire on them with rifles. This was a novel manoeuvre in the desert, and the unfamiliar fusillade checked ibn Rashid's leaders and confused them. They retreated, and paused for consideration, and advanced more subtly; but time after time they were met by rifle fire. The fighting continued all day, but the oasis held, and the antagonists never met within a sword's length; and at dusk ibn Rashid withdrew to his camp, perhaps more puzzled than injured by his upstart enemy's tactics.

In the following dawn ibn Saud expected the attack to be renewed; but on the contrary, the opposing army was seen to be striking camp, and during the day the whole of it disappeared towards the north. It seemed as though ibn Rashid had made up his mind to turn his attack to Riyadh, but he had not. After that single indecisive fight, he retreated the whole of the enormous distance he had come, and went back to his siege of Kuwait.

Perhaps the prodigal use of ammunition had made him believe that ibn Saud's resources were greater than his own. Certainly he cannot have known the truth: that ibn Saud had blazed off almost every round that he and his Bedouin possessed, and could have been forced within an hour or two to fight it out with swords. The freshly recruited Bedouin had brought not only their camels and rifles, but all their ammunition with them; but when it was used, in the course of that one exultant day, neither they nor ibn Saud could afford to replace it. It was another ten years before ibn Saud could save up enough to repeat his successful barrage, and in the meantime the battles he fought reverted to traditional forms of fighting. But by bluff and luck, he had been able to claim a victory, the first which the Saudis had won for a generation.

The whole of the rest of that campaigning season was spent in feints and manoeuvres. Ibn Rashid bore heavily on Kuwait. The ruler of Kuwait, feeling himself in danger, sent riders to ibn Saud to ask for help. Ibn Saud was tempted out of his southern fastnesses and led his army up to Kuwait to relieve the ally who had given sanctuary to his family in its exile. As soon as ibn Rashid heard he was coming, he broke off his siege and retreated towards his own dominions; but somewhere out of sight of the spies of ibn Saud, he changed direction, and appeared without warning at the gates of Riyadh. This was a shrewd manoeuvre, but in shrewdness ibn Saud was at least the equal of ibn Rashid. Instead of hurrying back to Riyadh to relieve it, he marched into ibn Rashid's territory and began to plunder the camps and villages where ibn Rashid's warriors had their homes. News of his raids reached ibn Rashid's army, and the defenders of Riyadh watched it melt away; his Bedouin, no more reliable than any others, were going home to protect their herds and families. Seeing them so disorganised, the father of ibn Saud sent out the garrison of Riyadh to join in the plundering; and when the summer of 1903 drove all the contestants home to shelter from the heat, the House of Saud could claim to have had the advantage, and its fighters had collected satisfactory trophies.

It was about this time, in the intervals of battle, that ibn Saud began the expansion of his matrimonial career. He had already been married twice in Kuwait. The first time, he was fifteen and his bride was younger, but she died soon afterwards; he is said to have kept a sentimental memory of his first love all his life. The second time, his wife had two sons. The younger of them, Saud, who finally succeeded him as king, was born at almost the moment of the assault on Riyadh.

A passionate need for women was fundamental in his character, a part of the zest which gave him dominance over men and made him a ruler. As a ruler he had limitless chances to indulge it. The Koranic law on marriage was strict and specific, and truly to his precise Wahhabi faith, he obeyed it strictly; but interpreted to the letter, it offered a not unreasonable scope to its adherents. A man was only allowed to have four wives; but the marriage ceremony was a matter of minutes, with whatever witnesses happened to be available, and divorce was hardly more than a matter of seconds. A husband only had to declare to his wife three times that she was divorced, and that was that. Accordingly, ibn Saud never had more than four wives at a time. When Riyadh was settled, he kept them in separate houses there. But he made it a practice, before he set out on a journey, to divorce the one who was pleasing him least, in order to leave a vacancy which he could fill whenever he felt inclined while he was travelling.

Men who are not Moslems sometimes suppose it must be hard to choose a wife where women are always veiled from head to foot; but the amount of a woman which is revealed to men is a matter of custom, and ibn Saud chose his wives, or his emissaries chose them for him, by their voices and eyes and demeanour and antecedents, and whatever rumours he could hear of their beauty, as any strict Moslem should. Perhaps there is this to be said for the veiling of women: that the more there is veiled, the more there is left to unveil. Perhaps the western custom of near-nudity in public provides nothing quite so exciting as the moment when a Moslem bridegroom, overcoming his bride's pretences of modesty, unveils her face. It is not always, as one might suppose, the first thing he does; sometimes it happens long after the marriage is consummated, and it is said that ibn Saud never saw the faces of his less successful wives. If he was disappointed in them, he divorced them in the morning and sent them back to their fathers with thanks and a present; the father's displeasure was felt by the daughters, rather than by the king. Those who bore children were pensioned off and given houses, so that the children should be brought up well until they were six or seven, and old enough to join the rest of his family in his palace. Those who did not were free to marry again, with the added attraction of having once been married to the king; for divorce especially from ibn Saud, was no disgrace. The number of girls who enjoyed this honour grew. While he was in his thirties, he claimed with pleasure and pride to have married seventy-five, and said that he hoped to keep his health and strength to marry many more; and his hope was fulfilled. He is thought to have had about three hundred wives by the time old age overtook him, and when he died he still possessed his quota of four, and quantities of concubines and slave girls. In accordance with custom, his current wives were never seen by other men and he never spoke about them. What happened in the bedrooms of his palace, or in his tents at night, was strictly, and properly, his own affair, for a man's relations with his wife are as private if he has hundreds as if he has only one; but it was said that his domestic life was blissful. He enjoyed the company of his children, and had an excellent reputation as a father. Forty-four of them were sons who survived to grow up, and infantile mortality at the time was said to be seventy-five or eighty per cent. The number of daughters he had was never stated; possibly he never counted them.

Kings cannot always marry entirely for love, and some of the marriages he contracted on his journeys were political. In every kingdom, until the recent past, royal marriages were a means of uniting peoples or achieving national aims, but in monogamous countries their use was limited. Ibn Saud, however, was able to marry into every important tribe in his domains, and so bind them all to himself by family ties.

But politics and his own exuberant instinct were not his only guides; he was also capable of feeling a lasting love. His second wife, the mother of Saud who succeeded him as king, remained with him all his life. She was divorced, but was still his constant companion, so that as an old man, although frequently still a bridegroom, he was also, in affection if not in law, a faithful husband of fifty years' standing. He also showed a life-long devotion to his sister, whose name was Nura; and these two women, in later years, shared the duty of running his colossal and contented household. In a moment of confidence, when he was elderly, he explained to an English companion that a good Moslem would be allowed

33

fifty houris and one of his earthly wives when he came to Paradise; but he hoped that in view of his own exceptional career, God in his mercy would grant him six of his wives, because there were six he remembered with special and equal affection.

But during the years of his war against ibn Rashid, his life remained frugal, and although his weddings soon became frequent they never diverted him long from his plans of conquest. For two years, his generalship was perfectly successful. North-west of Riyadh, the desert ran eight hundred miles towards the borders of Palestine and Syria. Within it, there were three considerable towns: Buraida and Anaiza, lying close together a hundred and fifty miles away from Riyadh, and ibn Rashid's capital, Hail, another hundred and fifty miles beyond. Leading his Bedouin farther and farther into this wilderness, he drove ibn Rashid back to his own domains, and enforced his own sovereignty over the nomad tribes and villages. In 1904, he set his swordsmen to assault Anaiza, and captured it after a day of gruesome bloodshed.

By chance, a translation has been preserved of a letter written by ibn Saud himself to the Sheik of Kuwait to tell him the town had fallen. The letter came into British hands, and the translation is still in the archives of the British Foreign Office. Its Biblical language owes something to the Englishman who translated it soon after it reached Kuwait, but its wild and holy exultation in battle might have been expressed in Arabia at any time in a period of five thousand years.

"May God preserve you," he wrote to his patron. "We sent word to your Highness before this by the hand of your servant Madi that it was our intention to set forth on an expedition. So we proceeded ... and by the help of God and with your assistance, we halted our camels over above Osheziye at the break of day. And we abode there, we and the people of Kassim who were with us, for the rest of that day. And the people of Anaiza who were with us sent men to their friends furtively to announce our coming. And when it was the fourth hour of the night we bestirred ourselves and came to Anaiza.... And after we had said the morning prayer, we sent against them Abdullah ibn Jiluwi, with him a hundred men of the people of Riyadh to assist. And we marched against Majid, and when he saw the horsemen, God lifted his hand from off his men and helped us against them. And we broke them and slaughtered of them three hundred and seventy men. And God restored to us our kinsmen of the family of Saud who were prisoners in their hands.... And, by Almighty God, but two Bedouins on our side were slain. Then we returned to the villages of our friends. And they had taken the castle and laid hands on the family of Yahia and those with them and slain them, and emptied the houses of the family of Bessam. And, by God, there went away with Majid but some fifteen camels and seven mares; and the rest of their army and their horses and their arms and their tents and their furniture we took as spoil, by the help of God.... And our intention, by the Grace of God, is that we should speed to Buraida, if God wills. Thus far. Greeting."

The kinsmen who were restored to him in this battle were nine of his cousins. After it, they were given the collective nickname of the Araif, a word descriptive of camels which had strayed and been caught again; and they were to cause him disastrous trouble in future years.

Soon after Anaiza fell, Buraida surrendered to him, rather than suffer the same atrocious fate.

With the capture of these towns, the whole of the ancient kingdom of Saud was united again, excepting the Turkish stronghold in the Hasa; but it was a kingdom with no communications or administration or system of law, and ibn Saud's authority was slender. It depended entirely on the fickle loyalty of the Bedouin, and the loyalty of the Bedouin depended on more success in battle, and more reward in plunder. For the present, they were happy to be on the winning side, but ibn Saud could not stop fighting; fighting was all that held his new kingdom together. Like other successful military autocrats, he was bound to go on to find new victories, not merely for profit or glory, but also to satisfy the fighting spirit he had been at such pains to arouse in his army. Peace too soon might well have been fatal for him; if he had given his followers nothing to fight against, they would certainly have fought against each other, or turned on him.

Probably ibn Rashid, who was the same kind of autocrat and commanded the same kind of army, foresaw this difficulty and knew that his own territory would be threatened. So far, he seemed to have taken his defeat in a philosophical spirit. That was characteristic of the Bedouin. They always lived close to disaster – defeat, drought, hunger, sorrow and pain – and they suffered with resignation, believing whenever times were bad that, God willing, sooner or later, they would improve. He could afford to be philosophical while ibn Saud was merely recapturing what the previous generation of Saudis had so foolishly lost. But if ibn Saud went on, to try to capture what had always belonged to the House of Rashid, more drastic action to halt him would be needed. Accordingly, soon after Anaiza and Buraida fell, ibn Rashid asked the Turks for help, and in the spring of 1904, they ordered eight battalions of their own troops into the desert to support him. The war, which had been a family affair so far, had begun to spread its ripples overseas.

That Turkish army brought three unpleasant novelties into the desert: discipline, artillery and cholera. Ibn Saud had never encountered any of these three things, or any kind of army but his own, and so the approach of the Turkish forces did not seem to daunt him. When he heard they were coming, he marshalled his Bedouin and rode out to accept the challenge. But common sense may have suggested to him that fighters more efficient than the Bedouin existed, and that his leadership was facing its hardest test; for before he went out to battle he wrote or dictated an appeal for help and addressed it to the British Political Resident in the Persian Gulf, and dispatched a rider to take it towards the coast.

CHAPTER FOUR

THE BRITISH RESIDENT

The name of the British Political Resident was Percy Cox, and the letter he received in May, 1904, was the first communication between Riyadh and any foreign power, except the Turks, since Colonel Pelly's fruitless visit thirty-nine years before. Its request for help against the Turkish army posed a problem which Cox could not possibly have answered, and set in motion distant wheels of government which ibn Saud could not possibly have imagined.

The Political Resident was stationed at Bushire in Persia, on the opposite shore of the Gulf. He had two subordinates with the title of Political Agent, one at the court of the Sheik of Bahrain and the other, whose name was Knox, at the court of the Sheik of Kuwait. These three men served British interests throughout the whole of the Gulf, and for the next five years Cox and Knox were the only connection between ibn Saud and the western world.

Cox had only recently been appointed, but he had spent four years as Agent in Muscat in the south-east corner of Arabia; and there he had struggled with some success against the importing of slaves from Africa, and perfected his Arabic, and developed a natural affection and sympathy for Arabs. He was a tall, thin Englishman whose most remarkable feature was an extremely crooked nose; he had injured it in a football match. He was shrewd, gentle, tenacious, extremely patient and conspicuously silent; and of course, as a British civil servant, he was perfectly incorruptible. All these were unusual qualities in Arabia, where most men were loquacious, fierce and intolerant, and all governments maintained their power by bribery and violence. But his liking for the people he worked among was genuine, and many of them returned it with affection and respect.

Among these was the Sheik of Kuwait, Mubarrak. There could hardly have been two men with less in common: the abstemious uncommunicative Englishman, living alone with his devoted wife in such an alien land, the trusted servant of a king three thousand miles away; and the wily flamboyant Arabian autocrat with his well-stocked harem, who had won his throne by murdering his older brother and all his relations who opposed him. Yet they were friends. In British eyes, Mubarrak was a rogue, but a very engaging rogue. When Cox opposed those of his practices which he could

37

not approve, such as slavery in its basest forms, or trading in arms, or assassination, he always took the criticism well and seemed to make a genuine effort to reform; and when he relapsed, as he always did, he was apologetic and repentant. Cox recognised him as a shrewd and effective ruler, according to the precepts of Arab rulers, and he admired him for it. No one can say what qualities Mubarrak admired in Cox, but he undoubtedly did admire him. It was a strange reciprocal esteem; but it was not so rare, between the builders of the British Empire and their neighbours and subject races, as the critics of imperialism believe. Where the British lived in large communities, as they did in India and the settled parts of Africa, their behaviour and their air of superiority may often have been insufferable; but in the farthest outposts, where single administrators lived alone, a different facet of the national character was revealed, and many men spent their lives in perfect sympathy with the alien people who surrounded them. Cox was that kind of man.

From their outpost in the Persian Gulf, the British had been quietly watching events in Arabia for generations, and Cox's predecessor had sent some dry reports of them to London. In 1902, he reported the disastrous expedition which was made in the previous year by the Sheik of Kuwait and the father of ibn Saud: "The defeat sustained by Sheik Mubarrak at the hands of the Amir of Nejd (ibn Rashid) on the 17th March, near Anaiza, was decisive. As is not unusual in Arab warfare, he was deserted in the hour of need by certain Bedouins who had espoused his cause and who went over to the Amir's side, thus changing the fortune of the day."

"About the middle of January," the same report continued, "an event of great importance occurred in the capture by Abdul-Aziz of Riyadh, the old Wahhabi capital. Up to the present, the Amir of Nejd has taken no active measure against Abdul-Aziz, who has strengthened his authority at Riyadh and gained many supporters."

In the following year, 1903, the same officer mentioned "constant and conflicting reports" from the desert, and added: "It was generally expected that a decisive battle would have been fought ere this. No reliable news however of any encounter has as yet been received." In fact, ibn Saud had already beaten off ibn Rashid by his rifle fusillade at Dilam, but perhaps that story had not yet reached the coast.

These reports, and Cox's in later years, were not sent straight to London but were sent to the Government of India; for among the frontiers of administration by which the British had divided up the world, the line between the spheres of the British and Indian Governments happened to pass down the middle of Arabia. The Persian Gulf was under the wide dominion of the brilliant and formidable Viceroy of India, Lord Curzon; the Red Sea on the other side was under the Foreign Office. The domain of ibn Saud had its communications, such as they were, with the coast of the Gulf, so that British reports on his activities went first to Bombay and Calcutta, and thence to the India Office in London; and British policy on eastern Arabia was determined by the Secretary of State for India and transmitted back to the local officials by the same round-about route.

But the Hejaz, the domain of the Sherif of Mecca, which extended from the Red Sea coast to a vague frontier with ibn Saud, was regarded by the British as a part of the Middle East, together with Egypt, which was under British occupation, and the Sudan, where Lord Kitchener, only a few years before, had successfully slaughtered ten thousand ill-armed Sudanese in the Battle of Omdurman. Reports on the Hejaz therefore went by way of Cairo to the Foreign Office, and policy on western Arabia was determined by the Secretary of State for Foreign Affairs.

This curious division did not matter very much in the first decade of the twentieth century, when the two sides of Arabia were divided in fact by impassable wilderness in the middle. British officials from opposite sides of Arabia never met, except perhaps by chance on leave in England. Their reports, by their differing routes, did finally go to the same block of buildings in Whitehall, for the Foreign Office and the India Office shared a building; but the two departments did not always share the same interests or policy. Occasional memoranda passed across the courtyard, written in terms of strict formality: "The Under-Secretary of State for India presents his compliments to the Under-Secretary of State for Foreign Affairs, and begs to inform him. . . ." But neither of the departments always knew what the other of them was doing. By the time of the first world war, this dual interest had confused the Arab rulers and bedevilled their relationship with Britain; but it was shrouded in the red tape of generations, and it continued till 1924.

However, in 1904, ibn Saud had no idea of these complications. Almost certainly, the only British he knew of, apart from King Edward VII and Lord Curzon, were Cox and Knox. He left Kuwait before Knox was appointed. While he was living there, British warships had visited the harbour several times, and he must have seen them; but there is no reason to think that he had ever met an Englishman. The British had no interest in meeting him while he was merely the son of a wholly discredited exile. But his friend the Sheik of Kuwait had met them, and had made a treaty with them in 1899, and ibn Saud had undoubtedly learned from him that British power had to be respected, and might sometimes be turned to profitable use.

Kuwait had always been coveted by the Turks. If they had possessed it, their duties on imports to Arabia would almost have been a monopoly. They had constantly encouraged ibn Rashid, as their ally, in his fruitless attempts to reduce the town by siege. Early in 1904, a secret agent had given the British Ambassador in Constantinople a copy of a letter from ibn Rashid to the Sultan, in which he complained that the Sheik of Kuwait had been plundering his country and was clearly a tool of the British. The letter requested the Sultan's permission to attack. But whenever ibn Rashid's attack seemed imminent, the Sheik sent an urgent message to the British Political Resident, a British gunboat was quickly dispatched to anchor in the harbour of Kuwait, and the Turks, for fear of international complications, ordered ibn Rashid to withdraw. In the same year, 1904, Lord Curzon himself made a ceremonial tour of the Gulf, taking with him a number of warships and, for his own use, a gold and silver throne; and he landed at Kuwait and presented a sword to the Sheik. Finally, Knox was appointed as a permanent symbol of British interest. To send one officer to halt the expansion of a rival empire was an example of the splendid and insulting confidence of the British in that era; and it was perfectly effective. The Turks protested, but their threats, and ibn Rashid's, ended.

Such convenient protection must have been in the mind of ibn Saud when he sent his letter to Cox before he set out to do battle with the Turks. Evidently, the British did not like the Turks. If the Turks could send men and arms and money to ibn Rashid, there was a reasonable chance that the British might do the same for him. And indeed, if Cox had been able to follow his personal inclination, that naïve hope of ibn Saud's might partly have been fulfilled; for Cox knew that ibn Saud had already won the allegiance of the tribes in the central desert, and that Turkish attempts to reimpose the rule of ibn Rashid could only cause endless strife. But even in that age of power politics, no major power could risk a warlike act against another merely to help a worthy Arabian sheik. Ibn Saud's request was forwarded by Cox, and finally, by way of the India Office, it reached the Foreign Secretary, Lord Lansdowne. Of course, Lord Lansdowne refused it, with the comment that British interests in Arabia were confined to the coast and must not be extended inland. But he did go so far as to tell the British Ambassador in Constantinople to remind the Turks of an understanding reached some years before, that the British would restrain the Sheik of Kuwait if the Turks restrained ibn Rashid.

However, that moderate request revealed yet a third British point of view about Arabia. The Ambassador in Constantinople carried out his orders, but under protest. He replied that he thought it was unreasonable to try to dissuade the Turks from helping ibn Rashid, because ibn Saud, whom he called "the Wahhabi pretender", was clearly the aggressor. On the contrary, it was up to the Government of India to prevent the Sheik of Kuwait from giving any help to ibn Saud. He predicted serious but unspecified consequences if the Wahhabi dynasty were re-established. The Ambassador, in short, was backing ibn Rashid as strongly as Cox was backing ibn Saud; and the half-hearted protest he delivered had no effect whatever on the Turks.

Between these contradictory opinions, Lord Lansdowne took refuge in a statement that everyone should maintain the *status quo*; a policy on which Lord Curzon in India, whose tongue was always sharp and apt, had already made the private comment: "When you hear a Foreign Minister say anywhere that all he wants is to defend the *status quo,* you may guess in nine cases out of ten that he has no policy at all."

The acrimonious telegrams and letters conveying these divergent British views took quite a long time to pass between London, Constantinople, Calcutta and Bushire. But events in the desert could not wait on them. While all the formal phrases were being drafted, each superficially polite but shrewdly barbed, ibn Saud unaided had met the Turks in battle – and had lost.

CHAPTER FIVE

DEATH OF AN ENEMY

The defeat was inconclusive, for the reasons which made most desert defeats and victories inconclusive: in victory, the fighters turned to plunder, and in defeat they wisely ran away. The battle lasted all day on the 15th of June, 1904, in the height of the summer heat, and no less than a thousand men were said to have died in it. The scene must have been hideous; and yet in retrospect, from a distance in time and place, the battle seems a ludicrous affair.

It was fought without cover in the open desert, in a region of salt flats and sandhills, where the rival armies had pitched their camps within sight of one another. Ibn Saud was the first to attack. The Turks formed a defensive square, on which the mounted Bedouin swordsmen and snipers could not make much impression. One of ibn Saud's contingents, of the local tribe from the district of Anaiza, avoided the Turks and succeeded in scattering ibn Rashid's Bedouin, and overran their camp and stopped to sack it. But the main body of his troops faltered at the sound of Turkish cannon, a weapon they had never heard before; and at the height of the battle ibn Saud was wounded in the hand, and had to retire to his tent. By some accounts, he was also hit in the leg and left unconscious. Certainly he disappeared from the fray for a time; and in his absence his men lost heart, and he lost control of them. When he revived, he did not know of the success of the men of Anaiza, but assumed the day was lost. He abandoned his camp and escaped from the battlefield, and the Turks advanced to take their turn at plunder.

The men of Anaiza, returning laden with booty in triumph to the camp, were surprised to find it full of Turkish soldiers. But the Turks were no less surprised, to find a fresh rabble of Arabs approaching in their rear. They abandoned their loot and retreated. For the moment, the men of Anaiza had the upper hand; but they were weary and hot, and alarmed at the disappearance of their leader. So they also took to flight. The Turkish Army alone remained on the field of battle, still more or less intact as a fighting force; the army of ibn Saud was scattered and on the run. If the Turks, in addition to their discipline, had had the mobility and desert skill of an Arab army, they might easily have followed up their victory and made a rout of it, and put a final end to ibn Saud; but their movements were cumbersome, and no doubt they were exhausted by the heat. They retired within their own defended camp and contented themselves with tactical and moral victory; and ibn Saud was left alive and free to fight again.

The setback was serious, not only through the loss of his men and animals and the meagre equipment of his army, but also because it shook the faith of the Bedouin in his luck and skill; and the capriciousness of his followers' enthusiasm was always his weakness, as it had always been of every Arab ruler. For some weeks, it seemed his star was waning. But in spite of his wound, he started a series of hasty journeys to try to rally his scattered men and persuade other sheiks to send contingents to support him; and at that moment his personal charm was all that held his shaken domain together.

But he had one ally, though he may hardly have been aware of it, which was indestructible: the desert. The Turks were not desert people. The Turkish Government may have persuaded itself that sending its armies into Arabia was a civilising mission and a duty to the Arabs, just as the British, by convoluted reasoning, sincerely believed it was their duty to invade the Sudan. But to have sent the Turkish Army in the height of summer was merely cruel and stupid. As soon as the army started, it was doomed. There was really no need for ibn Saud to fight it. If he could have been patient and simply let it advance, and perhaps sent raiders to control the wells behind it, the desert would have won his victory for him with horrible certainty. Politically, the Turks had no right to be there at all; and yet in the campaigns of that summer it is the Turkish soldiers who merit sympathy. Many were conscripted peasants with memories of gentler countrysides in Anatolia. Before they reached the battle grounds of the rival Arabs, they had already marched for hundreds of miles on foot, beyond the last outposts of the world they thought was civilised, hungry and parched and surrounded by pitiless, outlandish enemies. They must have known that most of their comrades would never go home again, but would end as shrivelled corpses in the sand. They left no history of their suffering; but in trying to imagine it one marvels again that illusions of glory, and martial discipline, can make men resign themselves to lead such ignoble lives and endure such bestial deaths.

The British showed no reaction to the Turkish success. Perhaps they were wise enough to know it could not last, or perhaps they were too much absorbed in petty affairs of administration. The smouldering disagreement between the Foreign Office and the Government of India had flickered into a peevish argument over the appointment of Knox as Agent in Kuwait. It was Lord Curzon, advised by Cox, who had proposed that an agent should be sent there; and Lord Lansdowne, six months before, had agreed that Knox should go. But now, when Knox's work had only just begun, Lord Lansdowne instructed the Government of India that the agent should be withdrawn. Perhaps the Ambassador in Constantinople had talked him over. His vacillation annoyed Lord Curzon beyond endurance. Curzon consulted Cox, who told him the Sheik of Kuwait would be justifiably angry if Knox were taken away, and might transfer his allegiance to the Turks. A very long dispatch was sent from Calcutta to London, written in language so formally polite that it was blistering. Lord Lansdowne, it said, had never suggested before that the appointment was temporary. If that had been his intention, it would have been better not to have made the appointment at all. "But as a decision has been arrived at in the matter against which it would no longer be becoming for us to protest," the Government of India proposed a formula for saving face. Knox, they suggested, should tell the Sheik that until a proper house had been built for him he could not stay through the hot weather in Kuwait, and had therefore applied for permission to leave temporarily for reasons of health. This broadside, with its disingenuous diplomatic lie, was dispatched to London with the signatures of several officials of the Government of India, headed by those of both of India's biggest guns, Lord Curzon and Lord Kitchener, who was then the Commander-in-Chief. But they never had to order Knox to tell their disgraceful story. Nothing happened for two months; then a telegram came from the Foreign Office. Lord Lansdowne, it said, "while unable to admit the correctness of the inference, does not consider there would be any advantage in further pursuing the discussion of the subject. His Lordship sees no objection to the suggestion of the Government of India as to the means for effecting the temporary withdrawal of Captain Knox from Kuwait." Lord Curzon wisely left it at that; and Knox stayed where he was.

At the same time, a rather less angry argument was going on about a worthier subject: the traffic in arms. The British opposed the sale of second-hand rifles to primitive tribes, which was – and still is – a profitable trade in many parts of the world. For years they had tried to control it in the Persian Gulf. They knew that Kuwait was the centre of the trade on the Arabian shore, and that the Sheik himself was doing very well by importing weapons and selling them, at nearly three times the price, to ibn Saud and his tribesmen. The Turks knew it too. As a matter of general policy, the Foreign Office had to tell Lord Curzon the trade should be stopped; and while it continued it was always a trump card

44

for the Ambassador in Constantinople in his resistance to orders that he should calm the Turks.

But Curzon and Cox were reluctant to try to stop it. Cox said that if the Sheik of Kuwait could not help ibn Saud, he would lose his own popularity and power. Curzon said that if ibn Saud's supplies were cut, Arabia would simple be delivered to the Turks. Perhaps both of them also felt it was unsporting to try to influence the war in Arabia by such underhand means – in the phrase of Edwardian England, it was not cricket; for the ethics of sport were widely applied in the British administration, on the whole with success.

But Curzon had no need to press his argument. His position was strong. It would have been impossible to stop the trade entirely, however hard he had tried. Knox, single-handed, could not have controlled the whole flourishing market in Kuwait, and a few miscellaneous British gunboats could not have searched every Arab dhow. But it was possible, without provoking Lord Lansdowne, to avoid being too aggressively vigilant at sea, and to turn a blind eye to some things that happened in Kuwait. So the traders in arms went on thriving; and Knox was delighted when an innocent up-country Arab stopped him in the market-place and asked him what guns he had for sale, and refused to believe that a foreigner could have come to Kuwait for any other purpose.

So ibn Saud could still look to Kuwait to replace the weapons he had lost in battle, and the Sheik still had plenty for sale; and before the summer of 1904 was ended, ibn Saud was back in the field, confronting the Turks again, with his army reassembled and reinforced. It is impossible now to discover exactly what happened that autumn. Nobody was watching events with an eye for military history, and accounts which were given in later years were all different. It is only certain that by the end of September the Turkish Army was annihilated; and probably nobody even at the time, except men who were doomed to die, could have said how much was contributed to its downfall by ibn Saud, and how much by treachery, mutiny, starvation and disease.

The Turks had not advanced at all since they first defeated ibn Saud. They had only destroyed a few settlements near the old battlefield, some fifty miles west of the town of Buraida. The only place in that district worth attacking or defending was a town called Rass; and in front of Rass the two armies faced each other for several weeks, and neither moved.

Perhaps ibn Saud had understood by then that his wisest tactics were simply to wait for the Turks to exhaust themselves. But Bedouin armies were never good at waiting. It did not suit the Arabs' impatient temperament; and besides,

45

if the army did not move, its mares and camels ate the surrounding desert bare. Cholera, which the Turks had brought with them, spread to the rival camp, killed many of ibn Saud's men and undermined the courage of the rest; and it is said that after the first few weeks of inactivity, his army was on the edge of mutiny.

Yet the Turks must have suffered more. They were not fitted by inheritance or training for the heat. They wore uniform, instead of the Arab robe and headdress which European explorers had found the only comfortable garments in the desert. Above all, they were prisoners in their camp. The Arabs were only held there by the loyalty of the moment; they knew they could ride away and go home if boredom or necessity drove them to it; but the Turkish soldiers knew that if they ventured out of the camp alone, they would either die of thirst or have their throats cut.

But it was ibn Rashid who was the first to move. Some accounts said his Bedouin insisted on taking their camels to other pastures. Another said that he intended to march to Buraida, because he had received a letter to tell him that plans had been made to deliver the town to him; it seemed to be signed by a prominent merchant in the town, but had really been cunningly forged by ibn Saud. At any rate, this move by ibn Rashid gave ibn Saud his chance. For the first time that summer, ibn Rashid's Bedouin and the Turks were separated.

A part of ibn Saud's army attached the Bedouin as they moved, and caught them laden with the season's booty. He led the main part of his force in a mounted charge against the Turkish camp. He must have learned from experience that if his men could only get in among the Turks and fight them hand to hand the Turkish artillery would be useless. The charge succeeded. The Turks wavered and retreated, abandoning their camp and their guns and supplies; and without their supplies they could not survive in the desert. The Bedouin of ibn Rashid, seeing Turkish soldiers in retreat, broke off the fight and fled. Ibn Rashid himself was wounded.

The loot was tremendous. It is said that a chest of Turkish gold was found. Certainly, for the first time in its history, the House of Saud at last possessed artillery. Each man of ibn Saud's army was far too intent on snatching a share of the booty for himself to think of following the retreating enemy. But that did not matter much. Five hundred and fifty Turks were already dead, and for days afterwards, wandering and dying soldiers could be found and killed for the sake of whatever they were carrying. A few of them succeeded in surrendering, and a few escaped to Hail with ibn Rashid. That was all.

This victory was complete, and the reputation of ibn Saud among the Arabs rose higher than ever before. Yet rumours were heard in Constantinople which show the battle in a rather different light; and two months later they were confirmed by two Turkish survivors or deserters who staggered down to the coast and told their story to a British vice-consul. All these stories agreed that ibn Rashid himself, the ally of the Turks, had shot the Turkish commander because he refused to lead an attack on ibn Saud. Some of them added that ibn Rashid's Bedouin had turned on the Turks in the height of the battle, slaughtered a hundred of them and wounded ninety. It is not unlikely. Ibn Rashid and his men were Arabs, as purely bred as ibn Sadu and his; and probably the unhappy Turkish soldiers had been disliked as much by their allies as by their enemies. Anything could happen in Arabia, where loyalties, like the desert pastures, grew and withered quickly.

The result of the battle was also curious. Within a month of it, ibn Saud had offered his submission to the Sultan of Turkey and begged for forgiveness. He deputed his father to approach the Sultan; although the old man had abdicated in favour of his son, he remained the senior religious leader. His father wrote a series of cringing, obsequious letters, protesting that the members of the House of Saud were the true hereditary rulers of Central Arabia, and that the misunderstanding between his house and Turkey was only due to the calumnies of ibn Rashid, the usurper. "I am submissive to every desire and order of the Shadow of God," he wrote – and the Shadow of God was the Sultan; and again, "I am the obedient servant of our Lord the Great Caliph (God preserve his Throne till the Day of Judgment)."

The Sultan seemed to be baffled by the grovelling servility of the letters; perhaps it was overdone, so that even he, bemused as he must have been by a lifetime of flattery, suspected it was insincere. If he did, he was right; the submission was simply strategic. Ibn Saud had defeated one Turkish army, but even in his most ambitious moments he could hardly have dreamed of defeating the Turkish empire. He could not stop the Turks sending army after army into the desert if they decided to do so. They might never be able to beat him, but they might be a perpetual nuisance. Above all, so long as the Turks were allied with ibn Rashid, he could not come to grips with him; and ibn Rashid was the closer, more dangerous enemy. To break the alliance between them, it was well worth while to perform whatever humble antics would satisfy the Sultan.

Three months after the battle, in December, 1904, the Sultan decided to accept the submission; but at the turn of the year he changed his mind, and ordered a larger army to prepare to march into the desert. The Sultan was not the kind of ruler who had to explain his whims, and the reason why he changed his mind was not recorded; but he may have been influenced by his other vassals in Arabia. All the Arabian rulers were growing envious and apprehensive at ibn Saud's successes. The Sherif of Mecca certainly appealed to the Turks for a further effort to stop him before he went too far; and even the Sheik of Kuwait, whose friendship for ibn Saud had lasted exceptionally long, made surreptitious approaches to the Turks, and to his life-long enemy ibn Rashid, to preserve the balance of power in the desert.

But it was one thing for the Sultan to order his armies to prepare; quite another to launch them effectively into the desert. The armies seemed reluctant. It would be easy to say that the horrible fate of the first had made the others nervous; but a fairer judgment would be that the efficient professional Turkish officers knew it was futile to try to do battle with Arabs at the end of a line of supply five hundred miles in length across the desert. The main units of the new armies marched sluggishly to and fro in the northern part of ibn Rashid's country; and while they did so, ibn Saud bombarded the Sultan with more and more fawning letters, which the Sultan never answered.

In the spring of 1905, the Sheik of Kuwait arranged a meeting between a Turkish envoy and ibn Saud's father. Again the old man humbly begged the Sultan's pardon for his son, prudently adding that he would like to have it in writing; and as a further sign of submission, he said that his son would be happy to have a Turkish garrison in Buraida and Anaiza, provided only that ibn Rashid was kept away.

This cunning suggestion did deceive the Sultan, and a token force of the Turkish Army was dispatched and reached Buraida safely. Its commander's name was Lieutenant-General Sudgi; and a paraphrase of his dispatch on the entry into Buraida still exists, because the dispatch was intercepted, before it reached the Sultan, by the British Consul in Basra, whose name was Crow. It was triumphant, yet pathetic. Sudgi reported that sheiks hastened out of the town to meet him as he approached it. He presented robes of honour to them and appointed two as governors in reward for their fidelity and obedience. Eloquent prayers were read for the Sultan, the Turkish flag was hoisted on the towers, the Turkish army band struck up a march, and the troops were drawn up in line and cried "Long live our Padishah" – for this was one of the Sultan's many titles. Thousands of Arabs listened submissively, with folded hands; tears of joy were shed; a grand salute was fired.

48

Consul Crow's dispatches were often sardonic in their style. "The report ends," he wrote, "with dithyrambic praises of the Sultan and congratulations on this happy event, anticipatory of further victories and successes due to the pious devotion, clemency and power of His Imperial Majesty." The pathos of Sudgi's report lay in the fact that he had not won any victory whatever. The sheiks were certainly laughing at him and his robes of honour. He was no more than a live bait in a trap. His life hung on the mercy of ibn Saud, who could cut his lines of supply at any moment – a mercy which would not be extended a moment longer than political expediency demanded.

With the Sultan thus placated and his forces successfully muzzled, ibn Saud and ibn Rashid were left in the desert to fight it out alone; but it was over a year before they met again in battle, and the year was filled by intrigues and strange manoeuvres. Although ibn Saud had conquered Buraida and Anaiza, he had not yet persuaded everyone in the towns to accept his domination; on the contrary, the towns were divided against themselves, some factions supporting him and some supporting ibn Rashid, and some plotting against them both with the Sheik of Kuwait. Nobody supported Sudgi, and it was only ibn Saud's own presence within fighting distance which kept the towns in peace and kept ibn Rashid at bay. But he suddenly decided to leave them to themselves, and embarked on an expedition to the sheikdom of Qatar on the coast of the Persian Gulf, where the Sheik and his brother were fighting for the throne.

In his absence, of course ibn Rashid advanced. He occupied Rass, the town where he and the Turks had been defeated, and beat off the supporters of ibn Saud who sallied out to fight him from Buraida; and he governed the district so harshly that after a while the people united and begged ibn Saud to come back.

Long afterwards, it was said that ibn Saud had foreseen exactly what would happen, and had deliberately made his journey and left the towns alone to find out for themselves which ruler they preferred. If he did, it must have been a stratagem without any precedent. To allow an enemy to capture a part of one's country, merely to show the people how unpleasant the enemy would be, was a risk which no wise ruler would have taken; and ibn Saud was certainly wise in his fashion. But the early deeds of great men are often given a gloss in later years, and there are two more likely and on the whole more sympathetic, explanations of his journey. One is that he did not want to meet General Sudgi, whom he had foisted on the people of Buraida, and be forced perhaps to demonstrate in public the humble devotion his father had professed in his private letters to the Sultan. The other explanation is that he had run out of money. Later in his reign, he was often to suffer this common embarrassment. According to the British Agent in Bahrain, the general opinion there was that he had come to borrow from the sheiks on the Trucial Coast. The Sheik of Kuwait also said this was the reason for the journey, and told Knox he had written to ibn Saud to advise him that it was always impolitic for a ruler to confess a lack of funds. But the minor sheiks along the coast were alarmed at his approach, and probably in a mood to offer a loan, if that would persuade him to go home again in peace.

However, whether he intended this or not, his absence gave the people of Buraida and Anaiza a taste of ibn Rashid's lash, and brought them more solidly to his side. The pause in his operations gave him another advantage too: it reduced General Sudgi's force to the edge of starvation. In the summer of 1905, Consul Crow intercepted a second dispatch from the General, and it was pitiably different from the first. He wrote that his men were in great straits for want of money and supplies; they were on half rations and – a grimly suggestive complaint – they could not even buy shrouds for their dead. Their sufferings were confirmed by a party of twenty-five deserters who made their way to Kuwait in the autumn, with a story of deaths and desertions which had halved the number of men under Sudgi's command.

Ibn Saud also made use of his journey to send two emissaries to Bahrain, one to visit the telegraph station, and the other to visit the British Political Agent. The first sent a very long and expensive telegram, in his own name, to the Sultan. It began with the costly words: "Whereas my devotion, honesty, sincerity, friendliness, zeal and sense of honour do not allow me to discontinue tendering advice to my religion, my government and my Sultan, whether it is accepted or not ..."; and it went on to protest yet again the fidelity of the House of Saud to Turkey. The British Agent received a copy of the telegram before it was sent; his methods of espionage, like Crow's, were simple and effective. A few hours later, the second emissary came to see him with a totally contradictory proposal. Ibn Saud, he said, now felt himself strong enough to eject the Turks not only from his own domain but from the Hasa, the area of the coast of the Gulf which they had occupied for over thirty years; and after he had done so, he would like to make a treaty with the British. He would allow the British to appoint political agents in his domain, including the Hasa, and the British, in return, would protect him against a Turkish counter-attack by sea.

Such whole-hearted duplicity always seemed to delight the

British officials in the Gulf; there was indeed something charming about it. It revealed, by paradox, the disarming innocence of the Arabs; for all governments are guilty of double dealing in their international affairs, but sophisticated governments disguise it with a diplomatic mask. It was the lack of this hypocritical disguise, rather than any intrinsic difference, which made the bare-faced trickery of Arab governments seem like a caricature of diplomatic practice; and sinners who sin openly are sometimes more attractive than those who disguise their sins and pretend to be virtuous. So the British Agent received the proposal straight-faced, but forwarded it to Cox with glee and sympathy. Cox sent it on to India, and it reached the Foreign Office, where it was rejected as firmly as ibn Saud's first plea for help against the Turks.

As soon as ibn Saud returned to Riyadh he marched again, to hunt for ibn Rashid and bring him to battle. By then, the opponents were evenly matched in power; but ibn Rashid seemed reluctant to face the final test, and most of the winter of 1905 was passed in minor skirmishes. Only one thing distinguished the rival armies: ibn Saud's was inflamed with a puritan ardour which ibn Rashid had never attempted to inspire. Ibn Rashid might well have feared that spirit. He may also have been afraid, in a more prosaic fashion, that ibn Saud would use the captured cannons; but in fact, ibn Saud had nobody in his army who had learned to fire them.

In a report from Kuwait, Knox said that a truce had been made between the two; he called it a hollow truce. But no truce was mentioned in Arabian stories of that winter, and Knox's information was probably wrong; for ibn Saud was strongly bound by the Bedouin code of honour, and if there was a truce he was guilty of breaking it in a way which he himself would certainly have thought was dishonourable.

It was in April, 1906. Ibn Rashid was camped in an oasis less than twenty miles north of Buraida. He was on a raiding expedition, and he looted a caravan which happened to be carrying supplies to his ally General Sudgi. It seems that he thought ibn Saud was far enough away for his camp to be secure. But the spies and outriders with which the Bedouin armies surrounded themselves had failed him. Ibn Saud was close at hand, and the master of the looted caravan came to ask for his help in revenge, and told him that ibn Rashid's camp was loosely guarded.

It was a perfect opportunity for the surprise which Bedouin commanders always sought but seldom achieved. At nightfall, ibn Saud led his men on foot to surround the oasis. Some say his approach was hidden by a sandstorm. In the darkness, his army fell on the sleeping camp, to butcher ibn

51

Rashid's men as they awoke. Ibn Rashid made a desperate and gallant attempt to rally them. In the manner of an Arab prince in war, he proudly proclaimed his presence, shouting his battle-verses; and was shot to death among the palm trees in the early light of dawn.

PART TWO

THE PURITAN

CHAPTER SIX

RELIGION AND THE SWORD

In the belief of ibn Saud, all the battles he fought and the conquests he won in a reign of fifty years were fought and won for God, and therefore one should not try to understand his battles without a little understanding of his faith.

Islam is fortunate in having the shortest of all creeds: there is no God but God, and Mahomed is the apostle of God. It is fortunate again that the first and most important part of this creed has a musical ring in Arabic: *La illah illa Allah*. These four words, so simple that the simplest nomads believe they understand them, and yet so profound that scholars study them for lifetimes, are always on the lips and in the minds of pious Moslems. They form a mother's lullaby, a war-cry, a chant for manual labour, a confession of faith before death; and they imply not only that the God of Islam is the only true God, but also that God is the one and only cause of the universe and every event in it, that God rules the world and directs its smallest details. Few Christians are so constantly aware of the influence of their God as Moslems are of theirs. Men pray, and God in his isolation hears, but He never answers, He only rewards or punishes. Men do their best, but success or failure in any enterprise whatever is in the hands of God. *Inshallah,* if God wills, is a pious Moslem's only reference to the future, whether he is concerned with a trivial hope or fear or a matter of life or death; and past achievements and disappointments are equally ascribed to God. So ibn Saud believed without question that God gave him Arabia to rule and delivered his enemies to him; he himself could only do his best.

This plain uncomplicated view of God's omnipotence was a product of desert surroundings thirteen hundred years ago: Mahomed lived in the desert cities of Mecca and Medina. It was an expression in spiritual terms of the unity, simplicity and starkness of the desert scene, and the fierce intolerance of the desert people. Conversely, desert life since the time of the Prophet was a product of the simple faith; faith gave the Arabs the most conspicuous qualities of their character and society. It made them unusually free from superstition; where God was the arbiter of every small event, there was not much need for luck. It freed them also from despair and useless regret for the past. It gave them their sense of equality, because the greatest and the least among believers

55

were equally dwarfed by the majesty of God; yet it also gave them their conceit and renewed their intolerance, for unbelievers of any rank or eminence were far inferior to the poorest of the faithful. It gave them all the education they ever had, for the few of them who learned to read at all read nothing but holy books and Islamic histories. Above all, perhaps, it gave them courage in battle. Although so few of them usually died in their battles, all of them were ready to die and many were even eager, for the one certain way of triumphant entry into Paradise, as Mahomed had taught, was to die a martyr in the cause of God. Paradise was very real to them, and very simple. Primitive people's idea of heaven always expresses what they want on earth, and the Bedouin's heaven provided cool breezes and streams of water, rest and shade, delicious food and drinks and perfumes, and as many beautiful compliant women as even a desert Arab could desire. Heaven was a desert heaven; the creed was a desert creed.

The creed was expressed, once and forever, in the Koran, a book of about the length of the New Testament; and the Koran laid several duties on believers. The first was to testify that "there is no God but God." Another was to pray five times a day, at sunset, in the evening, before sunrise, at noon and in the afternoon. A third was to fast in the month of Ramadan; a fourth, at least once in a lifetime, if it were possible, to make the pilgrimage to Mecca. A fifth was to give alms, and in consequence of this injunction, and of the natural generosity of Arabs, nobody in the desert was ever allowed to starve.

But as the creed spread out to other more sophisticated people, into more gentle climates and more fertile lands, it naturally changed. Intellectual interpretations were added to it, and theology grew around it. It divided into sects, absorbed existing faiths and superstitions, developed rituals and adornments, and recognised shrines which were reverenced and saints who were almost worshipped; and while it branched and flourished in the outer world, it started to lapse in the desert, and the Bedouin began to slip back to paganism.

Ibn Abdul-Wahhab's reformation in the eighteenth century was lauched against both these heresies, the adornment of Islam outside the desert and the relapse towards paganism within it. No doctrine could have been more puritan than his. He believed flatly that all objects of worship other than God himself were false, and that all who worshipped them were deserving of death. It was false worship to use the name of a prophet or saint or angel in a prayer, or to seek intercession from any being but God, or to make vows to any other being. So death was deserved in his eyes not only for any man of any other faith, but also for the great majority of Moslems. By his doctrine also, it involved unbelief to profess any knowledge which was not based on the Koran, the Sunna – the sayings and manner of life of the Prophet – or necessary inferences from them. This final dictum, perhaps the most restrictive religious doctrine every proclaimed, had an obvious appeal to the ignorant Bedouin of his own time or of the first half of the lifetime of ibn Saud: if one is very ignorant, nothing can be more comforting than to believe that other people's knowledge is sinful. The doctrine fought a losing battle when the products of western knowledge began to be seen in the desert, but it was a battle, and not a capitulation: motor cars, telephones, radio, aircraft – each was held in its turn to "involve unbelief", and was strongly opposed by the strictest of the Wahhabis.

Ibn Abdul-Wahhab's reformation, aided by the skill in warfare of the House of Saud, burst out of the desert at the end of the eighteenth century much as the Prophet's revelation had burst out of it eleven hundred years before. Of course, it was not a matter of the same importance; it was not a new religion, it was only a renewal of an old one, with an added fervent intolerance. It swept down to the Red Sea and overwhelmed the holy cities, invaded Persia and even spread to India. It so alarmed the Turks with its spiritual and military power that they incited or ordered Mahomed Ali, the ruler of Egypt, to destroy it, and in the course of a long and difficult campaign his armies reached the Saudi capital and sacked it in 1819. The Saudi dynasty revived from this defeat, and moved their capital to Riyadh, a village close to the ruins of the old one; but most of their power was gone. Wahhabism lingered on in the desert towns, but the nomad Bedouin, without a powerful leader to hold them to the faith or lead them to holy war, fell back again to pagananarchy.

It was exactly this reformation that ibn Saud hoped to start again: to reconvert the Bedouin to the Wahhabi faith, and then to spread it into the outer world. It is said that he consciously modelled himself on the Prophet and on his own great ancestor of the time of ibn Abdul-Wahhab. In him, religious and secular leadership were combined. Mahomed had his military captains, and the previous Saudi had his preacher; but ibn Saud to a great extent was both. Yet he had a degree of intelligence, finesse and common sense which are not always found in autocrats and fanatics, and extremely seldom found in desert Arabs: he knew when to fight and when to call a truce, when to insist and when to compromise. In the course of time, and before it was too late, he learned a lesson of Islamic history. The Prophet's revelation had been spread by preaching and the sword at a time when it was only opposed by swords. The Wahhabi revival had been beaten back by the weapons of early nineteenth-century Turkey. A new revival in the twentieth century could not be spread far by the Bedouin's swords or even their ancient rifles; before it roused the opposition of twentieth-century powers, it would have to use discretion and subtlety as weapons.

Although ibn Rashid had been ibn Saud's fiercest enemy and was dead, the weakness of his own command of his tribal troops prevented him from following up his victory. Ibn Rashid's capital town of Hail was far away, a campaign to capture it would have taken the whole of the winter, and he could not have taken the risk of leaving his own domain so long for fear of revolt at home. So ibn Rashid's sons were left to fight for the succession among themselves; but while they did so, they were no menace to ibn Saud.

The Turks, on the other hand, were easily disposed of. Poor General Sudgi had fulfilled his purpose, by keeping the Sultan content while ibn Saud defeated ibn Rashid. Ibn Saud did not even pay him the compliment of fighting him. He simply told the sheiks on Sudgi's lines of supply to stop giving help or protection to his caravans; and the remainder of the Turkish force, its supplies cut off and its dispatches never answered because they never reached the outside world, withered like a plant uprooted in the heat. Knox in Kuwait saw a line of emaciated soldiers struggling northwards through the desert behind the town. Crow in Basra reported that the Turks had offered an amnesty to their deserters. The last of the Sultan's armies in the central desert vanished with hardly a trace. He never sent another.

Thus for the moment the active external enemies of the kingdom were defeated: the dangers which beset it next came from within. Many of the sheiks in the kingdom itself grew jealous of ibn Saud's success; and, as he might have expected, many of the men who had fought for him grew bored and quarrelsome when he could offer them nobody else to fight against and plunder. His campaigns of the next few years are extremely confusing in retrospect, and must have been almost equally confusing for their victims. The trusted allies of one moment became the objects of fiercesome punitive expeditions in the next; vanquished rebels, on the other hand, returned to the court at Riyadh as loyal subjects; and ordinary nomads, wandering with their families and their herds, must have found it very hard to know from day to day whose side they were on and who was fighting whom.

It would be tedious now to try to follow all the permutations of friendship and enmity among the score or so of

powerful tribes within the kingdom, and it would probably
be impossible to follow them exactly; but through all the
confusion, a single-minded purpose can be traced in the actions of ibn Saud himself. The jealousy of sheiks and boredom of warriors broke out in different ways. Sometimes they
refused to pay levies of money or goods or troops, which he
had begun to demand from them to support the meagre funds
of his father's house. Sometimes they ostentatiously paid
these tributes to ibn Rashid's heirs. Sometimes they shut the
gates of walled towns against his emissaries, or murdered
the men he had appointed as local governors; and most often
of all, they raided other tribes or families who had been conspicuously loyal to him, and robbed them of their herds.

To all these affronts ibn Saud reacted with whirlwind energy, appearing in person, unheralded, wherever there was
trouble in the kingdom, assaulting recalcitrant towns, leading
his own fanatical fighters against any forces which opposed
him, demanding the return of stolen property, imposing arbitrary fines, often being wounded in battle – but always winning, if not at the first attempt, then at the second or the
third. And yet when he won, and the beaten sheiks were
brought before him for his judgment, he never had them
executed – except on one notable occasion – and seldom
imprisoned, but usually pardoned them and put them back
in their positions of authority. Autocrats with less wisdom,
all through human history, have ruled by killing people who
opposed them; ibn Saud ruled by proving he was able to kill
such people, and then inviting them to join him and overwhelming them with generosity.

The reports of British consuls on the fringes of the desert,
and the stories told in Arabian history, show glimpses of ibn
Saud in this campaign to prove his mastery – a campaign of
over five years of almost continual travelling and strife. Buraida was still among the scenes of trouble: ibn Saud's appointed governor turned against him and declared the town
and district independent. Ibn Saud himself found the gates
of the town were closed against him. He forced an entrance,
seized the governor, warned him against such folly and re-
appointed him. The governor did precisely the same thing
again. The second time, ibn Saud could not force his way in,
and he laid waste to the neighbouring villages till some of
the townspeople lost heart and let him in. Again he forbore
to cut off the governor's head – undoubtedly to the governor's surprise, for that was the recognised punishment for
treason; but this time, he let the governor go to live in exile
in Iraq.

That was in 1907 and 1908. 1909 reveals a glimpse of one
of his less successful expeditions, when he went to impose

his will on a minor tribe on the north-west verges of the kingdom which had paid its tribute to the tax-collectors of the House of Rashid. His raid succeeded, the tribe acknowledged its allegiance, and he demanded the payment he thought was his due; but his own tribal troops, who had seized the tribe's possessions on his orders, disbanded themselves and made off for their homes with the booty, leaving nothing for their leader to collect.

Three months later, he was at the other extremity of the kingdom, besieging a fort on the borders of the Hasa, demanding reparation for robberies committed by the tribe of that area, and the surrender of thirty of their leaders or the payment of blood-money in their stead. The Turkish governor of the Hasa, strangely enough, was called upon to arbitrate. The tribe refused the demand, but ibn Saud attacked them in their fort, and forced them to comply. The reparation was made and the leaders were surrendered: to be given a stern lecture at the moment when they expected to lose their heads.

The lesson he was trying to teach by these unusual tactics slowly began to permeate the desert; skeiks great and small began to understand they would have to become his followers and serve him faithfully, whether they did it before or after he had beaten them in battle. Mercy in victory was characteristic of Bedouin, whatever their ruthlessness in battle or in anger, and the mercy of ibn Saud was also a far-sighted policy. The sheiks he defeated in this period were potential Wahhabis, and his aim was not to decimate the Wahhabis, but on the contrary to strengthen them against the infidels. Furthermore, the tribes could not be left without any tribal leaders, and would certainly have resented and probably murdered any puppet leader he tried to impose on them. Alive, the defeated sheiks might be persuaded to be helpful; dead, they would only have been remembered as martyrs, for whom their tribes, by Bedouin custom, would have had to seek revenge.

But there were some too proud to accept his domination. Among these, the most formidable were his own cousins, the Araif, the "rescued camels", whom he had welcomed after his capture of Buraida. There were nine of these men; and as soon as ibn Saud had rebuilt an enviable kingdom they began to lay claim to the throne and to rouse whatever dissatisfied tribesmen they could in their support. The strongest uprising led by these pretenders began in the south, on the edge of the Empty Quarter, in 1910.

A number of local chieftains there had already risen against the rule of ibn Saud, and he had already defeated and pardoned them. This was merely the kind of rising and repression and forgiveness which had almost become a routine; the hands of the Araif behind it were not apparent at the time, and it was only distinguished by the first use of a stratagem which ibn Saud found useful more than once. He drove the rebels back into their town; but he was not able to take the town by assault, for the walls of the towns of the desert, like the walls of the towns of medieval Europe, were proof against the weapons of roving armies. So he told the rebels he had driven a mine underneath their fort and was ready to blow it up. It seems very unlikely that he really possessed the skill to dig a tunnel in secret, or enough explosive to blow up a fort, or the knowledge to fuse it; but whether or not the mine existed outside his imagination, the threat of it was enough to make the rebels surrender. He took the leaders to Riyadh as his guests. This was a polite kind of imprisonment, and it gave an opportunity for what is now called indoctrination; but it did not last long, and they soon went home again.

It was then that the Araif made use of these men, by re-arousing their opposition to ibn Saud, to set up a rival government in the southern part of the kingdom. Ibn Saud was obliged to go down there again, taking a larger force. Without much difficulty, he captured the local leaders again, together with the oldest and most troublesome of the Araif, whose name was the opposite of his own: Saud ibn Abdul-Aziz. The rest of the Araif fled, one to Oman, and some to the Hasa, and the rest to the protection of the Sherif of Mecca.

This was one of the few recorded occasions when ibn Saud took cold-blooded revenge on an enemy who surrendered. The second revolt had overstrained whatever reasons prompted him to mercy. More than a dozen of the local leaders were paraded before him with halters round their necks, and then publicly beheaded in their own market-place. But he pardoned his cousin Saud. It is said that Saud had to watch the heads of his confederates falling one by one, and only received his pardon when the sword was poised at the back of his own neck. That may be fiction, but it has a ring of truth, for Arab punishments were forceful; and Saud remained loyal and held high office under his cousin's rule for the rest of his life.

By 1911, these energetic tactics had dazed the desert people and imposed a kind of peace on them, or at least a pause in their habitual state of tribal war, and for a few years he was free to give less of his energy to fighting and more to the other pursuits of kingship. He could hunt, and encourage sports, and pay more attention to the needs of his many wives, and enjoy the stimulus of a fresh one as often as he wished; and he could play with the older children of the colossal family he was founding, and continue to rebuild the palaces in Riyadh which ibn Rashid had destroyed in his régime. And so effective was his building, both of family and palaces, that a traveller reported, in 1914, that no less than a third of the whole of the town of Riyadh was taken up by the houses of his relations: his wives and concubines and children, and the multitudinous cousins who had thrown in their lot with his.

During these years ibn Saud had some leisure at last; and perhaps one may presume that he used it to think about what he was trying to do, and what direction his life's ambitions were to take. He was still only twenty-six. In four years, he had won a kingdom which in mere physical size was almost as big as France, and had spread his puritan ideals all over it. But so far, it was only a kingdom in name – if indeed it should even be called a kingdom, for he did not assume the title of king until twenty years later. It still had no system of government or law. It still only existed because the sheiks in it either admired him or feared him; and he still knew that any or all of them would turn against him if ever they lost their admiration or overcame their fear.

As for the humble subjects of the kingdom, they had no conception of an orderly society, and certainly would not have liked it if they had. Such a thing had never existed in the desert, and few of them knew it existed anywhere else. Being illiterate, and being totally isolated by the desert and their own intolerance, they had no reason to try to imagine Edwardian England, or America under Theodore Roosevelt, as societies which co-existed with their own. A civilised rule of law would have ruined their sports of raiding and robbery, and the archaic custom of feuds between rival tribes; and when it destroyed these sports, it would also have undermined the Bedouin concept of honour and chivalry. Submission to a man-made set of laws would have reduced a Bedouin, in his own eyes, to a status no better than his slaves'.

And yet, on the other hand, no kingdom could ever be stable while its citizens lived the violent lives of Bedouin. Many Arabian rulers before ibn Saud had created kingdoms in the desert as large as his; but most of the kingdoms had broken up as soon as the rulers died, whether they died by violence or were cunning or lucky enough to die in their beds. Very often, the kingdoms had been destroyed by quarrels within the vast families of rival sons that polygamous rulers begat. That had happened when ibn Saud's grandfather died, it had happened not ten years before in Kuwait, and it was happening at that very moment not only in Qatar, but also in ibn Rashid's kingdom; for on ibn Rashid's death, all his sons hurried home from the battlefield, each hoping to be the first to seize the throne, and four successive occupants of it were murdered in the next two years.

Even at the height of the power of the Arab empire a thousand years before, when Arab influence spread from Spain to China, Central Arabia had remained as lawless as ever. The splendid flower of Arab civilisation was rooted in the desert, but it only achieved its splendour on the margins of the area it covered, where Arab energy impinged on older civilised societies. In the desert itself, the energy was dissipated even then in tribal quarrels and the endless struggle to win a living from the land. So, however far back one searched in the desert's history, it was hard to find stories of any government which was more than ephemeral.

But that was what ibn Saud had begun to hope to create. While he was still in his twenties he had conceived the ideal of a law-giving government and a stable kingdom which would exist and support itself without depending on his personal authority. Not only that; he had also discerned the only possible means to achieve this revolution. The Bedouin, or some of them, must give up their nomad lives and turn from herding to agriculture; for a nomad may make his own laws, but a man who has tilled a plot of land and planted a crop on it must always have an interest in stable government from one harvest to the next. To invite the Bedouin to submit to law in their present kind of life was useless, but some might be invited to accept a piece of land and be tempted to a life of more comfort and less hunger; and having accepted that, they might find that law and order were desirable. Ibn Saud thought of building settlements in the oases of the kingdom, where men would be drawn from many different tribes, to be united by their Wahhabi faith instead of their tribal loyalties, and to give allegiance to God and him instead of their tribal sheiks. These religious yet secular communities were to be called the Ikhwan – the Brotherhood.

It is hard to say how such ideas, in the intervals between primeval battles, came into the head of this remarkable young man. He had been given more education than most of his people, but it was only an education within the fanatically narrow limits of Wahhabi doctrine. He had no experience of any ways of life except those of the desert and the desert towns. He had never seen a civilised city or a well-cultivated countryside, and had never met anyone who had travelled farther than Cairo, Baghdad or Bombay. He cannot have read about the civilised countries of his day, because he only read Arabic and his reading was confined to the Koran and a few religious works of puritan merit. Even picture books, which might have given him some impression of the achievements of civilised life, are unlikely to have come into his hands, for Wahhabis so detested the worship of images that they distrusted photography and drawing, especially of any human figure. It seems indeed that his plans to civilise his unruly countrymen were not derived from any teaching, but solely from his own spontaneous thought, and perhaps from the distant example of Mahomed himself. To rise in such a manner above one's circumstances might well be accepted as a mark of genius; and if it is, ibn Saud was certainly a genius.

With these origins, it is not surprising that the system of government he devised was crude and autocratic; it is only surprising that he devised any system at all. It is not surprising that the methods he used to achieve his aims seemed bloodthirsty to Europeans half a centry later; it is only surprising that he succeeded. In all his actions, martial and marital, he lived in accordance with the morals of his place and time, and to judge him by any other moral standard would be wrong.

Having established some form of military security ibn Saud could make an attempt to put the financial affairs of the kingdom into order. These were always extremely precarious, for the only sources of revenue were levies and tolls on the sheiks and merchants, who had little enough themselves. The kingdom had nothing to export, except camels and horses, and its needs in cotton cloth and rice and coffee and ammunition had to be bought abroad. Most of this elementary trade was carried on by barter, and the amount of money in circulation was minute.

What there was of it was in Maria Theresa dollars. These large silver coins were originally an Austrian currency, but were popular throughout the east, largely, it is said, because they bore a portrait of the Empress not merely unveiled, but displaying a splendid bosom in a low-cut gown. She died in 1780, but the coins have been minted almost ever since, still bearing the date of her death. Towards the end of his life, when oil had made him a multi-millionaire, ibn Saud recollected with wry amusement the time when he could carry the whole of the kingdom's treasury in silver dollars in his saddle-bags.

As soon as he had achieved some degree of peace within the kingdom, he started to realise his idealistic plan: to found the Ikhwan settlements. Some authorities see these settlements as the greatest of his achievements; for the battles and diplomatic intrigues were merely the means of building a kingdom: the settlements were a means of giving it permanence. The first stage had often been achieved in Arabian history, but the second never.

Puritan though he was, there were people in the kingdom
64

far stricter than ibn Saud himself. Religious authority existed in parallel with his own secular authority, and he always had to take care that it was on his side. Religious power lay largely in the hands of the Ulema, the Learned Men, elders whose main concern was to see that the Wahhabi interpretation of the precepts of the Koran were observed to the very letter, together with those of the Sunna. Ibn Saud used religious fervour as a source of courage and recklessness among his fighting men; but the same fervour could have been turned against him by the Ulema, who critically watched every move he made and every opinion he expressed. Ibn Saud was the ruler, under God, but the Ulema looked on themselves as the guardians of the people's conscience, and they guarded nobody's conscience more carefully than his.

To satisfy the more bigoted of these fanatics sometimes strained what little patience ibn Saud possessed. He was too intelligent and wise and humorous to follow all their extremes of zealotry. He administered strict, cruel punishments for crimes, which he believed were necessary in ruling Bedouin; but he cared much less about the punishments the Ulema inflicted for minor sins – the ferocious public floggings in the market-place of Riyadh for smoking a cigarette, or singing, or being late for prayers. He sympathised least of all with the attitude of mind which makes it a sin to enjoy life, or seem to enjoy it – an attitude the Ulema shared, though they did not know it, with puritans of other religions than their own. Ibn Saud openly enjoyed all the pleasures his faith allowed him: sex and battle and sport, political intrigue, heroic and bawdy stories and practical jokes, generosity and hospitality, and above all, perhaps, the fulfilment of ambition. But merely by enjoying life frankly, he risked the enmity of the Ulema.

One object of the Ikhwan settlements was therefore to keep the Ulema contented and tie them to himself by a common interest. Among Bedouin, the Ulema's successes in preaching were hard to win and harder to maintain. The Bedouin would accept Wahhabism with a cruel zeal so long as they could put the name of heretic to the people they wanted to slaughter anyway; but they would discard the faith as quickly whenever it failed to suit their changing lusts and purposes. As a practical matter, when Bedouin were scattered sparsely through the desert, the preachers could not keep them under constant influence. But to bring the Bedouin into settlements gave the Ulema entirely new chances to plant their faith and see that their converts never lapsed from it; and so it helped to ensure the Ulema's support for ibn Saud, whose strength was the only guarantee of the peace which the settlements needed to put down their roots and grow.

Thus the settlements were firstly designed to be religious, a brotherhood in God; but their secular purposes were essential too. After God, their allegiance was to ibn Saud, and he meant them to provide a corps of troops whose loyalty would not be subject to the whims of minor sheiks. In this purpose, they almost succeeded too well. For more than the first decade of their existence, they formed the backbone of his army; but a time was to come when their fanatical brutality put him to shame, and he had to quell the monstrous faith he had given such power to.

The first settlement was founded in 1913 at wells called Artawiya, between Kuwait and Buraida. The Ulema sent preachers, and ibn Saud scraped up the money to pay for new mosques and extra wells for irrigation, and Artawiya grew and flourished quickly. It had its troubles. The Bedouin who accepted plots of land found farming was harder work than they expected, and the puritan teaching did not give them much incentive for growing rich. They began to degenerate into idle paupers, and the books of religion had to be searched for words which commended the earning of riches and the pleasures which riches could buy. But that phase was overcome. Within ten years, Artawiya had grown to a town as large as Riyadh, and sixty other settlements had been founded. It was said that by then, if ibn Saud had called out all the Ikhwan, he could have brought together sixty thousand men, each eager to kill or to die for their God and for him. But he never encountered a crisis which needed an army of anything like that size. Instead, the Ikhwan gave him a great reserve of power, from which he could always draw whatever force he needed; and it was a force of men who were always fresh and always changing, with a lust for battle and plunder, or reward in Paradise, which was always new and sharp; men far more ruthless and far more terrible than the tribal levies of his earlier days; men who spread fear and respect for the justice of ibn Saud, and gathered stories of courage and atrocity; in some eyes the heroes of the faith, and in others mere mad and wanton slaughterers.

So the settlements gave the Ulema new fields for the harshest extremes of their Wahhabi faith, and gave ibn Saud, in the end, a military strength which no other ruler in Arabia could resist, except those who had British support. But their importance was greater still. In them was created a new class of citizen in Arabia, a class between the merchants of the towns and the untameable men of the desert. This new class, by its very existence, tipped the balance from barbarity towards a kind of civilisation. For the first time in the desert's history, the proportion of men who were settled and more or less amenable to law was enough to form the foundation of a stable state; and it was on that foundation that the state of Saudi Arabia began to grow.

But it had not been able to start its growth in total isolation. Just before his execution of the traitors in the south, ibn Saud had been back to Kuwait to visit Sheik Mubarrak, and while he was there he had dined with a young Englishman whose name was William Shakespear.

CHAPTER SEVEN

SHAKESPEAR

This notable dinner party was held in the first week of March, 1910. Shakespear had taken over from Knox as Political Agent. Ibn Saud accepted his invitation, and also brought his brothers Saad and Abdullah to dinner, and his eldest son Turki, who was nine. Shakespear reported afterwards that his guests were "very pleasant"; and that extremely inadequate comment provides all that is known of ibn Saud's first meeting with a Christian. One would have liked to know what they talked about, and what ibn Saud thought of Shakespear, and even what they ate: whether Shakespear provided sheep roasted whole on heaps of rice and ate them with his right hand on the floor, or whether he made ibn Saud sit down at a table with the profusion of cutlery and the eight or nine courses of an Edwardian English dinner. But nobody recorded these things, and everybody who dined that night is dead or has forgotten.

William Shakespear indeed appears in the history of ibn Saud's Arabia as a tenuous character. His middle names were Henry Irvine, but in spite of the doubly theatrical air of his names, he had become a captain in the Indian Army. He died young, so that his qualities are remembered more dimly than those of most of his contemporaries; but he played an important part in this history, and if he had lived a little longer he might have achieved as much in Arab warfare as another man of his generation on the other side of Arabia: T. E. Lawrence. He was about the same age as ibn Saud: both were just over thirty when they met. His colleagues spoke of him, after he was dead, as a man of energy and humour. He was an expert in boats, and sailed the Persian Gulf in a small steam pinnace which belonged to the agency. Cox remembered watching him on a dirty night at the head of the Gulf from the dignified deck of the steamer which plied between the ports. The pinnace was punching into a steep head sea and taking it green. It hove to, the steamer altered course to see if he needed help, and Shakespear leant out of his boat with a megaphone and offered the steamer a tow. He became an expert camel rider too, and made very extensive journeys in the desert. Above all, to judge from his rare dispatches, he had youthful enthusiasm and a spirit of adventure; and these were qualities which might have endeared him to ibn Saud, who certainly shared them.

He had just come back from a month in the desert when he asked ibn Saud to dinner. Knox had made journeys too, but none so ambitious. Perhaps he had never had time. His five years in Kuwait had mostly been spent in patiently build-ing a solid relationship with Sheik Mubarrak. To set a formal seal on his success before he left, he had made a presentation to the Sheik on behalf of the British Government: a portrait in oils of King Edward VII, and two saluting guns, a quick-firing Hotchkiss three-pounder and a brass muzzle-loading six-pounder. The Sheik mounted the muzzle-loader in front of his palace gates, and the Hotchkiss in the bows of a steam yacht he had recently acquired – a yacht complete with a Scottish engineer. He also hung the portrait in his palace; but one may suppose he preferred the guns, for within a few weeks a requisition had to be sent to India for extra ammuni-tion. Kuwait in fact, was safely within the British orbit, and it was Knox's pioneering work which enabled Shakespear to leave his post so long.

He travelled with half a dozen Arabs, including a falconer whom the Sheik had insisted on sending with him – perhaps more to report on what he did than to offer him sport – and he covered 450 miles: the first European to penetrate so far inland from the coast of the Gulf since Colonel Pelly in 1865. He was soon caught up in the feuds and raids of the border-lands where Sheik Mubarrak's territory merged with ibn Saud's. At some wells, his followers advised him to approach by night, in order to avoid a dominant local tribe; at others, they insisted on going by day for fear of outlaws who might be there at night. On one evening, Shakespear had the full-blooded experience of a Bedouin raid. The dust of horsemen was seen; his own men ran to defensive positions in the dunes; the horsemen, twenty or thirty strong, galloped towards them in a semicircle, shouting and firing wildly. His men fired back; their shooting, he said, was execrable. The raiders took no notice of the defenders or their fire, but galloped through them towards the camels which they meant to seize. As they passed, Shakespear's Arabs recognised the war-cries of a tribe which happened to be friendly at the moment with Sheik Mubarrak, and they stood up and shouted back and waved their head-cloths and their rifles. Soon the raiders were drink-ing Shakespear's coffee, laughing at their comical mistake, and instructing him in the arts of raiding: telling him, for ex-ample, that Bedouin in winter could go for three days with-out water and two without food, but that their mares needed water after thirty hours. Shakespear described this minor ad-venture to ibn Saud; and ibn Saud, he reported to Cox, "ex-pressed considerable surprise at the length and distance of my tour, and still more that I had enjoyed it."

This was the best introduction he could have had to ibn Saud. The Victorian explorers of Arabia, with the exception of Colonel Pelly, had disguised themselves as Moslems; but the explorers of the twentieth century, of whom Shakespear was among the first, discovered that if a man was willing to live in the Bedouin fashion, and if he sincerely sympathised with Bedouin aspirations, most of the Bedouin would accept him as a friend and let him remain an infidel. Ibn Saud himself, when he was older, had to learn to deal with Europeans and Americans who made no concession to Arab customs or manners or beliefs; but it was lucky that the first European he met was a young soldier, an enthusiast, a man flexible enough in mind and tough enough in body to take to the desert ways, and ready to see the joke when he was shot at.

The two men did not meet again till the following spring, when Shakespear made another long journey into the desert and, whether by luck or design, found ibn Saud and his army on the march. This journey, like the first, was a remarkably adventurous undertaking. For all that he could have known, he was putting his head into the Wahhabi lion's mouth. His status as a British official would have protected him from an overt violence; but accidents often happened in the desert, and if they did not happen they were perfectly easily arranged. But the journey went well. In the diary which he kept meticulously, Shakespear excelled his previous reticence. All that he wrote, on 6th March, 1911, was: "Camped with ibn Saud. Raining." But this time, when he returned to Kuwait, he did write a dispatch which gives the first glimpse of ibn Saud through European eyes.

"Ibn Saud," he reported to Cox, "gave the impression of being endowed with a particularly straightforward, frank and generous nature. He treated me most hospitably and in the most genuinely friendly manner. He and his brothers did not show a trace of the fanatical spirit which might have been expected from the ruling Wahhabi family, and his advisers and the leaders of his forces also treated me and my men with the most cordial friendship. I feel convinced of the correctness of this impression, for I frequently discussed matters of doctrine custom and religion which are held to be anathema by the Wahhabi sect, and was always answered with calm and intelligent reasoning without a trace of fanatical heat. I was habitually addressed as 'brother', and if I had been one in fact I could not have been treated more as one of the family."

Fanatics often become more placid when their fights are won, and it is a sign of the growth of ibn Saud's self-confidence at that stage of his career that he could show such friendly feelings for a Christian foreigner, without caring what other Wahhabis would think about it. It must have cost him some thought to overcome the religious scruples he was heir to, and some effort to make his followers do the same; for none of them had ever seen anybody so outrageously infidel as Shakespear in his sun-helmet and his British uniform. Ibn Saud himself had reasons for being friendly with the British in a diplomatic sense, but he was never enough of a diplomat and an actor to make much show of friendship face to face unless he felt it – his duplicity to the Sultan had all been expressed by letter or by his father; and his followers in camp knew nothing of his politics. So one can only conclude that something in Shakespear's behaviour really endeared him to them all.

Ibn Saud was determined to talk politics. He told Shakespear that in secret, without telling anyone but his father, he had just sent an emissary to try to see Cox in Bushire. He still wanted the British to accept the idea he had put to Cox six years before: that he would turn the Turks out of the Hasa, the British would guarantee him against a Turkish counter-attack by sea, and he in return would welcome British political agents in his kingdom. Shakespear, of course, knew that the British Foreign Office had firmly turned this proposition down when it was made. He protested to ibn Saud that he had not come to talk politics, but simply to enjoy a desert journey, and to meet him on his native hearth and see how an Arab chief lived in the desert. He said he had no sort of authority to discuss political problems, but he was sure the British Government would not support ibn Saud against the Turks. They had always confined their interests to the coast, and they were on amicable terms with the Turkish Government and would be averse from anything like an intrigue against it.

But he could not escape by pretending to be an innocent traveller. Ibn Saud told him the whole history of the past century in Arabia from the Wahhabi point of view, to convince him, though he needed no convincing, that the Saudis were the true hereditary rulers of the central desert; and he said that all the Princes of Arabia were in correspondence with each other, making plans to attack the Turks simultaneously and drive them out of the country for good and all.

His proposition about the Hasa seemed much more reasonable, in the way he expressed it himself, than the bare request for British protection had seemed when Cox received it. The Saudis, he said, bitterly resented the Turkish occupation of the Hasa, but they thought an expedition against it would be fruitless if the Turks could bring in unlimited troops by sea. They could only do that if the British let them through. Yet the British had kept the peace at sea in the Persian Gulf for

71

a century, and stopped anyone sailing on it with warlike intentions; surely, therefore, they would not allow the Turks to do so. By turning the Turks out of country which had always belonged to Saud, he would become the ruler of part of the coast of the Gulf; all he asked then was that the British should treat him as they treated all the other rulers – Sheik Mubarrak, the Sheiks of Bahrain and Qatar and the Trucial Coast, and the Sultan of Muscat, most of whom would certainly have been overrun by the Turks or Persians if the British Navy had not been vigilant. He finished with a piece of flattery which probably expressed a perfectly sincere belief: he was appealing to the English, he said, because they were always for peace and justice and could be trusted to keep their promises.

This proposition must have appealed to Shakespear; but knowing his own government, and having some idea of other points of view, he did not let enthusiasm run away with him. He promised ibn Saud to pass on what he said to his superiors, but he warned him he did not think he would get the answer he wanted. Then he rode back to Kuwait to draft a dispatch to Cox. He was young, and still on one of the lowest rungs of the ladder of his service, and he expressed his own opinion with formal diffidence. "I venture to think," he wrote, "that with ibn Saud established in the Hasa and in friendly relations with us, our position would be considerably strengthened." Any British official in the Gulf would have recognised this as a splendid understatement.

Shakespear's dispatch was important enough to go almost the whole way up through the hierarchy of British government, collecting minutes as it went; but the higher it went, the less enthusiasm it aroused. Cox was just starting on a journey and had no time to comment, except to remark that the emissary of ibn Saud had indeed reached Bushire, but had been sent away again without a conclusive answer because he had brought no letter of authority. But Cox had often expressed his own opinion. He would have welcomed more friendly intercourse with ibn Saud, and would much have preferred ibn Saud to the Turks as a ruler of the Hasa. But he was still unconvinced about making a specific treaty because he was still uncertain whether ibn Saud was a match for the Turks in the long run.

In 1911, the world was still in the railway age, and railways were the backbone of strategy. Observers of Arabian affairs were obsessed by the importance of two railways which the Turks were building, one to Baghdad and the other – which achieved a kind of fame unique among railways when Lawrence destroyed it – through Palestine and the Hejaz to Medina, with an extension planned to Mecca. Three years before, Cox had noted that ibn Saud's domain was clear of Turkish troops, but he had added: "The Hejaz railway is gradually outflanking it from the west, and the darkening shadow of the Baghdad railway threatens it from the north. It is difficult to see how, in the absence of some diversion in its favour, Central Arabia is to escape ultimate absorption by the Turks." There is no reason to think that he had changed his mind, and he was right to reserve his judgment. He had not yet had Shakespear's experience of meeting ibn Saud, and had not felt the strength of his confidence or the force of his personality. And indeed a "diversion" did save Arabia from the fate he had foreseen: no less a diversion than the first world war. But in the meantime, while this doubt remained, ibn Saud's hope of a treaty with Britain was doomed; for to back a loser is the classic mistake which all diplomats hope to avoid.

Nevertheless, the India Office was tempted by the idea. A draft minute to the Foreign Office, which was never sent, went so far as to say "It is worth thinking of, in case they drive us to extremes"; and "they" were the Turks. But the minute which actually passed across the Whitehall court-yard, from the Under Secretary of State for India to the Under Secretary of State for Foreign Affairs, was rather more guarded and very much more verbose. "Objections to a policy of adventure in Central Arabia," it said, "are not less strong than when the question was under consideration in 1904. But in view of the intractable attitude of the Turkish Government in the Persian Gulf it is important that His Majesty's Government should leave none of the weapons at their disposal unexamined. It is evident that one of the most powerful of these is such a response to the overtures now made by Abdul-Aziz ibn Saud as would render the position of the Turks on the Arabian coast of the Gulf untenable." After the reference to weapons at the government's disposal, a separate and still more cautious hand, using red ink, wrote in the addition: "though the question of employing one or more of them at any particular time must require separate consideration."

So Shakespear's zealous dispatch reached the desk of Sir William Lee-Warner, who was a councillor in the India Office; and his comment was a masterpiece of damp discouragement.

"I think we must be very careful not to be drawn into Arabian affairs," he wrote. "There is no reference to the railway in this conversation, but the line to Mecca may well make all the difference to Turkish strength. Again, if the Turk should be turned out of Europe he will become a dangerous customer in Asia. Abdul-Aziz under feelings of hostility to

73

the Turks speaks friendly and would welcome a British political (agent), but remove the Turkish pressure and he would want to sweep away Muscat and rule to the sea. Behind Turkey may stand Germany, and with the uncertainties of the future I hope that neither from Aden, nor from Muscat, nor from Kuwait shall we be tempted to interfere or even directly interest ourselves in Wahhabi or Central Arabian affairs."

Such ponderous caution is never so charming as the youthful impulsive hopes it extinguishes; and when youthful judgments are proved by events to be right it is only too easy, in retrospect, to scorn the maturer judgments which were wrong. Shakespear turned out to be right, and Lee-Warner to be wrong. The railway made no decisive difference, and it never reached Mecca; when the Turks were turned out of Europe, they were turned out of their Asian empire too; and Muscat was never swept away by ibn Saud. And yet, looking back from so far away in time, it is only right to admit that a policy of adventure may build an empire, but a policy of caution is needed to maintain it. Perhaps Lord Curzon was the only man of his time who might have torn this memorandum into shreds, with all its unjustified assumptions and suppositions, and its red herring of Germany. The Foreign Office, consciously correct, suggested that if the Government of India wanted to propose a change of policy towards Arabia, they should state a case for it; but Curzon had left India, and the Government of India never tried.

In spite of such disappointments, or perhaps as a solace, Shakespear continued his desert explorations in the intervals of desk-work in Kuwait, and in February, 1914, he left the town on his longest and most adventurous journey. In three months, he rode right across Arabia and reached the northern end of the Red Sea coast near Aqaba, and he made a long detour to visit Riyadh. He camped a mile outside the town, and went into it several times to visit ibn Saud – the first European who had seen the place since Colonel Pelly. While he was there, he watched ibn Saud assembling his men and camels for a raiding expedition, and wrote in his diary that he had had the awe-inspiring experience of seeing the great man lose his temper.

In the latter part of this tremendous journey, Shakespear crossed the tracks which Lawrence was to follow three years later, during the war, in leading the Arab revolt; and when Lawrence passed that way, he met men who had travelled with Shakespear, and heard "tales of his magnificence and of the strange seclusion in which he kept himself day and night."* Shakespear's wish for seclusion is understandable;

* *Seven Pillars of Wisdom*, chapter xlv.

74

Lawrence shared it, and it was only conspicuous by contrast with the gregarious habits of the Bedouin, who in Lawrence's phrase "usually lived in heaps." But Lawrence's choice of the word magnificence only adds to the enigma of Shakespear's character. Shakespear always travelled light, with an escort so small that the least of Bedouin sheiks would have been disgraced by it. Furthermore, by the time he reached Lawrence's country he was almost penniless; he had nothing left which he could offer as a gift to sheiks who gave him hospitality and, when he needed a guide, he had to bargain parsimoniously because he could not afford the usual fee. There was certainly no physical magnificence, in his appearance or accoutrements, sufficient to impress the Arabs and stay in their memories and add to their camp-fire stories. Perhaps it was magnificence of personality.

One may guess that ibn Saud talked politics again when Shakespear passed through Ryadh. Shakespear made no mention of politics in his diary; but apart from his usual reticence, this was a matter of commonsense discretion, for travelling in Arabia was still precarious, and if he had died or his diary had been stolen, political notes might have embarrassed ibn Saud, or the British Government, or both. It is also fair to guess that they talked again about the Hasa, and that something Shakespear said persuaded ibn Saud that the British were never likely to give him the protection at sea he had asked for so many times; for within two months of Shakespear's visit, ibn Saud had decided to act without British help. He took the warpath again, for the *coup d'état* he had waited ten years to perform: the ejection of the Turks from the last of his father's kingdom.

The principle town of the Hasa was Hofuf: a larger place than Riyadh itself, with a wall and a very strong fortress. Ibn Saud's assault was a mixture of the tricks he had used in the capture of Riyadh and the attack on the southern rebels. In May, 1914, he led a mere hundred bravados into the town by night, and crossed the fortress walls with palm-trunk scaling-ladders, and drove the Turkish commander and most of his officers and a few of his men to refuge in the mosque; and there he threatened them with a real or imaginary mine beneath the mosque, and offered the alternatives of being blown up or surrendering and accepting his safe-conduct to the coast. There was some hesitation. It was hard to believe the Wahhabi leader would commit the sacrilege of blowing up the mosque; but he persuaded the commander that he meant it. The Turks surrendered, gave up their arms, and submitted to being escorted to the coast and embarked for the voyage home. No British help was needed. A feeble counter-attack from Bahrain was repulsed, and within a few weeks, with little bloodshed, the last of the Turks had left the Hasa, never to return.

It was none too soon. Five months later, Britain and Turkey were at war, and the Persian Gulf, which had always been a backwater of trade and diplomacy, had become a main channel for British troopships. If the Turks had still been in the Hasa then, it would have been the British, not ibn Saud, who turned them out. Probably the British would have returned the Hasa to its historic owners; but possibly they would have discovered what nobody yet suspected: that this dreary stretch of sand concealed immeasurable wealth.

CHAPTER EIGHT

DEATH OF AN ENGLISHMAN

After his journey, Shakespear went home on leave. He had hardly arrived in England when war was declared between Britain and Germany. Three months later, Turkey was dragged into the war on the German side, and an expeditionary force of the Indian Army had landed at the head of the Persian Gulf to begin the long and costly campaign of Mesopotamia; and Kuwait, where Shakespear had served so long alone, was full of the clamour of a passing army.

This was a good example of the way in which wars between major powers spread, involving countries which have no part in the original dispute, reviving old irrelevant enmities, and setting men to slaughter other men whom they have never heard of, for causes which they cannot understand. The governments of Britain and Turkey had no real reason to fight each other; still less had the people of Britain and Turkey; and still less again the people of Turkey and the Indians, on whom much of the suffering of the fighting fell. In 1908 revolution had broken out in Turkey, and in 1909 the old Sultan had been deposed in favour of his younger brother; and since then, relations between the governments had been cordial, or at least quiescent. Most of the Turks who knew anything at all about the British rather liked them, but many senior officers of the Turkish Army had been trained in Germany. In 1913, these officers overthrew the government; and soon after the outbreak of war, under German pressure, they had involved their country in such openly war-like acts that the three allies Britain, France and Russia inevitably declared themselves at war with her. By then, the Indian Army was already on its way to the Gulf; and so, because Germany had challenged Britain in Europe, British, Indian, and Turkish soldiers were thrown into battle in a land which was foreign to them all.

Such civilised and complicated war contrasts with the wars which ibn Saud had fought. The archaic Bedouin battles, deplorable though they were, were direct expressions of the primitive instinct to fight which many men still possess. The Bedouin fought hand to hand, against an enemy they could see personified, in support of a leader they admired and knew; and everybody had a good time, except the people who happened to be hurt. The same might be said of football, but it could not be said of the impersonal slaughter and deluded loyalties of modern wars.

77

The first world war, however, had very little effect on the lives of ibn Saud's people. It surged round his frontiers, but his deserts and his towns were left in peace, or in their usual state of homely tribal conflict.

To follow his fortunes in that war, one must glance at its strategy. The accession of Turkey brought Germany immense advantages. Turkey controlled the Dardanelles, and could cut off the Russian Black Sea fleet; through Palestine, she could threaten Egypt and the Suez Canal; and through Mesopotamia and Persia she could stir up trouble in Afghanistan, and might even threaten the north-west frontier of India. Above all, Germany expected that the Sultan, in his capacity as Caliph, would proclaim a Holy War, unite all Islam against the British, and cause revolution amongst the millions of Moslems within the British Empire. Although Britain was a Christian country, the British Empire was by far the largest Moslem community in the world. In India alone, there were many more Moslems than in the whole of Turkey and Arabia, and they included so many of the troops of the Indian Army that revolt among them would have crippled Britain in the East. But this last expectation, of course, was never fulfilled. The Sultan did proclaim a Holy War, but it had no consequences anywhere outside Turkey. The Moslems under British rule put their secular loyalty first, and the Arabs took no notice of the proclamation.

In 1914, there were only four aircraft in India, and the military use of motor transport was experimental. The movement of an army to any battlefield was a matter of ships or railway trains or mules and horses – and of colossal route-marches by the infantry. By these means, there were only two possible battlegrounds on which the British could come to grips with Turkey on its Asiatic side: roughly speaking, the top of the Red Sea and the top of the Persian Gulf. Between these two was the desert; and it was elementary that whichever of the two belligerents could win the desert Arabs to its side could use them to harass the flank of its enemy in both the impending campaigns. In the west, so long as the Sherif of Mecca was loyal to his Turkish overlord, the whole of Britain's traffic through Suez and the Red Sea was sailing uncomfortably close to an enemy shore for nearly a thousand miles. In the east, the routes of communication from the head of the Gulf to Baghdad were the rivers Tigris and Euphrates; and the Euphrates was vulnerable to anyone who emerged from the desert to attack it. So the Sherif of Mecca and ibn Saud, and to some extent ibn Rashid (the son of the ruler ibn Saud had killed), found themselves in the strong position of being wooed by each of two wealthy enemies. Of the three, ibn Saud was uncommitted, though certainly not very fond of Turks in general; the Sherif was under Turkish domination but far too ambitious to be satisfied with that inferior position; and the House of Rashid, having always been cut off from British influence by the territory of the other two, inevitably started on the Turkish side. The desert allegiances, in fact, were nicely balanced, and the only consideration which weighed with the Arab rulers was their own self-interest.

To say this is not to be critical. The justice of the British war, whatever it was, had nothing to do with the Arabs. The British were convinced that right was on their side, but so were the Turks. As allies, from the Arab point of view, there was something to be said for either. The British had a reputation, at least in the Gulf, for honesty and fairness: the Turks had a reputation everywhere for barbarous cruelty. On the other hand, the British were Christians and the Turks were fellow-Moslems. Both of them were willing to promise the Arabs immediate bribes, and also to promise them independence when the war was won. So the choice of the Arabs could only depend on the size of the bribes, and on which side they thought was going to win. Whenever British campaigns were going well, the Arabs' support was ardent: after such disasters as Gallipoli and the Siege of Kut, it noticeably cooled.

It was the Turks who first reached Riyadh, in 1914, with offers of money and armaments. The Government of India, with its three-man establishment in the Gulf, had nobody qualified and free to go to see ibn Saud, and it was fully occupied in putting its armies ashore at the mouth of the Tigris and Euphrates – an urgent operation, because the British already possessed an oil refinery at Abadan on the Persian shore and could ill afford to lose the fuel it provided for their fleet, which was in the process of being converted from coal to oil. Shakespear was the only man who knew ibn Saud, and he was in England. He was summoned back; but while he took ship to Bombay, ibn Saud was left without advice from Britain.

Of course, he accepted the Turkish gifts; he had always been in need of arms and money. As Moslems, the Turks had also brought him a plan of campaign against the British infidel. He and ibn Rashid were to be reconciled. He was to come to the defence of Basra in Mesopotamia, ibn Rashid was to help in attacks against Suez and Egypt, and the Sherif of Mecca, together with the ruler of the Yemen, was to see to the defence of the Red Sea coast against British invasion. But when ibn Saud had safely received the presents, he contrived to avoid committing himself to the plan. He played for time, by explaining that nothing could reconcile him with

79

the House of Rashid, and he must therefore stay and defend his own domain until ibn Rashid had actually started his advance against Egypt.

Thus, when Shakespear reached the Gulf and entered the desert again, in the last few days of 1914, none of the Arab rulers had made any positive move. He found ibn Saud in war-camp between Kuwait and Buraida: in spite of the Turkish plan, he was hunting for ibn Rashid again to bring him to battle. Shakespear was welcomed as an old friend. Although the Turkish emissaries were still in Riyadh, ibn Saud assured him he was entirely on the British side. But he still wanted a definite treaty with Britain. Unless he was given that, he said, there was a danger he might be forced into actions which would seem to be friendly to the Turks. Ibn Saud, in fact, had understood the strength of his new position, and was ready to enjoy it; and he and Shakespear sat down there and then to draft the treaty he had waited for so long. The draft was very much like the ancient treaties between the British and the sheiks on the coast of the Gulf. Britain was to recognise and guarantee the independence of ibn Saud, and ibn Saud was not to have dealings with other foreign powers. But hard cash was also mentioned. Britain was to pay, in arms and money, for any action ibn Saud could take against the enemy; and the enemy, to ibn Saud, meant ibn Rashid.

This document was sent to the coast for transmission to Cox and so to the British Government, and Shakespear waited with ibn Saud for the answer. At that moment, he must have felt his position was enviable and his future was bright. His contemporaries in the British Army were being decimated as platoon and company commanders on the Western Front; but he, in spite of his youth and his junior rank, had been brought all the way from England as the only Englishman friendly with ibn Saud. Within a few days, single-handed, he had achieved what he had been sent to do; he had found ibn Saud was eager for his advice, and had drafted a treaty which would bring a third of the desert to the British side. Above all, he was doing a thing no Englishman had ever done before: he was honoured guest of an Arab prince at war, marching with a Bedouin host to battle.

The battle was imminent: ibn Rashid was close at hand. Nothing would have made Shakespear miss the chance to witness a kind of war which no other British officer had ever seen. Ibn Saud, indeed, tried to persuade him to keep out of harm's way, but he insisted not only on seeing the battle but on doing something useful. Ibn Saud had one Turkish cannon with him, and one man who could fire it, rather uncertainly. Clearly this was something a British officer could help to do; and accordingly, on 24th January, 1915, Shakespear entered battle among the Bedouin forces, still wearing his British uniform and sun-helmet, with the gun.

Except for his presence, it was a perfectly typical Bedouin fight, in which the final issue was decided by the troops' insistence on treating battles merely as sporting events. Ibn Saud led out his cavalry to seek the enemy. Shakespear and his gun sallied forth with the infantry. Scouts reported ibn Rashid's forces were approaching, and the gun was set up on a knoll. When the enemy came in sight, the gunner opened fire, and Shakespear stood on a higher eminence, using a pair of field-glasses and shouting corrections of the gunner's aim. As the masses of Bedouin infantry charged each other, Shakespear was hit by a rifle bullet in the thigh, but he went on directing the gunner until the armies met and mingled sword to sword. Then, with no more targets, the gunner sat down to watch the fight.

It went against them: the infantry began to break and run. The gunner, understanding Arab warfare, knew they had lost. He hastily buried some parts of the gun in the sand and ran away, calling to Shakespear also to run for his life. But Shakespear stayed where he was. Looking back in his flight, the gunner saw ibn Rashid's camel corps approaching, and he saw Shakespear stand up to face them before he fell and the camels overran him and trampled him into the sand. Two months later, when the gunner went back to look for his gun, Shakespear's body was still lying on the hillock.

Such sudden lonely death must always leave a fruitless speculation. Perhaps Shakespear could not have run, with the wound in his thigh; but the gunner said he did not try to run. Perhaps for all his sympathy with the Arabs, he had not understood the rules of Arab war; perhaps in that final moment, as an officer of the Indian Army in the pride of Kipling's era, he could not bring himself to do as the Arabs did. The Indian Army, in adversity, stuck to its guns and did not run away.

As usual, the battle settled nothing. One of the tribal contingents of ibn Saud had broken off the fight at the crucial moment to loot the enemy's camp, and made off for home with its spoils. With this desertion, ibn Saud was unable to protect his own camp, which was looted by ibn Rashid; and both commanders were left with their armies mauled and scattered and their stores and equipment stolen. Yet, inconclusive though it was, this ridiculous battle, and Shakespear's death in it, had an influence on the whole of the conduct of the world war in the middle east. It was eighteen months before any new effective leadership was offered to the Arabs, and then it was offered not to ibn Saud but to the Sherif of

81

Mecca, in Lawrence's campaign of genius in the west. Before Shakespear died, he had shown the rare ability, which Lawrence shared, to win the Bedouin's affection. There is no reason to doubt that if he had lived, he would have organised British support for ibn Saud, and led ibn Saud and his Ikhwan and Bedouin, who were much better fighting men than the Sherif's, either north towards Baghdad or west towards the Mecca railway; and Lawrence's campaign might never have been possible or necessary, and his masterpiece might never have been written.

Ibn Saud wrote to Cox. "Alas," he said, "that our cordial friend and well-wisher was hit from a distance and died. We had pressed him to leave us before the fight, but he insisted on being present, saying: 'My orders are to be with you. To leave would be contrary to my honour and my orders. I must certainly remain.' Pray inform His Majesty's Government of my sorrow."

Ibn Saud asked Cox for another officer to take the place of Shakespear, but Cox seemed to be discouraged by Shakespear's death, and nobody was sent. Arabic-speaking officers with the stamina for desert life were not very common in the Gulf; the army needed them all in its struggle through Mesopotamia, and the High Command, for the present, had lost all interest in ibn Saud. He could only have been of use, in a military sense, if he had been able to harass the Turks along the Euphrates or the Mecca railway, or at least deprive them of the help of ibn Rashid. But all the reports and rumours the British could glean from the desert appeared to agree: ibn Rashid and ibn Saud, they said, had both claimed a victory, but the cost of it in men and materials had put ibn Saud out of action. And furthermore, the same thing had happened to him which had happened so often before in his moments of weakness: one of his own tribes had taken the chance to revolt. This time it was in the Hasa, and for a long crucial period ibn Saud was engaged yet again in the weary and bloody pursuit of tribal strife.

It was in this revolt that ibn Saud was wounded in the thigh and a famous camp-fire story was created. According to this celebrated tale, while ibn Saud lay suffering in his tent, a rumour spread that the bullet had hit a much more vulnerable spot and finished him as a husband and a father. This was a dangerous belief. Alarm and despondency grew, and claimants to the leadership began to count their chances. But, warned in time of what was being said, ibn Saud sent men hot-foot to the nearest villages, with orders to find him a suitable bride at once: luckily, he had a vacancy in his quota of four. A maiden was brought, and he married her the moment she arrived; and, to the joy and relief of his followers, disproved the mischievous rumour there and then.

The treaty which Shakespear had drafted was sent on its leisurely way to London, and came back, months afterwards, with the British Government's approval. A mere messenger took it to ibn Saud: the British could not spare an emissary, or did not think it was worth the trouble to find one. Ibn Saud signed the document, with some reservations; and so at last he bound himself to Britain. Nearly a year after Shakespear's death, in the last week of 1915, he met Cox by arrangement on the shore of the Hasa, and the treaty was ratified. But this event, which he had striven for so long, had lost its savour by the time it came. The British gave him a subsidy of £5,000 a month, which he badly needed, and a gift of a thousand rifles. But they did not even bother to suggest that he should use these gifts, as Shakespear had intended, to intensify his war against ibn Rashid. The Government of India no longer cared about his active support. The campaign in Mesopotamia had gone too far, and he seemed to have fallen too low, for his help in it to be worth soliciting. Their bribe was merely reckoned to keep him quiet.

CHAPTER NINE

LAWRENCE AND THE SHERIF
OF MECCA

All through the years from 1911 to 1915, while ibn Saud was engaged in the east of his country ejecting the Turks from the Hasa and bargaining with the British, he was aware of a menacing rival behind him in the west: the Grand Sherif of Mecca. To trace this rivalry, one must go back some years before the world war began.

Sherif Hussein was a member (as the title of Sherif implied) of a family which traced its descent from the Prophet: he was also, in that period, a mere minion of the Turks. He had spent eighteen years as a more or less honoured prisoner in Constantinople, but in the course of the revolution there in 1908 and 1909 he had come into favour and been appointed ruler of the Hejaz and guardian of the holy cities.

Both he and his domain were different from ibn Saud and his. The Sherif was not a Bedouin: he was a sophisticated city Arab, and his mother was Circassian. His kingdom was not mainly a desert kingdom, although it had deserts and desert people in it: it was urban in its politics and outlook and its power was concentrated in the cities of Mecca, Medina and Jidda. Compared with ibn Saud's impoverished domain, the Sherif's was economically sound. Its riches derived from the somewhat ignoble trade of fleecing pilgrims. Almost all the inhabitants of the holy cities and the Red Sea ports, like the inhabitants of tourist resorts in later eras, lived by selling something to the visitors at inflated prices: accommodation, transport, food or souvenirs, or their own services as guides, or even water; while those who had nothing to sell became touts for those who had. The Bedouin near the pilgrim routes were paid to resist the temptation to raid and rob the pilgrim caravans; for pilgrims who had already been robbed by Bedouin would have brought no profit to the more ingenious robbers in the towns. On the proceeds of the pilgrimage, the city people indulged in all the luxuries and carnal pleasures which Wahhabis regarded with disgust. A Scottish Arabist of that period wrote: "The fanaticism of the Meccan is an affair of the purse; the mongrel population (for the town is by no means purely Arab) has exchanged the virtues of the Bedouin for the worst corruption of Eastern town life, without casting off the ferocity of the desert. The unspeakable vices of Mecca are a scandal to all Islam, and a constant
84

source of wonder to pious pilgrims." Thus, although the city was the centre of the Moslem world, it was also the prime example of the moral decadence which Wahhabis were sworn to reform.

The difference between the open desert and Mecca's devious alleys may also be seen as a symbol of the difference between their rulers. Shakespear had used the words straightforward and frank to convey his first impression of ibn Saud, but an exactly opposite impression was made by the Sherif on most of the British who met him. He could be charming, he was certainly well-read, and his manner was polished and courtly; but he seemed to the British unable to be frank. On the contrary, he seemed to delight in being oblique, ambiguous and obstinate, fantastically subtle when no subtlety was needed, and madly suspicious even of his friends. He was a much older man than ibn Saud – probably fifty-five in 1910 – and as he grew older his habit of mind grew even more tortuous, until nobody could discover his true opinions or intentions through the webs of circumlocution he wove around them. It is only fair to add at once that before he died he had ample reason to be suspicious of the British, and that the British may have inclined to exaggerate his faults. But it is clear that the only quality he shared with ibn Saud was a vast ambition: an ambition, always implicit and sometimes expressed, to become the king of all Arabia. Ibn Saud's ambition was finally almost satisfied: the Sherif's was thwarted and led him to the edge of madness.

With this shared ambition and contrast of character, the Sherif and ibn Saud were bound to clash. It was only a renewal of an ancient rivalry. Ever since the Wahhabis had captured the Hejaz a hundred years before, the sybarites of Mecca and their rulers had felt a lingering fear of the fanatics who had descended on the city from the east and might descend again. They had watched ibn Saud's successes with concern. In 1904, the Sherif's predecessor had asked the Sultan to put a curb to ibn Saud, but the Sultan had not succeeded; and in 1909 Sherif Hussein had many incentives to try where the Sultan had failed. A success against ibn Saud would have furthered his own ambition, and allayed his people's fears, and pleased the Turks who had appointed him. In 1911 he had an opportunity. Merely to lead an invading army into the desert could never have succeeded; but when the Araif, the pretenders to the throne of ibn Saud, escaped from execution after their unsuccessful revolt and fled to Mecca to ask for the Sherif's protection, he saw a chance that they might seize power if he helped them, and then might remain his vassals.

Another stroke of luck gave him added encouragement:

he captured Saad, the brother of ibn Saud. Saad had been sent, in the course of ibn Saud's campaign against the Araif, to try to recruit some tribesmen along the vague boundary of the Hejaz. By chance, the Sherif was also there, recruiting the same tribe for his own service, and Saad was taken by surprise. The Sherif saw his value and took him back to Mecca.

With Saad as hostage and the Araif as willing candidates for glory, the Sherif wrote to the Sheik of Kuwait, and to the current occupant of the Rashidi throne, to ask for their support against ibn Saud; and having thus, as he hoped, united everyone behind him, he embarked on an expedition into ibn Saud's domain, relying more on subtlety than force, and taking only three hundred Bedouin with him.

He penetrated more than a hundred miles beyond his borders before his plan began to come to grief. Then he learned that no help was coming from Kuwait, or from the House of Rashid. Both rulers indeed, as ibn Saud had told Shakespear, were plotting at that particular moment to drive the Turks out of Arabia, and were not inclined to help the Sherif, who was the Turks' supporter. He also learned that ibn Saud was on the march to meet him with a far superior force; and when this news reached his own three hundred men, they began in the prudent manner of Bedouin troops to melt away.

Nevertheless, with Saad in his hands he still had the power to bargain, and ibn Saud did not dare to attack him. The rivals halted, with two days' march between them. The Sherif sent a letter, explaining that he had not come for war, but only to reassert his own and the Turks' authority over the province of Kasim, of which Buraida was the centre – an historical authority, he said, which had merely been in abeyance for the past few generations. Specifically, he demanded that out of the revenue which ibn Saud collected from the province, he should pay him a yearly tribute of the equivalent of £6,000. He also insisted that ibn Saud should promise always to help the Turkish forces with men and supplies when they were needed – and in that context, the Turkish forces meant his own. The letter implied that Saad would be sent as a prisoner to Turkey if ibn Saud refused.

Ibn Saud replied by sending munificent gifts. Riders galloped from one camp to the other with further letters: the two rulers never met: and finally, Saad was freed, and ibn Saud took him back to Riyadh, while the Sherif returned to Mecca, taking – as he believed – ibn Saud's acceptance of his humiliating terms. His diplomatic victory was widely published in Turkish and Egyptian papers. But when the terms of it came to Cox's knowledge, he remarked that even if ibn Saud had made such promises, they were most unlikely to be observed; and as usual he was right. Not a penny was ever paid, not a man was ever lent to the Turkish forces, and ibn Saud, in a later talk with Shakespear, denied that he had ever promised anything: the Sherif had only made his claims, he said, to save his own face at the end of an absurdly unsuccessful expedition. Indeed, in retrospect, the Sherif's foray does have an air of absurdity, like many of the Arab's warlike gestures. It was only his first attempt against ibn Saud, and he was not the man to be deterred, either by passing defeat or ridicule; but before he could try again, the world war had transformed the political surroundings of Arabia, and given him a chance of fame he would never have had without it – a chance which was fundamentally caused by the arbitrary line that British imperial administration had drawn down the middle of Arabia.

Shakespear saw a glimpse of what this division portended when he crossed Arabia just before the war began. His journey was more than a pioneering work of exploration; it was also the first direct link across Arabia between the separate hierarchies of British power. In crossing Arabia from coast to coast, he had also crossed from the sphere of the Government of India to the sphere of the Foreign Office; and when he emerged unheralded into Egypt, he became the first British official from the Persian Gulf to discover that British officials in Egypt totally disagreed with him. In Cairo, he reported to Lord Kitchener, who was then High Commissioner in Egypt; and after that formidable audience he wrote to Cox. The "local bigwigs," he said, seemed disposed to exaggerate the influence of the Sherif; their information on Central Arabia – in other words, on ibn Saud – was "much more sketchy" than he had expected. One senses the dismay of a captain who finds he disagrees with a field-marshal, but one cannot tell whether Shakespear saw the importance of the fact he had discovered. The fact was that at that critical moment of history, on the brink of war, the British in Egypt were much too inclined to look at Arabia through the Sherif's eyes, accepting him and his ambitions at his own valuation, and regarding ibn Saud as uncouth and unimportant; while the British in the Persian Gulf, prejudiced in the opposite direction, saw in ibn Saud the best of Arab aspirations and in the Sherif the worst of Arab decadence.

By 1915, the difference of opinion had not narrowed, it had widened. At the very time when Cox and the High Command in Mesopotamia were giving up the idea of asking for Arab-co-operation, the High Command in Egypt was beginning to hope for it. Arabian affairs have always attracted intellectual Englishmen, and a number of men of extraordinary brilliance had assembled in Cairo and formed an office called the Arab Bureau. Among them, Lawrence was a junior. They were passionately convinced of the value of Arab help against the Turks. So far, they were right: the success of the campaign they sponsored proved it. But in choosing the Sherif as the Arab leader they were wrong: and this was proved by the chaos they left in Arabia. The choice was inevitable. The office of Sherif of Mecca was the highest in the Arab world, and his was the only important domain accessible from the Red Sea side of the country. They never seriously considered making use of ibn Saud; but if they had, the division of British administration would have stopped them. Lawrence once visited the Persian Gulf, before his campaign began, but he left in a huff when his advice was disregarded; for the division was even more than a matter of mere administration. It was the product of two separate traditions and two separate aspects of British mentality, typified in the characters of Lawrence and Cox. Lawrence and the Arab Bureau were dynamic, amateurish, self-confident, persuasive, and admirable even when they were wrong: Cox and the Government of India were cautious, sympathetic, professional, a little lacking in imagination – and, in this matter, right.

Apart from his mere proximity there were two diplomatic reasons for the support the British in Cairo offered to the Sherif -- or at least, there had been two reasons before the war began. One was that the Sherif and his sons had many friends among the sophisticated Arabs in Turkey, Syria and Palestine, who lived like himself under Turkish domination and already had ideas of Arab nationalism. To win the Sherif to the British side was expected to encourage these people's rebellious feelings against the Turks. The other reason was fear of the Caliph's influence on the Indian Moslems. These Indians had two religious interests outside their country: in the Caliph as the figurehead of Islam, and in the holy city of Mecca as the object of their pilgrimages. The support of the Sherif, as guardian of the holy city, was expected to counteract the hostility of the Caliph. But this second reason disappeared as soon as the war began, when the Indian Moslems proved to be perfectly loyal to Britain; and neither of the reasons had anything to do with the Arabs of Arabia itself.

For all these causes, the British in Cairo had no option but to choose the Sherif as the nominal leader of their Arab revolt against the Turks, and once having made their choice, to offer him ever-increasing rewards in gold and arms and power. The misfortune of Arabia was that they believed their choice of a man was right in Arab eyes. They did not allow for the fact that the high office of Sherif happened to be filled by a man who was foolish. The cash they poured into the Sherif's domain was enough, while it lasted, to buy the allegiance of every Bedouin in reach. But in doing that, it blinded the British to the fact that the Sherif had no personal following at all. His aspirations to Arab leadership had no support outside the sycophantic circle which surrounded him in Mecca; in spite of his holy descent, he was, after all, no more than a Turkish nominee imposed on the people of the Hejaz within the last decade. He began his revolt unaided and succeeded in pushing the Turks out of Jidda and Mecca itself; but then his troops lost interest, and his whole campaign stagnated for lack of a genuine leader. Lawrence stepped in to provide the leadership, making use of the Sherif's sons Abdullah and Feisal; and with Lawrence's genius and Britain's wealth, the revolt went from strength to strength. Yet it was always hollow: it was always an expression of Lawrence's will and of British power, and never of any permanent Arab aspiration. The further it went, the more trouble it inevitably stored. The Sherif grew more and more rapacious, and more and more convinced of his own high destiny; he demanded not only more gold, but more British promises of support for his own ambitions as King of all Arabia; and the British in Cairo, under the spur of war, and in the belief that the Sherif was the Arab's chosen leader, made him promises, either explicit or implied, which they could never have fulfilled – for they took no account of ibn Saud.

This was a miserable period in ibn Saud's career. He had trusted Cox and Shakespear, who stood in his eyes for Britain, and allied himself for the first time to a force he could not control. Now he was left, neglected and slighted in Riyadh, while rumours reached him of treasures and flattery lavished by Britain on the Sherif, whom he wholly distrusted as a rival and wholly despised as a man and as a Moslem. The stories he heard of camel-trains of gold on the road to Mecca made his own allowance of £5,000 a month seem meagre. His alliance with the infidel British had always been criticised by the extreme Wahhabis. Alone in Riyadh, without any moral support from Britain, surrounded by these narrow-minded critics, he can only have wondered whether he had been tricked, whether he might have driven a harder bargain, and whether his subsidy was only meant to tie his hands while the Sherif's power was built up to overwhelm him.

With fidelity which almost seems naïve, he clung to the image of Britain which Cox and Shakespear had created for him. He often wrote to Cox. His letters were dignified, and free from the querulous complaints one might have expected at the plain contradictions of British policy. Some of them even seemed humble, like the letters of a student to a man of respected wisdom. But they all expressed, with increasing urgency, the fear that the money and praise and weapons the British were giving the Sherif would encourage the Sherif, sooner or later, to attack him. What would happen then? he implied. The British had guaranteed his independence: now they were financing his rival, who made claims to all Arabia. Would they warn the Sherif to respect his independence? If the Sherif attacked, was ibn Saud to defend himself, as he was confident he could, or would the British consider their interests were involved? He was always ready, he said, to accept advice from Cox.

He wrote to the Sherif too, asking for reassurance; but the Sherif, already inflated by British patronage, replied with vainglorious scorn that nobody but a madman or a drunkard would have written such a letter. The suggestion of drunkenness, from the ruler of Mecca to the ruler of puritan Riyadh, was unforgivably insulting, as the Sherif undoubtedly knew; but ibn Saud merely copied the letter, and sent the copy to Cox.

Cox was an honest man and a conscientious civil servant, now compelled to carry out a policy he knew was not strictly honest. Ten patient years of his professional career had earned him the trust of the Arabs and made Britain the symbol of justness in the Gulf. His Government, through the India Office, had allowed him to make the treaty with ibn Saud: now he knew that the rival and richer department on the other side of the country was making promises inconsistent with the treaty. Sooner or later, the promises and the treaty were bound to clash, and either the Sherif or ibn Saud, or both of them, would rightly accuse the British of breaking faith. If Cox had found himself in this predicament in peace, he might have resigned or rebelled; but in war, short-sighted policies are often paramount, and what is right is often neglected for what is expedient. The worst thing that could have happened, from the immediate British point of view, was that ibn Saud in anger might have changed to the Turkish side and harassed the advance in Mesopotamia; the second worst, that he might have attacked the Sherif and interrupted Lawrence's campaign. To try to prevent these disasters, Cox was obliged to misuse the trust he had won, to try to soothe ibn Saud, to pretend that the British commitment to the Sherif was not so serious as it seemed – and to hope that somebody, after the war, would find an honourable compromise.

The Arab Bureau in Cairo suspected the danger, and sent one of its learned Arabists, Ronald Storrs, by sea to the Gulf to discuss the problem with Cox. At Cox's suggestion, Storrs tried to reach Riyadh on camel-back to explain the Cairo point of view to ibn Saud; but he collapsed in the desert with sun-stroke and had to be carried back to the coast. The old city was still as remote from the world as it had always been.

Shortly after this failure, somebody in the British administration thought of making ibn Saud a British knight. This incongruous honour may have been meant to delay the impending crisis, for in those days British orders and decorations were given and valued almost all over the world, not only as recognitions of service but also as solaces for wounded feelings. Beside ibn Saud, there was another candidate for the honours list. Sheik Mubarrak had died in 1915, and an award was proposed for his son Sheik Jabir, to ensure, one can only suppose, that he followed his father's policy of friendliness for Britain. Accordingly a formal investiture or durbar – or majlis, to use the Arab word – was arranged in Kuwait, and ibn Saud was invited. Cox, as the representative of King George V, created Jabir Companion of the Star of India, and ibn Saud Knight Commander of the Indian Empire; and everybody, including ibn Saud, made speeches in praise of Arab unity. Henceforth he could have called himself Sir Abdul-Aziz if he had wanted to, but he never did.

This curious ceremony led to ibn Saud's first trip abroad, and his first encounter with the British in the mass. He went to Basra, which was the British base in Mesopotamia, and inspected the organisation of a British army, so fantastically complicated in comparison with his own. Artillery was demonstrated for him, and he was shown the bones of his own hand in an X-ray machine in a hospital. For the first time, he travelled in a railway train and saw an aeroplane; and for the first time also he saw something which possibly impressed him even more: a woman publicly unveiled who talked to him and everyone else as an equal – the formidable British traveller Gertrude Bell, who was then on Cox's staff.

He seemed to his hosts to be interested in everything he saw, but to judge from his comments afterwards he did not approve of it all. In particular, the mere existence of a person like Gertrude Bell offended his sense of decorum. The emancipation of women was a new and repulsive idea to him, an idea which would clearly have wrecked the Wahhabi social structure. The British who met him liked him and admired him, and he was still prepared to like the British; but he was certainly not prepared to condone their customs, which shocked him much more profoundly than his joyous polygamy shocked them.

Outrageous though Gertrude Bell appeared to him, she was in fact a very clever and perspicacious woman, and a secret report of his visit which she wrote for the Arab Bureau contained a vivid and feminine description of him which might perhaps have pleased him.

"Ibn Saud is now barely forty, though he looks some years older," she wrote. "He is a man of splendid physique, standing well over six feet, and carrying himself with the air of one accustomed to command. Though he is more massively built than the typical nomad sheik, he has the characteristics of the well-bred Arab, the strongly marked aquiline profile, full-fleshed nostrils, prominent lips and long, narrow chin, accentuated by a pointed beard. His hands are fine, with slender fingers, a trait almost universal among the tribes of pure Arab blood, and, in spite of his great height and breadth of shoulder, he conveys the impression, common enough in the desert, of an indefinable lassitude, not individual but racial, the secular weariness of an ancient and self-contained people, which has made heavy drafts on its vital forces, and borrowed little from beyond its own forbidding frontiers. His deliberate movements, his slow, sweet smile, and the contemplative glance of his heavy-lidded eyes, though they add to his dignity and charm, do not accord with the western conception of a vigorous personality. Nevertheless, report credits him with powers of physical endurance rare even in hard-bitten Arabia. Among men bred in the camel-saddle, he is said to have few rivals as a tireless rider. As a leader of irregular forces he is of proved daring, and he combines with his qualities as a soldier that grasp of statecraft which is yet more highly prized by the tribesmen. To be 'a statesmen' is, perhaps, their final word of commendation."

After the visit was over, Cox had a fleeting belief that some good had been done by it. Ibn Saud had renewed his promise to attack ibn Rashid and to leave the Sherif alone. The British had given him a sword of honour, and, which was more to the point, some extra money and four machine-guns, and they had trained four of his men to fire the guns. Indeed, the journey must have broadened the mind of ibn Saud: but Cox was too hopeful. Nothing happened. The journey had no apparent practical effect, either on the military situation or on Wahhabi society. A year later, the attack on ibn Rashid had still not begun. The machine-guns were stored and neglected in the fortress of Hofuf, three of them still in their boxes; and three of the trained men had died, while the fourth – the same gunner who had fought with Shakespear – had forgotten how the new-fangled weapons worked. Still left without a British envoy at his court to encourage him or persuade him, ibn Saud had returned to sulk again in Riyadh.

It was not till October, 1917, that at last a permanent British mission was sent to him, and by then it was too late to hope to reconcile him with the Sherif. The Sherif's armies under Lawrence had swept triumphantly into Aqaba on the way to Palestine; the Sherif had proclaimed himself King of

92

Arabia; and on the indeterminate frontier which divided the two domains, skirmishes had been fought between them in a war which could not be halted.

CHAPTER TEN

PHILBY

The head of the British mission was Harry St. John Philby, the strange and eccentric Englishman who later conceived a passionate hero-worship for ibn Saud and attached himself to his court for most of the rest of his life, and who also became the most widely travelled explorer of Arabia in his day and by far the most prolific writer on it.

Philby was one of Cox's assistants, a junior civil servant. Totally unlike Lawrence, he was neither a soldier nor a poet. Lawrence was always a heroic figure; Philby never was, although he lived much longer in Arabia and travelled farther. Lawrence found himself bitterly at odds with the British Government before his adventure ended, and so did Philby; but Philby was the kind of man who is always out of step, and always plaintively anxious to prove that he was the only man in step and that everyone else was out; and although, when he quarrelled with the British, and later with the Arabs, he sometimes had right on his side, his querulous self-justification often defeated itself. He had many friends and many enemies, friends who enjoyed his amusing conversation, and enemies he had embarrassed by tactless outspokenness or outraged by flouting their most dearly held beliefs.

He wrote at least a dozen books about Arabia, and in the last few years of his life he was working day and night on several more; and his books have the air of displaying more of his character than he intended – even more of it, perhaps, than he understood himself. They are naïve, verbose, pedantic, opinionated, and humorous in a manner which was old-fashioned even when they were written; yet they reveal the charm which endeared him to his cronies. They seem the books of a man who possessed an inquisitive mind, and a mass of unique information, and a passionate eagerness to impart his knowledge; but a man who could never see himself as other people saw him, and so was often unable to say what he wanted to say in a manner which other people would accept. His explorations were brave and genuine, and his geographical observations were admired by the American oil explorers who followed him twenty years later; but the few Arabs who have read his histories delight in disagreeing with them. If this curious man had remained a civil servant all his life, he might have remained a nonentity; but by breaking loose when the first world war was over, and devoting him-

94

self to following ibn Saud, he found a unique purpose for his life and won a vicarious fame beyond his true fame as an explorer. For luckily, ibn Saud was always among his friends, although they sometimes quarrelled. Ibn Saud enjoyed good-humoured argument, and Philby was the only man who almost always dared to argue with him. So, in the history of the last thirty years of the reign of ibn Saud Philby constantly intrudes. Wherever ibn Saud moves his court, from the early twenties to the end of his life, there is Philby too: a stocky bearded figure in Arab dress, fiercely and fearlessly argumentative, unalterably British and yet more Arab than the Arabs, always at hand to explain the western world to ibn Saud, and eager to explain ibn Saud to the western world – and conveying, in both directions, pictures which are highly coloured by his own peculiar personality.

However, in 1917, when Philby first went to Riyadh, he was still on Cox's staff, and as head of the mission his task was to further British aims, which were still the same as they had been three years before: to persuade ibn Saud to attack ibn Rashid, and not to attack the Sherif. These aims were still purely a matter of British strategy against the Turks. They took very little account of the wishes of ibn Saud or his people, or of the morality of inciting one Arab chief against another. Ibn Saud, in fact, would have liked to attack both his rivals: ibn Rashid because of the enmity rooted far back in the past, and the Sherif because of his claim to be King of Arabia, which was clearly a threat for the future. But those were political reasons, and politics were never the only reasons for action in the Wahhabi domain. The Ulema, and the Ikhwan imbued with their doctrine, had no serious feeling of enmity for ibn Rahid, who was rather less offensive in their religious eyes than the British themselves. But on the other hand, they were avid to march against the Sherif and purge the wickedness of the holy cities. So ibn Saud was urged in opposite directions by his British ally and his own religious leaders.

His decision was influenced by one thing the Ulema would never have considered: money. He had never been greedy for money for himself, but he could not hold his domain together without it. He needed it to maintain the Ikhwan settlements, and to mount and feed his armies in the field, and to subsidise his sheiks and sometimes to buy off his enemies, and above all to uphold the traditions of hospitality; for any of his subjects who came to him for justice or advice could claim to be fed and clothed at his expense and sent away with a present, and there were often a thousand or more of these supplicants encamped around his palace. Without enough money to do these things he could not rule:

the British were giving him £60,000 a year: and the whole of the rest of the national income, from taxes and customs duties, was not much more than that. He could not afford to refuse to do what the British wanted; without their subsidy, he was bankrupt.

At that moment of the world war, the attack on ibn Rashid seemed especially urgent to the British. Lawrence and his Sherifian followers had cleared the Hejaz and were ready with a British army under General Allenby for the final advance against the Turks in Palestine. So far north, they had ibn Rashid, not ibn Saud, on their right flank; and the advantage if ibn Saud could draw him off was obvious. In Mesopotamia too, ibn Rashid was a nuisance. The British and Indians had overrun wide tracts of fertile country, and Turkey was almost surrounded and blockaded, and was suffering from shortage of supplies; but goods were still being smuggled through the blockade from the Persian Gulf by way of the uncontrollable alleys of Kuwait and ibn Rashid's deserts.

In these conditions, it was not very difficult for Philby and ibn Saud to strike a bargain. Philby offered four field-guns and men to fire them, ten thousand rifles, £20,000 for buying camels and £50,000 a month for the three months which the British reckoned would lead to the defeat of ibn Rashid. Compared with the fortune sent to the Sherif from Cairo, this was a pittance; but as Philby pointed out, the Sherif had been called on for a greater effort.

The bargaining in the palace at Riyadh was ominously interrupted by rifle-shots of joy in the courtyard. These were in celebration of a victory against the Sherif. The Ulema, with or without ibn Saud's approval, had already sent their preachers to the Sherif's frontiers, and the people of one oasis had received their conversion with such impetuous zeal that they had thrown out the Sherif's governor and proclaimed their allegiance to ibn Saud. The name of the oasis was Khurma. Nobody outside Arabia had ever heard of it then: but within the next few years, it became one of those insignificant names which from time to time achieve a sudden diplomatic notoriety.

In spite of this sign of what was inevitably coming, ibn Saud grudgingly accepted Philby's offer. He agreed to prepare a final expedition against ibn Rashid; and Philby sent a messenger to Cox to inform him of the terms and ask for approval.

So far, Philby had been successful; next, he undid whatever good he had done by what seems an act of stupid irresponsibility. There had been a plan that Ronald Storrs, the expert from Cairo, should travel up from the Red Sea coast to join him in Riyadh; but the Sherif had disliked the idea of a conference between the British and ibn Saud, and he refused to let Storrs cross his kingdom, with the excuse that the journey into ibn Saud's domain would not be safe. Philby now persuaded ibn Saud to let him go to the Hejaz, and speak to the Sherif, and bring Storrs back with him. Ibn Saud was naïvely willing to prove to the Sherif that he was perfectly able to protect a diplomatic guest, and he agreed to provide an escort. Philby sent word to Cox of what he proposed to do, and set off without waiting for an answer. With good reason he suspected that Cox would have told him to stay at his post in Riyadh.

Afterwards, Philby wrote in one of his numerous books: "I should confess, perhaps, that my motives in making that proposal were of a mixed character, and not wholly based on the actual requirements of the situation, but that is a trifle and I have never regretted my action." It was far from a trifle, and much to be regretted. The fact was that he already pictured himself as a famous explorer, and longed for the achievement of having crossed Arabia from coast to coast; and he twisted his war-time duty to suit this personal ambition. If he had understood Arabia then as well as he understood it later, he would have foreseen the result. He had told ibn Saud he would be back within a month; but the Sherif, of course, politely refused to let him go back at all. He had to be sent to Cairo, and then to Bombay and the Persian Gulf to start again. At the crucial moment when ibn Saud was ready to take an active part in the war, and the British at last were ready to give him the means to do so, Cox found himself with nobody in Riyadh to complete the bargain. And when Philby returned four months later, in April, 1918, the moment had passed. The campaign in Palestine was finishing and the end of the war against Turkey was in sight; the British no longer needed ibn Saud's assistance, and their offer of money and guns had been withdrawn. Ibn Saud was furious. Philby was luckier than he deserved to be, for ibn Saud never guessed that he had tricked him with a half-truth; his anger was against the British in general, and the Sherif. To calm him and prevent an attack on the Sherif, Philby lent him £20,000 on his own responsibility, for the gold the British Government had provided was still in his hands; and with that as a means of persuasion, he launched him on an expedition to ibn Rashid's capital town of Hail.

The expedition was a failure, for lack of the British guns to assault the walls of the town; and by the time when ibn Saud returned to Riyadh, the world war was over. Through Philby's foolish journey, ibn Saud had lost not only a useful sum of money, but also his final chance of British help against his life-long enemies. Worse still, he emerged from the war not, like the Sherif, as an ally of the victors, but with a reputation in British eyes for indecision. The Sherif seemed forceful: ibn Saud seemed ineffective. But this was misjudgment. These were the qualities not of the rival rulers, but of the British departments which had sponsored them and offered them advice. The forcefulness was due to the Arab Bureau and Lawrence, and not to the Sherif: the indecision to the Government of India and Cox, and not to ibn Saud. The five years after the war, when British influence was more remote, showed both the rulers in a different light.

CHAPTER ELEVEN

FALL OF THE HOUSE
OF RASHID

At this low ebb in ibn Saud's affairs, he also suffered personal tragedies. The world-wide influenza epidemic of 1919 ravaged Riyadh. Three of his sons died in it, including the eldest, Turki: so did his wife Jauhara. A monogamist can hardly estimate what grief Jauhara's death may have caused him. One would suppose a man with unlimited numbers of wives could never experience heights of love, or therefore depths of sorrow. Ibn Saud was quoted once as saying that no woman was worth too much lamentation, because there were always attractive women left; but this was said to comfort a man in mourning. Jauhara, however, had been his wife for an unusually long time, and was said to have been his favourite. She was among the six he hoped to meet in Paradise.

The death of Turki may have grieved him more, or differently; for wives might come and go, but the relationship of a father to his eldest son remained unique. Ibn Saud was thirty-nine and Turki was twenty when he died; they were men together, and in the exclusively masculine society of Arabia ibn Saud could have felt an intimate affection for his son which he would never have wanted to offer to any woman. Turki is said to have been extremely handsome, but to have taken less interest in women than his father, although of course he was married several times. His passions were hunting and war, and these were arts he had learned from ibn Saud. Ever since he was seventeen, he had acted as commander-in-chief in his father's absence, and had led successful campaigns. Ibn Saud regarded him as the heir to his domain, the future bearer of the Wahhabi standard; and he was the only one of his sons, so far, to whom he had given any authority. Some of his highest hopes must have ended when Turki died.

But if action is a cure for sorrow, ibn Saud can seldom have sorrowed long. The Khurma oasis was still demanding his attention, the House of Rashid was still as turbulent as ever, the Sherif was still unbearably insulting, and worst of all, the victorious allies at the Versailles conference were making proposals which filled him with foreboding.

As an active ally, the Sherif was represented at the conference by his son Feisal: ibn Saud was not invited, and all he could do was send his own third son, who was about fourteen and whose name was also Faisal,* to London to congratulate the British on their victory. But the decisions of the conference satisfied neither the Sherif nor ibn Saud. Yet another contradictory aspect of British policy came into prominence. The British in the Persian Gulf had guaranteed ibn Saud's independence: the British in Cairo had encouraged the Sherif's dream of an Arab kingdom: but the British in London, overruling both, had made a secret agreement with the French and Russians, as early as 1916, which nullified an important part of the Sherif's hopes. He had supposed that his promised kingdom would include the greater part of the "fertile crescent", the predominantly Arab lands on the Mediterranean shore and in Mesopotamia. But the secret agreement had already divided these countries – Palestine, Syria and Lebanon, together with Transjordan and Iraq – into French and British "spheres of influence". Lawrence and his seniors in Cairo had not been told of this agreement when they led the Sherif into his revolt; nor had Cox. When Lawrence heard of it, he felt he had been cheated and misled into cheating the Sherif; but by then the revolt had gone too far to stop, and he merely determined to make it so resoundingly successful that his own government would be ashamed to neglect the Arabs' claims.

Yet these claims were swamped in the world-wide bargaining of Versailles. The crude idea of spheres of influence was modified, by the new concept of mandates under the League of Nations, but still without fulfilment of the Sherif's expectations. Syria and Lebanon became French mandates: Iraq, Palestine and Transjordan, which was newly created a state, were assigned to the British.

Mandates were an idealistic plan, attributed to General Smuts and President Wilson. They intended that what have since been called emergent nations should be given provisional international recognition, but remain under the instruction of the mandatory power until they were able to stand on their own feet. But the plan took too little account of human fallibility. It was difficult for the mandatory powers to maintain such a high disinterested purpose, or to seem to maintain it; and it was difficult for the small mandated nations to accept such patronising help. Naturally, the people of these nations thought they were ready for total independence long before anybody else thought they were; and naturally, the foreign forces and advisers in their countries seemed to them suspiciously like colonising agents, and wounded their national pride. The mandates in the middle east, before they ended, became a far greater burden for Britain and France than either had expected, and although they probably pre-

* The difference in spelling is a western convention

100

vented more strife than they caused, they always remained a source of intense ill-feeling.

The mandate of Palestine was the most unhappy of them all, because it embodied the ancient Jewish longing to return to Zion. The British Government had formally given its support in 1917 to the proposal to make a national home for Jews in Palestine, with the condition that it should not prejudice the civil or religious rights of non-Jewish communities already in the country. But as there were only seventy thousand Jews there at the time, and seven hundred thousand Arabs, the condition was impossible to fulfil. For over a quarter of a century, the British as the mandatory power were to pursue the hopeless task of trying to reconcile the Arabs and the Jews, and were only to be rewarded in the end by the antagonism of both.

Like every other Arab, ibn Saud was bitterly opposed for the rest of his life to the settlement of Jews in what he regarded as an Arab land, but it concerned him more as a matter of abstract racial justice than of practical politics. He had no frontier with Palestine, and he always remained so purely a Bedouin that anything beyond the frontier of the desert seemed to him remote. Problems on his frontiers and inside them took all of his time and energy.

At the end of the war, the most pressing of all these problems was in the oasis of Khurma. Since the people of Khurma had declared themselves the subjects of ibn Saud, the Sherif had sent a series of expeditions to teach them otherwise. Each time they had beaten him off; and each time they sent impassioned appeals to ibn Saud for help. His hands were still tied by his promises to Cox, and by the fear that if he fought the Sherif, who was still a British ally, the British might cut off his subsidy and leave him helpless for lack of money. But the Ikhwan, the fighting men of his settlements, knew nothing of this restriction. The appeals for help from Khurma only fanned their ardour against the Sherif to a fiercer heat; and ibn Saud could never have begun to explain to them that he depended on pay from an infidel foreign power. This could only have seemed to them an unforgivable disgrace. So his own fighters were puzzled and offended by what seemed his indecision or faint-heartedness. Clamour against him grew, in angry tones which threatened insurrection. At last he was forced to follow the Ikhwan's wishes, which were also his own, and to risk his alliance with Britain. He promised the Khurma people his protection.

At about the same time, a conference was held in the Foreign Office in London to discuss the obscure oasis, for ibn Saud and the Sherif had each complained to the British of the other's aggression there; and it was thus that the name of Khurma found its way into diplomatic archives. Lord Curzon was chairman of the meeting, but it was a long time since he had left India, and the Foreign Office was still under the influence of Lawrence's valuation of the Sherif's army; so the conference decided that Khurma belonged to the Sherif – not, it is said, for strictly historical reasons, but partly because they believed the Sherif would win if the rivals fought for the place. With this decision, they settled the fate of Khurma in a way they had not intended. The Sherif, with the assurance of British approval, sent his son Abdullah with a powerful force to assert his right to the oasis. Ibn Saud, unable to break his promise to protect it, let loose the Ikhwan in defiance; and Abdullah's army was routed and slaughtered. Only Abdullah himself and a few of his staff escaped to Mecca, bringing stories of fierce Wahhabi fighters which caused panic in the holy city and agitation in the British Foreign Office. Philby says that an angry telegram was sent to the British representative in Iraq, who made the monthly payment to ibn Saud, telling him to stop it forthwith – but that he wisely put the telegram in his pocket and forgot it until the Foreign Office had simmered down.

This victory was proof of the efficiency of the Ikhwan: it was also proof of their danger. Religious zeal and ignorance have always been a dangerous combination, and seldom have men so supremely ignorant been infected with such a blinding faith. Ibn Saud had created the Ikhwan, by setting Wahhabi preachers to fertilise Bedouin minds, and the settlements still fulfilled their purpose in the State by providing a passably stable base for law; but the fighters' ambitions were running out of hand. In the eyes of these ferocious men, the desert and its towns and settlements seemed the enlightened centre of the world; ibn Saud was their acknowledged leader under God, so long as he led them in the direction they had been taught to want to go; and the world beyond the desert, which none of them had ever seen or been able to imagine, was merely the dark and heathen field God willed they should conquer for Him. In terms of Arabian history, this state of mind may be seen to be recurrent, for that part of the world had given birth to three great religions, and undoubtedly to many more which failed and were forgotten. A religion so primitive and militant as the Ikhwan's was doomed to failure in the twentieth century; but before its extremes were moderated, it drove its simple adherents to a kind of madness, in which they sacrificed themselves like lemmings in the sea, or moths in an irresistible blaze of light.

Ibn Saud still believed in his mission to purify Islam; but he was the only man in his domain who understood the subtle political webs which enclosed it, and almost the only man whose ardour was restrained by common sense. He saw plenty of enemies round him, each ripe for conversion or war; but he knew that all except one were protected by Britain. That one was ibn Rashid: and so he set all his power of persuasion to turn the Ikhwan's reforming rage away from the Sherif, and towards his other neighbour.

He had already sent his preachers to the outlying tribes of Rashid, and they had found enthusiastic converts; and at the very moment when he needed a human quarry for his troops, a fresh episode in the bloodthirsty family feud of the Rashidis gave him his chance. One day in 1920, the current ruler went out with his cousin for some target practice, and while the ruler aimed at the target the cousin aimed at the back of the ruler's head and shot him dead. The cousin himself was instantly chopped to pieces by loyal slaves, another cousin involved in the plot was thrown into prison, and the remaining claimant to the uncomfortable throne was a boy of eighteen whose mother was a negro slave. All this was nothing new in Hail. In the past century, only two of the heads of the ruling family were known to have died by nature. One other had committed suicide, one had been killed in battle by ibn Saud, and all the rest, at least a dozen, had been murdered by their own relations. But under the new young ruler, the domain was divided in its loyalty and largely ready to rally to a new creed and a more inspiring leader.

It was twenty years since ibn Saud had first fought an ibn Rashid. In all the successes and reverses of that long dynastic war, he had only once reached the gates of Hail, and then he had been repulsed. Now its own dissensions made it fall, as easily and unexpectedly as the Hasa had fallen when at last he had tried his strength against it. Ibn Saud advanced into Rashidi territory with his armies and his preachers. Rashidi tribes revolted, either to join him or to declare a short-lived independence. The young ruler in desperation released the cousin who had been imprisoned. The cousin, still impelled by family hatred, turned against the ruler, and the ruler fled from his own kinsman and threw himself on the mercy of ibn Saud. The cousin rallied some forces, fought a large but of course an indecisive battle, and at last was driven back within the city walls.

When ibn Saud had seen those walls before, he had not been able to breach them for lack of the guns the British had offered him. He still had no British guns, but his men had hauled his ancient Turkish cannons across the three hundred miles of desert from Riyadh. He did not fire them. Perhaps by then it would have been foolish to try, because the cannons and their ammunition had been in the careless hands of his gunners since he captured them seventeen years before. Perhaps, on the other hand, he preferred not to damage a town he was certain would soon be his, and not to affront its people who would soon become his subjects. But the cannons were effective as a threat, and the threat was combined with the lures which were also part of any Arab siege. There were three main gates in the city wall of Hail, and each had a separate body of men to defend it under a captain. Bribes were offered to each of the captains of the gates. After three weeks, the people of the town began to lose their nerve, one of the captains fell to temptation and opened his gate at night, and the city fell in ignominy. The usurping ruler held out for another month in the fortress of the city and then surrendered, and the twenty years' war was finished.

As ever, ibn Saud was chivalrous in victory. He prevented his troops from looting the city, and distributed his army's supply of food to the hungry city people. He took all the remaining members of the family of Rashid as his guests to Riyadh, where they lived out their lives at his expense, in reasonable freedom, within his crowded court. The captains of the Rashidi army were absorbed into his own; the two captains of the gates who had refused his bribes were promoted more quickly than the one who had accepted. He married the principal widow of his murdered rival and accepted the orphan children as his own – a practice in the aftermath of Bedouin battles which was both benign and shrewd, for it both ensured that the children would not suffer, and eliminated them as rival heirs. In course of time, the imprisoned cousin himself, who had held the fortress in the final stand, joined the numerous and honoured company of fathers-in-law of ibn Saud; and the House of Rashid, having lost its power in war, surrendered its independent existence in ibn Saud's receptive marriage bed. Henceforth, the whole of the central desert of Arabia belonged to him; and in a solemn conclave of the sheiks and the Ulema, led by his father, he was now proclaimed Sultan: the first formal title he had had.

PART THREE

THE KING

CHAPTER TWELVE

RULE OF LAW

Neither the increase in his territory nor the title of Sultan made any notable difference to ibn Saud's behaviour, but they can be seen in retrospect to mark an epoch, the end of what had been no more than a swollen sheikdom, and the beginning of a nation. They provide a convenient moment to turn aside from battles and intrigues, and see how he maintained the power he had won.

Although his domain was now twelve hundred miles long and six hundred wide, as nearly as anyone could define it, he still governed it single-handed in the manner of any Arab sheik. That was the only kind of government he knew, and at that time he had never doubted it was perfect. Superficially, his rule was unmixed despotism; but in the desert, Arab despotism, either a tribal sheik's or a sultan's, was always under control, simply because life was so cheap and the Arabs so independent in spirit. A Bedouin expected three things of his ruler: to keep order with a strong hand, to protect the poor against the rapacity of the rich, and to defend the grazing grounds against marauding neighbours. If the ruler was weak, and murders and robberies grew common, and the poor were oppressed and neighbours invaded the land, the people murdered the ruler and chose another without any hesitation; and if the ruler himself oppressed the poor and weak, beyond the limits of oppression which were recognised, his fate was just as swift. It was a primitive system, but it suited the desert and the Arabs very well. An Arab despot was given the power of life or death over his people, but his people retained the power of life or death over him; and if ibn Saud had ever lapsed from his people's idea of a ruler, he would have died as quickly as so many of the House of Rashid died.

In the desert, he ruled through tribal sheiks, and in the towns through local governors. The sheiks were still chosen in the traditional manner by their tribes, but the governors were his own appointments, and some of them were survivors of the cousins and boyhood friends who had captured Riyadh with him twenty years before. Abdullah ibn Jiluwi, for example, who had been first through the postern gate of the fortress and had killed the Rashidi governor, was now himself the governor of Hofuf in the Hasa, and had grown up to be a much more ruthless man than ibn Saud himself.

At about this stage of his career, he also began to collect

a few advisers round him. Most of them were foreigners from other Arab countries, because nobody in the kingdom had any more knowledge than he had of the problems of government on a national scale. The senior of them was Sheik Hafiz Wahba, an Egyptian with a wide experience of the middle east, who was later his ambassador in London. A Lebanese called Fuad Hamza was another, who organised in the course of time the nucleus of a Foreign Office. The only native of the country who held what might be called a ministerial status was Sheik Abdullah al Sulaiman, a man of Anaiza who began by keeping the box of Maria Theresa dollars which was the nation's treasury under his bed, and still used much the same simple methods twenty years later, as Minister of Finance, when there were golden sovereigns by the million in the treasury. Philby might also be said to have been an adviser, in so far as he was always ready with advice; but it was several years after the fall of Hail when he first joined his fortunes to ibn Saud's, and at his own wish he never held any paid or official position in the court. The older sons of ibn Saud were growing up, and when Hail was taken Saud and Faisal, the oldest two, were already commanders in his army; but he had not given either of them any other responsibility. Saud was twenty and Faisal about seventeen: Saud a man of action, keen on hunting and popular with the Bedouin, and Faisal already something of an intellectual with an interest, since his visit to London, in the outside world.

But none of these men was anything more than an adviser. None of them was given authority of his own. Ibn Saud's was the only authority in the kingdom, and on one subject, the handling of the tribesmen who were still the great majority of his people, he never asked for anyone's advice, because he believed with justice that nobody knew as much about it as he did. The essence of any Arab rule was that any Arab had a right of access to his ruler. This principle had evolved in small ephemeral kingdoms and in tribes, but ibn Saud clung to it all his life; and even when his subjects numbered millions, any man among them, rich or poor, expected to be allowed to walk freely into his majlis – his reception room or tent – and hail him by his first name and be welcomed, and sit down on one of the carpets or benches along the walls and tell him his troubles and complaints. The complaints might be against a neighbour or a rival, or against a governor, or even, if they were tactfully phrased, against ibn Saud himself; and justice was permanently promised.

As the number of his subjects grew, the time he spent in his majlis receiving them came to occupy most of every day; and in later years, when he had to negotiate with foreign
108

ambassadors, these dignified people always had to seem content to be interrupted by any ragged Bedouin who wandered in. But by then, as they all observed, ibn Saud had developed a most unusual ability for dealing with several different matters all at once. The Bedouin would enter, and the negotiations be broken off; while the ambassador hid his wounded pride, ibn Saud would listen to the Bedouin, announce his decision, explain his reasons for reaching it, and gossip for the time which good manners demanded; and then return to the negotiations precisely where he had stopped. In the pauses of a conversation, he could also dictate two letters sentence by sentence to two secretaries simultaneously: a convenience in a language which had never been reduced to shorthand.

Towards the end of his life, when his kingdom was an international power of some consequence, his subordinates tried to save his time and his waning strength by discouraging the flood of people who wanted his personal advice, and dealing with some of the minor complaints before they reached him. By then there were posts and radio telegraphs in the country, so that he was even more accessible than before; complainants did not even have to make the journey to Riyadh or sit in his majlis. But when he heard of this well-meant protection, it provoked one of the last of his formidable rages, and the very last of the royal decrees he issued. The decree was dated June, 1952, but it was still the expression of a simple Arab sheik.

"Whereas we have been informed," it said, using the royal "we", "that some complaints addressed to us through wireless or post offices are withheld from us, we hereby order that any complaint submitted to us by any person whatsoever shall be sent to us literally without any change. Those concerned shall not delay it or reveal its contents to the person complained of, whether he be a governor or a minister, of low or high rank." The decree ordered punishment for anyone proved to have delayed or stopped the delivery of any complaint for any reason, and commanded all governors to proclaim the order to all citizens. "We inform all our subjects," it ended, "that we are always ready to receive any complaints; if any person submits his complaint to us, he who has been done an injustice will undoubtedly be given his full rights, and he who causes this injustice will be punished as he may deserve. By so doing, we discharge the obligation before God of a sovereign to his people. We pray God to bestow success and blessing on all of us." The document ended without any of the pompous flourishes which monarchs are apt to use, both in the east and west. It was signed, quite sufficiently, "Abdul-Aziz."

Long before those days of posts and telegraphs, in the seasons which were best for travelling, spring and autumn, visitors crowded round his palace by hundreds or even thousands every day, bringing not only complaints but greetings, homage, congratulations and reports; but in spite of the ever growing numbers, each man who came to see him expected gifts. This also was an ancient custom, easy enough to maintain when sheikdoms were small and travel was difficult and dangerous; but ibn Saud observed it all his life, even when any of his subjects could reach him in Riyadh by thumbing a lift in a truck or buying a ticket, if they could afford it, in a regular airliner. The fundamental gift received by every man who ever went to see him for any purpose was a ceremonial cloak. He also gave money whenever that was appropriate, and presents in kind when it was not: jewelled daggers, swords, horses, women's clothing for his visitors' wives, necklaces of pearls from the Persian Gulf, rings, carpets, slave girls occasionally, and gold watches in his later more sophisticated years. His visitors were always fed at his expense, and provided with food for their journeys home, and many who were once given money also received a right to demand it every year. By custom, they never thanked him for these gifts. Indeed, the gifts were not a sign of favour, but on the contrary, to omit them was a sign of his serious and dangerous displeasure. When foreign visitors began to come to Riyadh, towards the end of his life, he extended the same fantastic largesse to them: diplomats, business men, journalists, technicians, airline pilots, army officers, all went away with his cloaks and daggers, or his jewels or his fine Swiss watches – but not with his slaves.

Apart from his visitors, thousands of other people expected his bounty. Tribal sheiks were regularly given stocks of food, and annual gifts of money which in practice provided a salary. People who suffered disasters, fires, accidents or illhealth; those who ran into debt, or could not afford a dowry, or owed blood-money which they could not pay; those who had once been rich but had fallen on evil times, or those who were destitute and yet ashamed to beg; his own defeated enemies; even those who had twice been convicted of theft and consequently, in accordance with the ancient penal code, had had both their hands cut off and so become incapable of earning a living – all turned to ibn Saud for support and received it. Wherever he travelled, he provided feasts for the people he travelled among, and threw handfuls of silver coins to the poor, and when local sheiks gave him feasts in return they sent him the bill, and were disappointed if he paid much less than twice what the party had cost them.

To any outside observer, it would have appeared that thousands of the lowest good-for-nothings in the land were contentedly sponging on their Sultan, and so they were; but ibn Saud knew perfectly well what was happening, and was perfectly satisfied with it. Generosity and hospitality are real pleasures to an Arab, in addition to being enjoined by his religion; and it is no part of perfect generosity to consider whether one's beneficiaries deserve it. Ibn Saud could not have curtailed his gifts because tradition demanded them, and because his power partly depended on them, but he would not have curtailed them if he could. He enjoyed them.

This tradition runs all through a purely Arab society, from richest to poorest. There is a popular story of a very poor Bedouin who owned almost nothing but a splendid and valuable mare. A sympathetic friend, to relieve the poor man's want, had offered a very high price for the mare but had been refused. A time came when the mare was all that stood between the Bedouin and destitution, and the friend sent a message that he was coming again to make another offer. He came, and was entertained to the feast which hospitality demanded. It was the mare; and the Bedouin of this story is not considered foolish, but wise and good, by other Arabs. A poor Bedouin whose family is hungry will camp away from caravan routes, because the moral obligation to feed frequent travellers might reduce him to penury and his family to the edge of starvation; but even he will grind the last of his husks of coffee for a stranger, for he never knows when he may need help himself. Every true Arab likes to give and entertain according to his means or a little beyond them. Ibn Saud's means were the most capacious in the country, and so therefore was his giving; and it was only a part of tradition that this giving should often leave his treasury empty, as it did.

Thus while strength of character, self-confidence and fighting skill were the sources of his power, accessibility and generosity were two of his methods of wielding it. A third was the exercise of justice. His majlis was more than a reception room, it was also a court of law; he was the judge, and the gaolers and executioners were his slaves, and no professional advocates intervened to complicate issues with pleading. Yet the exercise of justice provided another control over Arab despotism. The court and the prison and executioners were his, but the law was not his, it was God's. The Wahhabi Ulema, in discarding the complexities which time had added to the simple Moslem faith, had also discarded most of the subtle interpretations which had been placed on the holy Koranic law since the time of Mahomed, and all the extensions from Greek and Roman law which had been added to it. They believed the code of law of Wahhabi Arabia was

111

the pure essence of the law which God revealed to the Prophet thirteen hundred years before. Ibn Saud's own conscience would never have let him twist the Prophet's revelation to his own ends; and if he had tried, the Ulema would soon have corrected him and sooner or later, if he persisted, have overthrown him.

In general, under this simple and ancient code of law, few deeds were defined as crimes, but punishments were drastic. Murder and theft were the principal crimes which had prescribed rewards. For theft, a hand or a foot was cut off in public by the executioner's sword, and hung up in a prominent place as a warning. For murder, the sentence was death or the payment of blood-money, and the family of the victim had the right to make the choice. If they chose death, they also had the right to be the executioners, so that honour was perfectly satisfied and no family feud was started. By tradition, they used the method the murderer had used, but by custom one relative was chosen to shoot the convicted murderer; and it was thought an act of grace if he raised his gun to shoot, and let the convicted man wait a second or two for death, and then forgave him.

The punishment for treason was entirely at ibn Saud's discretion, and although he could have executed every rebel, he seldom did so. Whenever he did proclaim a sentence of death or amputation it was carried out immediately. But most of his judgments were a matter of equity and Arab common sense. Malicious wounding or damage of property, for example, were simply punished by the payment of recompense. For wounding, there was a kind of tariff according to the nature of the wound, and offenders who could not pay were shut in a dungeon until their family raised the money. When motor cars appeared in the country, the same rigorous tariff was applied to drivers, and after a collision both drivers were put in gaol until a court had decided who should pay.

Much later in the reign of ibn Saud, when oil was found in his country and Americans came to live there, his punishments, especially the amputations, seemed to them to be barbarous. Once or twice, they reported thefts to his authorities, but they were shocked when their employees were convicted and lost their hands or feet, and especially shocked when they died of blood-poisoning or gangrene. Consequently, they began to suffer thefts in silence, and Arabs began to understand that they could rob Americans in safety. Next, the Americans asked permission to treat the stumps of thieves convicted in their neighbourhood, so that their wounds would heal, and that was granted. Finally, they asked to be allowed to give pre-operative treatment, but the thought of his convicts coming drugged and careless for their punishment was too much for ibn Saud. He refused, and replied in effect that if he condemned a man to have his hand cut off, he did it with very good reason, and expected the man to know it was happening. The Americans' feelings, indeed, were understandable but illogical. It is not very long in western history since punishments for theft were even sterner. Society must be highly organised, and possess an effective police force, before it can dare to moderate punishment as a deterrent and replace it by a sufficient risk of detection. Bedouin society only began to be organised under ibn Saud, and he had no detective police force. It was only fear of inexorable punishment which had brought the Bedouin out of anarchy and made the desert safe. Without these punishments, the Americans could never have developed the oilfields in peace, unless they had tamed and ruled the Bedouin themselves.

As ibn Saud, between his warlike expeditions, spent so much of his time in his majlis, his most familiar aspects in peace are those of host and judge. The few people who went to visit him from abroad in the 1920s were received by a series of chamberlains or delegates: first at the coast, to welcome them, and then at intervals on their journeys through the desert, to ensure they had all they needed, and finally at the gates of the rambling, primitive, mud-brick palace in Riyadh. Thence sheiks of the entourage led them by the hand, past bodyguards in gold and scarlet robes, through crowds of suppliants in the courtyards, by labyrinthine corridors where Bedouin and slaves and soldiers sat waiting for the Sultan's bidding, and holy men in shadowed archways endlessly recited the Koran; and finally through ante-rooms where close companions of the Sultan and some of his elder sons were ready with their greeting. The influence of ibn Saud pervaded this throng of people, and news of what he was doing was constantly passing among them; and since his people referred to him among themselves as the Shuyuk, which is the plural of sheik, the news of him was given in the plural: the Shuyuk are praying, are hunting, are dining, have gone to rest, are angry.

After this evidence of far-flung autocratic power, some visitors were surprised by the simplicity of the Sultan's dress and manner. Only two things distinguished his clothes from the Bedouin's: one, that they were always clean, and two, that a gold wire was woven into the fillet he wore round his head-cloth. His Wahhabi austerity of dress contrasted with his liberal use of scent; but scent was an indulgence approved by the Prophet and always enjoyed by the Arabs, and ibn Saud himself had been heard to say that he followed the Prophet in three things, prayer and scent and women.

113

The majlis of the palace of Riyadh was a large undecorated room divided by a line of pillars down the middle, for desert architecture was restricted not only by Wahhabi taste but also by the length of the palm trunks which could be used for rafters. The room was shadowed, in contrast to the brilliance of the sun, so that visitors, whether by design or not, could be seen approaching before they could see inside it, and found themselves confused by the gloom for a moment before they saw the tall silent motionless figure waiting for them. He stood up courteously to receive the humblest of his callers, and led those whom he wanted to honour, holding them by the hand, to a seat beside him. After the formal inquiries which Arab etiquette demanded, his conversation was forceful and to the point, and he emphasised his words by gesturing with a camel-stick which he always carried. Arabic scholars found his homespun desert dialect confusing, and he is said to have had a habit of explaining that his argument could be placed under three headings and then elaborating six or seven; but he had the proficiency in discussion only possessed by people who know exactly what they are talking about, and the astutest diplomats came away with an impression of his wisdom.

Meetings with ibn Saud, as with any Arab, were punctuated by the serving of coffee, the other universal indulgence of the Arabs. This habit, not nearly so ancient as the use of scent, was unknown in the Prophet's time. Accordingly, when coffee was first introduced to the desert it was passionately denounced by the puritans of the day, and people were executed for drinking it; but in the course of time the most extreme Wahhabis succumbed to the addiction and forgot the religious argument. When ibn Saud called for coffee, the call was taken up by slaves and soldiers and shouted in fearful warlike voices to the distant room where the coffee-makers sat; and some of his guests, who did not understand what was happening and perhaps were a little nervous in the presence of a man who had the power to cut their heads off, were alarmed by this sudden commotion. On the other hand, not one of his western visitors left him without a recollection of his smile, and several of them used the word which Gertrude Bell had used to describe it: sweet. The oddness of this effeminate word, applied to such an extremely masculine man, is a measure of the impression his smile had made on them; many people only half convinced by his arguments were persuaded to accept them by his smile. Far fewer people, fortunately, saw him in his rages, which were rarer. Those who did were terrified.

Conversation was not only a way of conducting business, it was also the only kind of intellectual entertainment in Wah-

114

habi Arabia, where science and all the arts, the theatre, music, painting, sculpture, even writing except of religious tracts and histories, were condemned as immoral. Accordingly, after the evening prayers, when ibn Saud had nothing else to do, he simply sat and talked. Usually he had half a dozen companions with him, but most of the conversation was a monologue except when Philby was there to argue with him, and anyone used to a wider choice of pleasures would have found the evenings unbearably tedious. It took a particular kind of determination to argue with ibn Saud, and he was not used to being contradicted; but on the other hand his sycophants could go too far and he often rejected flattery, saying he knew himself better than the flatterer knew him, or that no being but God possessed such qualities: a small but engaging streak of modesty. The subjects of conversation were limited. In his serious moods he talked of religion and desert politics and the art of ruling, and sometimes of astronomy. Any man who lives in the desert studies stars, but ibn Saud's astronomy was closer to religion than to science, and he never quite lost his belief that the earth was flat. In lighter moods almost all the talk was of women. At his gayest, he devised and perpetrated practical jokes and "dares" which were boyish in essence but often had macabre Arab overtones. Any schoolboy, for example, might have thought of one bet which Philby recorded: a bet that one of ibn Saud's companions would not spend a night in a cave supposed to be haunted by jinns. The macabre element was that one of the prizes was a negro girl who was taken, terrified, to share the companion's vigil, and was given to him although he lost the bet.

The only public amusements allowed in Riyadh were feasts and picnics, and falconry and races. Ibn Saud avoided most of the feasts, and when he had to attend them he did not seem to enjoy them very much. They were held to celebrate weddings and welcome important guests, but the food at a feast only differed from everyday food in quantity. All Arabs who could afford it ate rice and boiled mutton twice a day, and feast days mainly involved the slaughter and boiling of larger numbers of sheep – except on very special occasions when a whole boiled camel formed the centre-piece, the camel being stuffed with sheep, the sheep with chickens, and the chickens with eggs. Feasts therefore gave the pleasure of hospitality to the hosts, but little pleasure to guests unless they were poor and hungry. Among the hungry guests, the feasts were a race against time. Talking during meals was not expected, and they sat round the vast dishes on the floor, moulding the mixture of rice and greasy mutton into balls with their right hands stuffing it into their mouths, as quickly as good manners would permit. Far more food was provided than the invited guests could possibly eat. When the guests of honour had eaten all they could and sat back praising God and the host, it was impolite for others to continue, and that was the reason for their haste. When they had retired, inferior people, slaves and the household of the host, had their opportunity; and finally beggars and onlookers and children from the streets were allowed to fall upon what remained and eat what they could if they wished, or stuff the rice and bones and solidified gravy in their skirts and carry it away. During the 1920s, ibn Saud himself withdrew more and more from these banquets. He ate very little, his own private meals were hasty and irregular, and he perpetually worried about his digestion and dosed himself with medicines his doctors concocted for him. He never learned to use a knife or fork, but about 1930 he installed some chairs and tables in his dining-room, and when he had western guests he used a spoon.

Picnics, falconry and races pleased him more than feasting. All of them, like the feasts, were purely masculine entertainments, but he took his small children and the adopted children of the Rashids to the picnics in the groves of palms round Riyadh, each child attended by the slave appointed to serve and protect it day and night; and he seemed to enjoy and succeed in the role of father. Races, on horseback and camelback, were arranged on the spur of the moment, and sometimes the guests at the picnics competed in target shooting; and ibn Saud, of course, was expected to give the prizes. Falconry had more of the qualities of sport, since it needed some patience and practice; but the patience belonged to the men who were employed to train the hawks, not to the rich men who owned them. It was not a sport to suit most modern western taste. When gazelles were the quarry, they had their eyes pecked out, and the hunters only had to follow on horseback, in order to reach the blinded creatures before they were killed by the hawks; for a Moslem could not eat an animal which had not been killed in a ceremonial manner with a prayer. Nevertheless, the gallops across the desert for this purpose were exciting. This kind of hunting defeated itself when cars were brought into the desert. Ibn Saud and his sons and companions discovered they could kill more game by being driven at top speed across the desert with relays of rifles and men in the back of the cars to load them, and other cars behind to collect the corpses; and within a few years, the remaining gazelles had taken refuge in the mountains, the desert ibex was almost extinct, and nothing could be found to hunt within hundreds of miles of Riyadh.

From public duties and pleasures he disappeared at night, and in the afternoon siesta, to his harem. Unfortunately, very little can ever be known of what he did there. His domestic secrets were always respected by the few Arab men and the many women who shared them; and Philby, who had a longer and closer friendship with him than any other westerner, loyally kept to himself whatever backstairs gossip he may have heard, and only published the scraps of information he was given by ibn Saud himself. The rest is surmise and deduction.

It is difficult for monogamists, thinking of the problems of a man with three hundred wives, to follow a middle course between shocked disapproval and hilarity; but if these extremes cannot be avoided, hilarity is probably the more appropriate of the two. Philby, in one of his most felicitous understatements, said that ibn Saud had "a marked tendency to uxoriousness", and so he had; but he only indulged it within the limits of a moral code which has survived without the slightest change for thirteen centuries. It is possible to disapprove of this ancient moral code, but there is no logic in disapproving of people who are born to it and observe it conscientiously. On the other hand, one comes nearer to an understanding of the Arabs' outlook by admitting that ibn Saud's achievement has a comic aspect, because most of them found it amusing.

One guess that may be made with confidence is that ibn Saud's harem was nothing like the conventional western picture of harems. Dancing girls in what are recognised as harem trousers do not fit the Wahhabi scene. If such creatures exist or existed anywhere, it might have been in Persia or Turkey or Egypt. Ibn Saud's uxoriousness was not licentiousness, and it needed no artificial stimulation. On the contrary, his own sparse comments on it give an impression of rather dull respectability, only relieved by frequent changes of partners. He once told Philby that his conversation with his women was never more than small-talk; and it would certainly have been unreasonable of him to expect intellectual companionship from his wives, because he also said, on another occasion, that women could be permitted to listen to the reading of holy books, but that other reading, and especially writing, were unsuitable accomplishments for them. But intellectual companionship was not the point. Like ordinary Bedouin men – and probably women – he frankly thought sex was the greatest of worldly pleasures. He is said to have told the Sheik of Kuwait that the thing most worth living for was "to put his lips on the woman's lips, his body on her body and his feet on her feet"; and although some misunderstanding or fault of translation made him seem to describe a difficult posture for a man of six feet three, his meaning was perfectly clear.

Each of his four current wives, except the more ephemeral

of them, was given a house and slaves and attendants of her own, and as the Koran enjoins a husband to treat all his wives with equal consideration, he visited each of the houses strictly in its turn. He also had a house of his own which was run by his concubines, who had a status which could hardly be distinguished from his wives'. He said he restricted himself to four concubines and four favourite slaves, making twelve in all; but of course he changed the composition of this team whenever he liked. Sometimes he freed a slave who really won his heart, and once or twice in this way he married a girl he had originally bought. One or another of his dozen demanded his attention every night, and he seemed to feel that this was a minimum duty his reputation depended on; but he admitted he seldom indulged them more than once a night, and never in the morning, which he thought was unhealthy. The last few of his children were born when he was 67, and Philby believed his failure to have any more preyed on his mind after that and made him more morose and illtempered than he had been in his prime. Perhaps the most notable of all his remarks to Philby was that he had never seen a woman eat or drink.

Three hundred wives, of course, is a round figure. Some authorities put it higher. Nobody ever knew precisely how many he had married. He lost count himself, and his own estimates of the number depended on whom he was talking to. In 1930, he told Philby and some of his other companions that he had married 135 virgins and about a hundred others, but had decided to limit himself in future to two new wives a year. If he kept his resolution for the next twenty years of his active life, it would have brought him to 275. But on the other hand, when he was talking to western acquaintances later in his life, he was much more diffident in his claims. In 1947 he told a party of Americans he had had thirty wives. One of his brothers-in-law who was present disagreed with him, and said the number should be forty or fifty, and after a good-humoured argument they compromised on forty-five. Evidently he distinguished in his own mind between wives of long standing and the wives of a night or two he married on his travels – those whose faces he was said to have never troubled to unveil. Certainly, although he was equally legally married to all of them, there was a wide distinction. To some he was very faithful. One of them, whose name was Munaiyir, bore him seven sons and several daughters and was still married to him when he died.

Ibn Saud's achievements in legal marriage were unique, at least in modern times. Few other Moslems would have had the stamina, or even perhaps the wish, to rival him. Most Arabs were well within the quota of four wives – not merely
118

four wives at a time, but four for a lifetime – and the Prophet probably never considered that any man would make such a literal and liberal use of the marriage law as ibn Saud. Yet the law was perfectly precise. It followed the principle one may trace in the whole of Koranic law: that law should restrict a man as little as possible, but punish him harshly if he acts outside it. Islam admits that man is polygamous in his instinct, and believes that life-long sexual fidelity to one woman is an unnatural standard, contradictory to his nature. God who gave man his instinct also gave him the law by which he must govern it. Hence, Moslem marriage law gives sufficient scope to the instinct man is provided with, and defines the rights of wives and children; and having given so much scope, it punishes transgressors very severely. When wives are plentiful, and divorce is easy and no disgrace either to man or wife, adultery is a temptation most men can be expected to resist, and punishment for it is correspondingly stern: it is the ancient Biblical practice of stoning to death. Christians are sometimes shocked by the harshness of the punishment, and by the laxity, as it appears to them, of the marriage law. Moslems are equally shocked by the unnatural restriction, as it appears to them, of enforced monogamy, and by learning that in Christian countries adultery is not a crime at all. But both, to some extent, misunderstand the other, for the harshness of punishment must always be in proportion to the liberty the law allows. In practice, in Wahhabi Arabia, few adulterers were stoned. Few people committed the crime. Men's wants were satisfied, and they seldom saw other men's wives; while if a wife fell in love with another man, only the stubbornest husband would refuse to divorce her. Moreover the law demanded four reputable eye-witnesses as proof of adultery, and adulterers, one may suppose, would be exceptionally careless to commit their crime in view of so many people. The ghastly penalty was therefore seldom suffered except by people who insisted on pleading guilty in remorse.

Not even Philby, in thirty years of friendship with ibn Saud, ever saw any of his wives, and not even an Arab could generalise with any certainty about the characteristics of Arab women, because he never met any except his own close relations. One tends to think of such hidden, veiled, uneducated women as downtrodden creatures who had very little will or character of their own, but what evidence there is suggests that they had quite as much as anybody else. In public affairs they played no part whatever, but they certainly had their influence behind the scenes. Perhaps in one respect their lack of education was an asset; as girls they wasted no time on academic studies, but spent it all on learning a single lesson: to handle
119

men. It is said that ibn Saud's wife Munaiyir was such a capricious and self-willed young woman and led him such a dance that he divorced her and let her marry someone else; but then found he was so miserable without her that he caused her second husband to divorce her and married her again. There was another girl he married three times; she had a baby by him each time, and by three of her four intermediate husbands. It is also said of Munaiyir that after he died, when her seven sons were grown-up princes with homes and families and dignity of their own, she insisted that all of them should still dine with her every day unless they could give her an extremely good excuse. Many Arabs who prided themselves on their manly independence were really under their mother's thumbs, and matriarchal pride was recognised in the custom of naming women after their eldest sons. Munaiyir, whose eldest son was Prince Tallal, was usually known as Umm Tallal, the Mother of Tallal.

Nevertheless, by any standards except the standards of this strangely masculine society, it was quite unfair that the law restricted women more than men. A man could have his wives and concubines and slaves, but a married woman committed a capital offence if she had sexual relations with anyone but her husband. A man could divorce his wife in a moment, but a wife could only divorce her husband by a legal process. The veiling of women and their confinement in the harem were matters of custom not of law: the Koran only demanded that they should be modest in their dress. It was only custom also that they should never be given the slightest education. But both customs were as rigid as the law, and self-perpetuating. The whole relationship between the sexes was based on the concept that a woman's only pleasure is to please her lord and master; but as Arab women were brought up with that idea and in their ignorance never heard of any other, there was nothing to make them dissatisfied with their status, and there is no reason to think they were less happy than other women. The wives of poor men suffered from overwork, and the wives of rich men suffered from boredom, and some of them, rich or poor, suffered from unpleasant husbands; but all of that could be said of women anywhere, and women in Arabia had at least the compensation that they were never left to fend for themselves: whatever happened, poverty, sickness, widowhood or divorce, their nearest male relations always took care of them. The wives of ibn Saud undoubtedly thought themselves the luckiest of women. Their security of tenure was frail, and they had to share him with at least eleven others. But when their marriage to him ended, they carried the honour of it with them all their lives, and while it lasted he was handsome and powerful and generous and, if a man can learn from experience, must have been the most talented of lovers.

Slavery was an institution of ibn Saud's domain which was less defensible than polygamy. He himself owned hundreds of slaves all his life, and slavery was an essential part of his social system. It had always existed in Arabia, and Wahhabi Arabia was so isolated that the revulsion against slavery which spread through the civilised world in the nineteenth century did not penetrate the desert until a century later, if indeed it has even reached it now. Meanwhile Arabia was and perhaps still is the centre of a trade which spread its tentacles far over Africa and Asia.

Most of the slaves in the desert and the desert towns were the sons and daughters of generations of slaves, but others were brought into ibn Saud's domain by many routes. The traders of Muscat bought or abducted them on the coast of East Africa and the far shores of the Persian Gulf. A smaller and more specialised trade overland brought light-skinned boys and girls from the north, Georgians and Circassians and Armenians who were valued for their beauty. Negroes and Ethiopians were brought in caravans across the Sahara and smuggled through the British patrols on the Red Sea into the Hejaz and thence to the central desert; and stocks in the Hejaz were also replenished by the pilgrims to Mecca themselves, some of whom were tricked into slavery when they were destitute, and some of whom deliberately brought their own surplus children or servants and sold them to pay the expenses of the journey. By this means, Indians, Javanese and Malayans were found in the desert markets. Cox and his colleagues and predecessors, and the British Navy, played a lone hand against the trade by sea. Nobody helped them, and they were even opposed by the French, who were still allowing some Arab slavers in the first decade of the twentieth century to fly the French flag and so avoid being boarded by the British. The British efforts never succeeded in stopping the seaborn trade, although they made it much more dangerous and so increased the price of the slaves who were smuggled through; and the trade overland was hardly controlled at all.

Probably ibn Saud never gave a serious thought in his life to the morality of owning or buying slaves, and probably nobody ever questioned it in his presence. He knew, of course, that Cox disapproved of it, and that the Turks, among others of his neighbours, had tried to abolish it in their own country, and he was irritated by a right which the British claimed to set free any slaves who escaped to their consulates. In 1936, the British persuaded him to make a decree forbidding the import of any slaves by sea, and forbidding their import by land unless their owners could prove they were already slaves

121

before the date of the edict. But that decree, which was totally ineffective, was the only step he ever took against the custom. In his eyes, slavery was simply a part of the natural order: slaves were a race which existed somewhere between the human race and the camels, and when he gave a pretty girl to one of his favoured friends he no more considered the feelings of the girl than those of the handsome mare he might give to another. If his conduct had ever been called in question, he would probably have defended it as other slave-owners have often defended theirs. Such people can always claim that slaves may be better fed and housed and clothed by their owners than they would be by their own free efforts. Certainly his own male slaves, and those of many other Arab autocrats, were ready to defend their owners to the death. Throughout the kingdom, in households great and small, slaves could be seen in positions of trust and some degree of honour, like the positions of contemporary British butlers. The attitude of the masters was perpetuated, as it so often has been, by the attitude of the slaves, who had never heard of a world without slaves and accepted their lot without question, taking a pride – again like the British butlers – in the family they served and their own place in it. It was true that young slave girls were expected to satisfy their owners' roving lust before they were married off to other slaves to provide a new supply; but they expected this fate no less than their owners did, and probably very few of them, unless they were viciously treated, had either the intelligence or the sensibility to resent it.

None of these arguments, of course, can excuse the practice of slavery anywhere. Most slaves in Arabia may have been treated tolerably well, even with casual kindness and affection; but they had no rights whatever and no protection, and the penalties were dreadful if they tried to escape and were caught. The worst of all the misery was not among those who were born to be slaves, but in the distant villages where children were sold and abducted, on the caravan routes where they were shackled together, and in the markets within the kingdom itself, where men, women and children were auctioned like animals, and husbands and wives, or parents and children, were sold separately if bids were too low for them as families. This cruelty and degradation were condoned by the Moslem religion, and always had been; yet they only continued because the religious leaders shut their minds to them. If the slaves had been infidels, a logical argument for slavery might have been founded on the Koran and the teaching of Wahhab, but they were not. All of them were either born Moslems or compelled to accept the faith, and many became as devout as any of their masters. It should therefore have been admitted that masters and slaves were equal in the sight of God, unless it were denied that slaves were men at all. It was indeed considered an act of grace to free a slave, but when it was done it was often done to earn merit in Paradise, rather than through compassion for the slave. Slavery was so firmly entrenched in desert society that no religious leader had ever tried to uproot it, and ibn Saud and his successors were equally blind to its evils. It was still as active as ever long after his death, and long after the country had joined the United Nations and learned of the Declaration of Human Rights. It was only in 1962, when the monarchy which ibn Saud had founded was on the defensive against the attacks of neighbouring Arab republics, that slavery at last was declared illegal; but even then the declaration seemed to be made unwillingly, and brought no signs of rejoicing among the slaves or remorse among their owners. Slavery is still too fundamental a part of the life of the desert towns to be abandoned in a day, or even in a generation.

However, at the time of the fall of Hail, the first breath of self-criticism in the desert was a whole generation way. Ibn Saud presided over his archaic kingdom, always accessible during the day and always closeted in his harem at night; almost always generous but sometimes cruel; almost always jovial but sometimes furious; perfectly satisfied that the way he governed was the best if not the only way to govern, and sincerely believing his work was divinely ordained. This belief was the final control of his despotism. Praise and power never corrupted him, because he never lost his acute awareness of the power and presence of God.

CHAPTER THIRTEEN

THE FIGHT FOR MECCA

The capture of Hail brought new expanses of desert into ibn Saud's domain and new grandeur to his court. But it did not bring much money; if anything, it left him poorer than before. Soon after it, he asked for another meeting with Cox, who by then was the British High Commissioner in Iraq. Perhaps he hoped to have his subsidy increased, as a kind of reward for his victory. During the war, he may have reflected, the British had offered to pay him to beat ibn Rashid, and now he had done it for nothing; he could hardly have understood that the moral and financial outlook of western governments was different in peace and war. Perhaps, on the other hand, he only hoped for advice. Cox was his only friend with any worldly wisdom.

Cox agreed to meet him, for reasons of his own. While ibn Saud was engaged with ibn Rashid, the British dispositions of the fertile crescent had been completed, in a manner which Cox knew ibn Saud would very much dislike. The British Government had installed the Sherif's son Abdullah – the same prince who had lost his army to ibn Saud at Khurma – as Amir of Transjordan, and supported him, under the mandate, with a British air force. And in 1921, at a conference in Cairo, Mr. Winston Churchill as Colonial Secretary had caused another of the four sons, Feisal, to be installed as the King of Iraq.

This king-making was a sop to the Sherif and to Lawrence; and although nothing could have satisfied the Sherif, it did at last set Lawrence's demanding conscience almost at rest. It was also successful, for both the monarchies outlived the mandates and continued long after the countries were independent. In Transjordan, Abdullah ruled for thirty years until he was murdered in 1951, and his grandson King Hussein still rules in 1964. In Iraq, Feisal lived until 1933, and his dynasty lasted until his grandson was murdered by the forces of the dictator, General Kassem, in 1958. In the turmoil of middle eastern politics, both governments deserve to be called long-lived.

By the capture of Hail, ibn Saud acquired long frontiers with both Transjordan and Iraq. When they were added to his existing frontier with the Hejaz, there were several thousand miles of desert borders, unmarked and ill-defined, between him and the family of his rival. These gave unlimited possibilities of trouble, and Cox's aim in meeting ibn Saud was to try to persuade him to accept the two new kingships and recognise their frontiers.

An urgent point was added to the meeting by the maddest so far of all the Ikhwan's exploits. After the capture of Hail and the subjugation of its tribes, fifteen hundred members of the Brotherhood pressed on towards the north, intent on further holy desolation to earn themselves credit in Paradise. With or without the permission of ibn Saud, they crossed the frontier into Transjordan; and there they massacred the inhabitants of a village within twenty miles of Abdullah's capital, Amman. By any standards, this was a crime. In the wildest of the Bedouin wars and raids, nobody ever deliberately injured women or children, or old men who had given up carrying arms; but the Ikhwan's lunatic blood-lust on that expedition made them slaughter every human being in their way, and their ignorance of the outer world made them do it almost in sight of the British air force stationed under the mandate in Amman. Consequently, these men, who had never seen a machine of any kind, found themselves attacked in the open desert by aircraft and armoured cars. Some escaped, but the Arabs on their line of march were as shocked as the British by their wanton act and had no mercy on them. Few men of the fifteen hundred returned to the villages where they had started, and these survivors found no sympathy even there. Ibn Saud threw them all into prison, to teach the Ikhwan not to fight without his orders.

The meeting between ibn Saud and Cox had a double importance, apart from renewing their respect for one another. For the first time, ibn Saud agreed to limit his kingdom by a line on a map, and for the first time a significant word was used in his part of Arabia: oil. They met in the winter of 1921, in the village of Oqair on the shore of the Hasa where they had met to sign the treaty in 1915. Cox landed on the beach from a naval pinnace: ibn Saud arrived, as usual, at the head of a camel-mounted army of miscellaneous followers. This was the first of their meetings attended by any chance observers; and among these was Ameen Rihani, an American poet of Syrian birth, who watched the proceedings with a humorous western eye.

As it happened, Rihani met ibn Saud in the desert and rode with him the last few miles towards Oqair, and unlike Shakespear he wrote about that rare experience: the earliest description by a foreigner of a scene too familiar to the Arabs to merit description. The caravan marched in the coolness of the night, which was the usual practice of the Bedouin of the central desert; and in the dark and silence, outriders could be heard as it approached, chanting the personal cry of ibn Saud to proclaim his passing, so that travellers might either approach him in respect or flee in awe. Rihani believed the cry was *"Ya su'aiyed,"* which is the diminutive of happiness, implying that the ruler offered happiness, but that great happiness could only come from God; but he probably misunderstood it, for the usual cry for the Sultan's progress was simply *"al Saud"*. Ahead of the column, servants drove flocks of sheep, and camels laden with tents and carpets and waterskins and the cauldrons used for boiling the sheep and the mounds of rice. The column itself was led by ibn Saud: much taller than most of his men, he also rode a taller camel, selected from a famous breed from Oman, so that nobody could fail to know him even in the darkness. On that occasion, his journey was leisured, which meant that the caravan only moved at a herdsman's pace; and as the camels shueffld through the sand, he discoursed on religion and politics to the minor sheiks and the captains of the army who rode beside him. Behind was a press of mounted soldiers, a dozen or fifteen abreast, and his slaves dressed in scarlet cloaks and armed with swords, and among his train were some of the recently conquered Rashids. They seemed morose.

At Oqair, ibn Saud was host to Cox, and with an Arab's hospitality, he had simply instructed his agent in Bahrain, who knew the English, to provide whatever an Englishman might need to make him feel at home. The tents for Cox and his party were pitched at some distance from ibn Saud's; and while ibn Saud's were only furnished with carpets and the camel saddles against which it was the custom for an Arab to recline, the Englishmen's contained chairs and tables, cutlery and linen, camp beds and a portable bath. The lavish provisions included cigars and whisky; a Wahhabi would still have been flogged for tasting either. Everything Englishmen reputedly needed, sinful or otherwise, was there; but not everything that an Arab's franker tastes demanded. Cox was three days late, and the entourage of ibn Saud was restive. One of them said to Rihani: "We Arabs cannot endure severance and long absence." A second, to explain this enigmatic statement, simply said: "We desire women all the time"; and he added, no doubt with awe: "And he whose desire is strongest of all desires is the Imam." The English, when at last they all arrived, were true to a tradition more admirable than absurd: they dressed for dinner.

The line on Cox's map which ibn Saud accepted at Oqair defined most of his frontier with Iraq and Kuwait. There were two places where he and Cox, who was representing Iraq, could not agree, but there they hit on the novel idea of drawing two frontier lines, with a neutral zone between them where herdsmen from either side would be free to look for grazing. They also promised that neither country should fortify the frontier. It was a simple and sensible agreement, and the neutral zones they drew have been respected ever since and still exist to-day.

A photograph also still exists of ibn Saud and Cox at this encounter, sitting on chairs in the sand outside a tent. Ibn Saud is massive and erect, in his robe and his chequered head-cloth. Beside him, Cox looks wan and tired and small. He is dressed like a middle-aged English gentleman of his period on his way to his London club, in laced boots, a lounge suit, a bow tie and a trilby hat. But standing behind them both, with a hand on the back of each chair, symbolically like a puppeteer who holds the strings controlling the monarch and the administrator, is a fat man in European clothes and a sun-helmet, contentedly smiling; and this is Major Frank Holmes, who had been pretending to be a butterfly collector, but had just revealed himself as the representative of an oil-prospecting syndicate.

Holmes was a New Zealander, much tougher than he looked. His employers were a small concern called the Eastern and General Syndicate, which had been formed in London a couple of years before. During the war, internal combustion engines had been shown to be the thing of the future, but nobody had been able to do much prospecting for fuel supplies. Immediately after it, therefore, financiers good and bad formed numerous syndicates and companies, some able to work the oilfields if they found them, and some merely hoping to get in first, to buy concessions from land-owners and sell them again at a profit. Everyone in oil knew that the Persian Gulf was a possible hunting ground. What little was known of Arabian geology suggested it; the Anglo-Persian Oil Company had been working productive wells in Persia since 1909, and there were seepages of oil on the surface in the island of Bahrain and the desert of Kuwait. Major Holmes had already been in both places, trying to bargain with their rulers on behalf of his syndicate for concessions to search for oil; and he had wormed his way into the conference at Oqair by sheer stubbornness and patience and by insisting that a unique kind of butterfly inhabited the Hasa. He pitched a small tent of his own between the Arab and British camps; and finding him there, both ibn Saud and Cox were too well-mannered to send him away again.

Nevertheless, his presence was embarrassing for them both. Holmes wanted a concession to search the Hasa, and Cox knew that Anglo-Persian was interested in the Hasa too. Anglo-Persian was much larger and more effective than Eastern and General, and the British Government had a major shareholding in it. As a civil servant, Cox could not become too deeply involved in commercial competition, but on the other hand he could not refuse to give ibn Saud sincere advice when he asked for it; and the only advice he could give was that if ibn Saud were to sell a concession to anybody, he would do better in the long run with the larger state-supported company, which was equipped to work an oil-field if it found one, and would not merely sell it to somebody else.

Ibn Saud's embarrassment was worse; not only a question of whom to sell a concession to, but of whether to sell one at all. He was desperate for money, and Cox had not offered him any; but with the Ulema and the other extreme Wahhabis behind him, he very much disliked the thought of having foreigners in his country. To admit unbelievers to the birthplace of Wahhabism was the very opposite of his hope to spread his doctrine farther and farther abroad. It threatened the moral basis of his realm with influences he did not understand, and might not be able to control, and therefore feared.

But poverty forced his hand: his need was immediate, and his fear was more remote. He did not believe there was any oil underneath his desert; if he had, he might have hesitated longer. He had no idea how much he ought to be paid for what he felt sure would be a wasted search; but he made up his mind at last, unwillingly, to sell the right to the highest bidder. Holmes was there, and Anglo-Persian was not; and after some months of hesitation, ibn Saud accepted Holmes's offer of £2,000 a year.

In retrospect, this sum of money seems ludicrous, for hundreds of millions of pounds' worth of oil have flowed from the Hasa since then. The very tents at Oqair were surrounded by fantastic hidden fortunes. But something even more ludicrous occurred. The syndicate sent some geologists, but they did not discover any oil at all. None of the major companies would buy the syndicate's rights, and after two years it failed to pay its rent and allowed its concession to lapse. More than another decade had passed before the search was renewed, and in the meantime ibn Saud was left as poor as ever.

For the next few years, indeed, he was poorer. The British, far from wanting to increase his subsidy, were impatient to stop giving money to him, and to the Sherif of Mecca. The subsidies had been cheap as a weapon of war; in peace, they seemed extravagant. Britain, having defeated the Turks, had left Arabia with numerous independent rulers, great and small, and had guaranteed nearly all of them against aggression; now she was in the absurd position of having to pay them all to refrain from committing aggression against each other. Perhaps people in government circles who knew of the muddled policies which had caused this situation might have regarded the payments as conscience money; but the average

128

British elector, faced perhaps with poverty at home and un-
employment, could not have been expected to care in the
least if Arabs wanted to cut each other's throats, or to see
any reason whatever why Britain should pay them to stop.
Sooner or later, a Member of Parliament would have asked
a question. Without waiting for that, the Foreign Office told
ibn Saud and the Sherif, in the autumn of 1923, that the payments would have to end the following spring.

That was the death-knell of the Sherif's kingdom: within
a year, ibn Saud was conqueror of Mecca. When the British
made the announcement, they invited both him and the Sherif
to send representatives to a meeting in Kuwait to try to re-
solve their differences, and Knox, who was then in Iraq, was
brought back to the Arabian scene as chairman of the conference; but argument lasted all the winter and settled nothing. Perhaps it would be unfair to say that the loss of £5,000 a
month determined ibn Saud to attack the Sherif. There were
other better reasons. But without that money, he had no reason to be afraid of British displeasure, and, which was even
more important, the loss of it brought him face to face with
financial ruin. Without the subsidy, or another source of income to replace it, he could not have held his kingdom together, and there was only one other source of income in
Arabia: the pilgrimage to Mecca. Whether or not he was
conscious of the choice, he had either to let his kingdom dis-
solve again in anarchy, or win the pilgrims' money for himself.

The other reasons for his action were provided by the
Sherif. An old man who causes his own downfall by his own
lack of wisdom is always a pathetic figure, and the Sherif
merits sympathy. He was on the edge of megalomania, and
although nobody now can diagnose the causes of his state of
mind, one cause of it was probably British policy. The British
had given him, or let him develop, an impossibly high ambition, and then stage by stage they had thwarted it. It is true
they never precisely promised in writing to support him as
King of all the Arab lands; but in a long correspondence
with him they had certainly guaranteed, at his request, the
independence of all Arabia and most of Iraq and Syria, which
then included Lebanon and Palestine, and they had even referred to this as the Arab Kingdom. Since they had given this
guarantee to him, as leader at least in name of the Arab Revolt, he had assumed they intended the vast domain to be his.
They knew this was what he believed, but while they needed
his help they had never dared to tell him firmly that his dream
was impossible, that all of Britain's power could never have
made him king of such a huge ungovernable entity; that
neither ibn Saud nor the Syrians nor Iraqis, and least of all

the Zionists, would ever have accepted him; or that he himself was absurdly incapable as a ruler. On the contrary, the British letters conveying the guarantee began with ridiculous flatteries which were neither British nor Arab in style, but might have been defined as Whitehall-Oriental. "To the excellent and well-born Sayyed," the first began, "the descendant of Sherifs, the Crown of the Proud, Scion of Mahomed's Tree and Branch of the Quraishite Trunk, Him of the exalted Presence and the Lofty Rank, Sayyed son of Sayyed, Sherif son of Sherif, the Venerable Honoured Sayyed, His Excellency the Sherif Husain, Lord of the Many, Amir of Mecca the Blessed, the Lodestar of the Faithful and the Cynosure of all devout Believers, may his Blessing descend upon the people in their multitudes!" There is some reason to think, from the Sherif's replies, that this struck even him as nonsense, but of course it made him think the British, in their own peculiar way, were eager to honour him. Instead of telling him the truth, once and for all, they let his hopes be slowly strangled by events. The Anglo-French agreement on spheres of influence, the British guarantee to ibn Saud, the appointment of his own sons instead of himself to rule Transjordan and Iraq, and above all the promise of Palestine to the Jews: these disillusionments, one by one, undermined his trust in Britain and left him so madly bitter that he came to believe the British consul in Jidda was trying to poison him.

The consul, however, far from being a poisoner, was a wit. He was Reader Bullard, and the chance combination of his sense of humour and the Sherif's antics provided dispatches which are still remembered in Whitehall as comic masterpieces: in Whitehall but unluckily nowhere else, for under the British Government's regulations even an official joke remains a state secret for fifty years. Afterwards, Bullard himself felt he had been unkind in making fun of the Sherif, but at the time when events in the Hejaz were coming to a climax, nobody in the British Foreign Office was taking the Sherif seriously.

His aged eccentricities were less amusing for his own subjects, and less amusing still for the pilgrims. He believed he had reformed the treatment of the pilgrims and stamped out the exploitation which had been a scandal under the Turkish rule. Everybody else in the Hejaz knew he had not. It was true that he had built a quarantine station and some hospitals, and covered some of the open water ducts in Mecca which had been a source of disease, and he believed and said that his hospitals were the finest in the world. But in truth they were so primitive that pilgrims preferred to die in peace outside them. He had also issued a tariff of maximum charges for the pilgrims' guides and lodgings, and their food and water – everything they needed except their camels, for which they were still supposed to bargain. But nobody took any notice of the tariff, and the bargaining and swindling were still as rapacious as they had ever been. He himself had increased the dues which pilgrims had to pay to him as ruler, and he insisted on payment in gold. Worst of all, he had lost control of the Bedouin. In Turkish days, they had been paid not to rob the pilgrims, but under the Sherif they found they could rob them and hold them to ransom without any risk to themselves, especially on the road from Mecca to Medina. To all this, the Sherif was happily blind. He was always surrounded by "yes-men" who, either through fear or greed, made sure that he stayed within the fool's paradise of his own delusions. So, while he regarded himself as the benefactor of the Moslem world, the Moslem world had begun to regard him as nothing better than a leader of robbers.

This reputation almost compelled ibn Saud to intervene. It incensed the extreme Wahhabis, and ensured that if ibn Saud attacked the Sherif and made himself the guardian of the holy cities, no Moslems would make any very strong objections. But the final impetus was given him by a single action of the Sherif's. For centuries, the Sultans of Turkey had been recognised as the Caliphs, the successors of the Prophet and the spiritual leaders of Islam. In the early part of 1924, Kemal Ataturk, the post-war dictator of Turkey, announced that the Caliphate was abolished, and the Sherif, who was visiting his son in Transjordan at the time, immediately proclaimed himself Caliph.

This was a pathetically foolish claim. The Caliph's had always been a controversial office, and sometimes in the history of Islam there had been rivals for it. But one certain thing about it was that no man could appoint himself Caliph, any more than a worldly prince, for example, could appoint himself Pope. There was not the slightest chance that Moslems in general would accept the Sherif's claim: on the contrary, it was certain the claim would turn his few remaining friends against him. This it did. The weekly newspaper in Mecca began to publish telegrams of congratulation from all over the world, but it was doubtful how many of them were real, because the paper's editor, and its most regular anonymous contributor, were known to be the Sherif himself. An outcry against him spread through the Moslem world. From that moment it was clear that somebody would depose him. It was only a question who would do it first.

Ibn Saud still hesitated. To attack and capture the Hejaz was not a military risk. He had been confident he could do it for years. But he probably knew it was quite unlike the

131

capture of Hail or the Hasa. The Hejaz was not simply another piece of desert; to add it to his kingdom was sure to change the character of the kingdom. His isolation would be lost, and his people exposed to foreign influence, and he would have to plunge into the international diplomatic world, for every country with a Moslem population kept a consulate in Jidda to take what care it could of its pilgrims. His simple skeikdom would have to become a nation.

There may also have been a more personal reason for delay: he was ill. Some kind of skin disease had infected his left eye with ulcers and blinded it. His own doctors had made it worse, and a surgeon summoned from Egypt had come too late to save it. For the rest of his life, that eye was shut, and it gave him a facial expression which was sometimes deceptively raffish and at other times forbidding.

Whatever the reason, he showed signs of a very uncharacteristic wish: to share the responsibility of deciding what to do. He called a meeting of the Ulema and other leading people, but it was his aged father who presided. The meeting sent a message to the Moslems of every country, drawing their attention to the Sherif's sins and proposing that the Wahhabis, on behalf of Moslems everywhere, should march into the Hejaz after the current pilgrim season and depose him: but it was ibn Saud's son Faisal, still not much more than a boy, who signed the message. There were very few answers, but the leaders of seventy million Indian Moslems approved the idea, and since they were British subjects, their approval gave the British Government a reason, or at least an excuse, for denying the Sherif the last shred of support that he might have expected.

The battle for the Sherif's kingdom began at the little town of Taif, and it might also be said to have ended there too. Taif was the nearest thing to a summer resort which existed in Arabia. Jidda, on the plain of the Red Sea coast, is unpleasantly hot and humid in the summer, even for Arabs; and Mecca, forty miles inland, is even worse, because it is shut in by hills which interrupt the breeze and seem to radiate heat at night; but Taif, another forty miles beyond Mecca, is high in the mountains which divided the rival kingdoms, and rich people of the cities of the plains had villas and gardens there. Ibn Saud, still cautious, allowed a band of his Ikhwan fighters to venture into the Sherif's territory, probably to see what opposition they would meet. Oh their way, they passed through Khurma, and the men of that oasis, still eager for revenge, came out to join them. Bedouin on the frontier left their families and herds in hope of loot or glory or excitement, and the reconnaissance force grew into a large but unorganised army. It marched towards Taif. Its leaders, the commander of the Ikhwan and the Sheik of Khurma, heard that the Sherif's son Ali was in the town, and were too impatient to wait for orders from ibn Saud, who was still in Riyadh, at least a fortnight's camel journey out of touch. They attacked the town, and the Sherif's garrison ran away with Ali in the forefront. The townspeople opened the gates after making some kind of truce, and the horde of Wahhabis entered unopposed. It is said that somebody who had not been told of the truce opened fire on them. Whatever happened, the bloodless conquest suddenly turned to a massacre: the Wahhabis looted and sacked and murdered. Wherever they could, they broke into houses and threatened the people until they confessed where their money was hidden, and then, having found whatever hoard there was, they cut the throats of all the men and boys, "sending them to Paradise" and laughing at those who showed their lack of faith by screaming. They pursued the religious leaders, the Ulema, into the mosque and murdered them there, for the mosque had domed tombs which made it a place of idolatry in Wahhabi eyes, and not of sanctuary. After a night of orgy, the commanders brought some order to their men, and all the surviving people of Taif, who had escaped by hiding or by successfully barricading their doors, were herded into Ali's palace outside the town. Two days later, they were released, but not allowed to go back to the town, which was so thoroughly pillaged by then that there was nothing left to be stolen; and they made their way to Mecca, taking frightful stories of the slaughter. Panic broke out in the holy city and thousands of people fled to Jidda. Thousands from Jidda took ship at once for Egypt, Africa or India. But the Sherif remained in his Meccan palace, declaring bravely that he would defend the city; bravely but foolishly, for his army had either disbanded itself or retreated to the coast.

Ibn Saud is said to have wept with dismay and disgust when he heard what had happened at Taif. The rumours of massacre were exaggerated, as rumours of horrors often are, especially in Arabia; but in fact three or four hundred people had been killed, and that was horrible enough. It was exactly what the people of the Hejaz had expected of the Wahhabis, remembering what had happened a hundred and twenty years before. The previous invasion had also begun with a sacking of Taif. But it would certainly not have happened if ibn Saud had been there. It was quite unlike his chivalrous treatment of the beaten people of Hail, and it was the worst possible beginning for a campaign of religious reform. He sent men on racing camels with orders to the two commanders forbidding further murder or looting on pain of execution, and forbidding also the sacrilege of fighting

133

in the precincts of the holy city; and he made ready to follow them with the bulk of his army as quickly as he could.

Mecca fell through fear. The merchants and the Ulema combined against the Sherif's hopeless show of courage, and forty of them sent him a formal request to abdicate in favour of Ali. No doubt they hoped by getting rid of him to turn away the wrath which they expected. He only gave in by degrees. At first, he agreed to abdicate but refused to appoint his son. A few days later, he agreed to leave Mecca, and finally he admitted his utter defeat and let himself be persuaded to nominate Ali to succeed him and leave the country.

He went with a preposterous kind of dignity. Deserted by all his sycophants, rejected by Islam, beaten in a day by ibn Saud, derided by the British, he loaded his family and all the possessions he valued into the half-dozen motor cars he had allowed to come into his country; and at the head of this ramshackle cavalcade, with his slaves beside him standing on the running boards, he drove out of Mecca through sullen hostile crowds. Even his enemies said he showed no sign of fear. In Jidda, he boarded an ancient coaster which he called his yacht, and people who saw his baggage said he personally supervised the handling of several soldered petrol cans, which were assumed to be filled with a hoard of sovereigns saved from his wartime subsidy or extorted from pilgrims. He sailed to Aqaba, in the far north of the kingdom, and after a while the British took him to exile in Cyprus. Six years later, he had a stroke, and was allowed to go to Transjordan to see his son Abdullah before he died: still a foolish embittered old man, still brooding on what he considered betrayal, still talking in riddles. Few people mourned him. His stubbornness had made him a nuisance to everyone, even his sons. Yet stubbornness always has a second aspect. It might also be said, and perhaps more truthfully, that even when his mind was least lucid he still remained true to his hopes and his beliefs, and it must be admitted that he was a victim of a time when British justice faltered.

Ibn Saud was taken unawares by the downfall of Mecca. His reconnaissance force reached the city long before he did, but the atrocities of Taif were not repeated. The commanders sent four of the Ikhwan into the city unarmed, in the ceremonial dress of pilgrims, to proclaim the safety of all who surrendered themselves to God and ibn Saud. The next day, two thousand entered, and manned the fort. They also were dressed as pilgrims, but they carried their rifles in spite of the holy law which forbids pilgrims in Mecca to be armed. The streets of the city were empty, the markets shut and the people barricaded in their houses. The Wahhabis set to work to purify the place, by demolishing shrines and tombs and orna-

134

ments on mosques, and destroying musical instruments and pictures of human beings. But there was no more looting, except of the royal palaces, and no more open violence. The city people began to emerge again, and began to think that the dreaded Ikhwan were not quite so bad as they had been portrayed. Perhaps they even began to understand that the Ikhwan themselves were in dread of a greater power.

A fortnight later, ibn Saud himself reached Mecca. He also put on the pilgrim dress, the seamless white cloths round the waist and shoulders, and on 13th October, 1924, he rode into Mecca bareheaded, repeating the humble formula of pilgrims: "Prepared for thy service, oh God, prepared for thy service." So he fulfilled the duty and life ambition he shared with every Moslem.

CHAPTER FOURTEEN

KING OF THE HEJAZ

With Mecca in his hands, ibn Saud turned to Jidda, its port, and Medina, the other of the holy cities. In Medina is the Prophet's tomb, and the Wahhabis who denied that even this was holy trained some artillery on it which the Sherif's army had left behind. But their aim was extremely bad, and before they managed to hit it there was time for the foreign consuls in Jidda to hear what they were trying to do, and to send a protest to ibn Saud, and for him to send an order to his troops to desist.

This was the first sign that he cared about foreign opinion. The second was that he did not attack Jidda at all, except by some desultory shooting from the same artillery. Ali remained for over a year in the town, while the Saudi forces surrounded it and reduced it by slow degrees to a state of starvation in which the poor were forced to beg for water and to sift the droppings of the horses of the rich for undigested grains of corn.

From the very beginning, Ali's stand was futile. Ibn Saud could have taken the town by assault whenever he liked, and was only deterred by the fear of offending or injuring the score or so of foreign representatives who lived there. The siege dragged on, because the foreigners and the citizens of Jidda were afraid of the wild Wahhabis, and because they liked Ali and sympathised with him, more or less, for having inherited a non-existent kingdom, so that even those who knew there was no hope for him could not bear to tell him so. The town filled with Syrian and Palestinian adventurers and mercenaries under a Turkish general who frequently promised Ali he was just about to chase the Wahhabi rabble out of the country. This makeshift army, wholly unqualified to fight, included several White Russians from Egypt who patched up and flew three old aircraft and dropped some home-made bombs from time to time; and there were also some armoured cars which had been made by an enterprising Syrian out of abandoned American army trucks and sheets of iron. As often happens in Arabian history, two contradictory stories are told of these armoured cars: one, that fanatical Ikhwan flung themselves at them until their mangled bodies brought them to a halt; and the other, perhaps more probable, that only one ever ventured beyond the walls of Jidda and came back shot through and through by rifle bullets, with the Russian driver angrily demanding compensation for a wounded eye.

A number of self-appointed peacemakers also turned up in the town with offers to mediate between Ali and ibn Saud, and among them was Philby. After a term as British Representative with King Abdullah in Transjordan – a post which Lawrence had also held before him – he had resigned from government service, because he was always disagreeing with British policy and disapproved in general of imperialism. He came to Jidda in the hope of winning ibn Saud's permission to explore the Empty Quarter, which nobody from the western world had ever entered. He had to postpone that ambition, because the British Government, through its consul in Jidda, forbade him to go beyond Jidda for fear that the Arabs would think he still had official standing; but he took a mischievous pleasure in dodging the consul and disobeying the Government, and succeeded by a round-about route in meeting ibn Saud on the edge of the forbidden zone of Mecca. He had promised Ali he would ask for lenient terms, but he found ibn Saud determined that no member of the Sherif's dynasty should remain. Nothing, indeed, that he or anyone could have done would have changed the fate of Jidda and Medina, or of Ali. Medina fell, and hunger and loss of trade made the people of Jidda turn against Ali and ask him to go. He offered his surrender to ibn Saud, with only two conditions, which were granted: that he and his family should be allowed to go in peace, and that the Ikhwan troops whom everyone dreaded should not be allowed in the town. A British warship took him to live in exile with his brother Feisal in Iraq, and in December, 1925, ibn Saud accepted the town from its leading citizens, extending his kingdom thereby from sea to sea. In the following month, in Mecca, he was proclaimed the King of the Hejaz.

While he had waited for Jidda to capitulate, he had established his own kind of rule in the rest of the country. It was much the most delicate act of government he had had to try. He started with the great advantage that everyone was terrified of him, but a mere reign of terror would never have satisfied him and would always have been too crude a way of ruling the holy land. For the lowest of economic reasons, he not only had to rule, but also to attract as many pilgrims as he could; and for the religious reasons which meant much more to him, he recognised a duty to help all Moslems, even those the Wahhabis considered heretics, to make the pilgrimage God desired of them. So he not only had to make the country safe for travellers, but also to moderate or repress the intolerance of the most extreme of his followers.

It took him a very short time to make the country safe –

much safer than it had been for centuries past – by means of his reputation for inexorable justice and, so far as is known, only one ruthless demonstration of power. One tribe decided to oppose him, and robbed a caravan and killed some travellers; and he sent his troops to surround the principal village of the tribe by night and slaughter every one of the two hundred men in it. Soon after this massacre, he met a European consul, and felt he had to explain its severity. He had to teach tribesmen the hard way, he said, because he understood them and knew that was the only way they would learn a lesson; "once we have punished them we shall not in the mercy of God have to do it again as long as we live." This he believed was not cruelty but mercy – more merciful than punishing evil-doers year after year in prison. At all events, whatever the logic of his argument, he promised that news of his retribution would spread through the desert and put an end to highway robbery; and so it did. On the pilgrim roads where Bedouin, for centuries past, had robbed and murdered and held to ransom, unless they were bribed to desist, travellers were able at last to go in peace, unarmed. For other crimes which had been common under the Sherif's and the Turkish rule, the full rigour of punishment prescribed by the holy law was brought back into use; amputations, beatings, executions by stoning and the sword in the squares and marketplaces. Justice in ibn Saud's domain was always seen to be done, and was soon respected in the Hejaz as it was in the lands he ruled from Riyadh.

The self-righteousness of his followers was less appreciated. Tens of thousands of Wahhabis who had not been able to make their pilgrimage during the Sherif's régime came out of the desert and desert towns to the holy cities, expecting to find them purged of heretical practices. These people, together with ibn Saud himself and his troops, inflicted their puritanism on the lax and easy-going people of the Hejaz. All tombs except the Prophet's were destroyed, even the mythical tomb of Eve on the outskirts of Jidda which women had always visited as an aid to conception; and at the Prophet's tomb Wahhabi soldiers were posted to stop people kneeling before it or reciting any prayer except the one which was officially approved. Smoking, drinking alcohol, making music, wearing gold or silk, all pleasures of the Hejaz, were forbidden, and attendance at prayers in a mosque five times a day was enforced by religious patrols who strode through the streets repeating the calls to prayer in fearsome voices and beating with canes on the doors and shuttered windows. An organisation called the Committee for Encouragement of Virtue and Discouragement of Vice, which was already active in the towns of the central desert, spread to the Hejaz to impose on every citizen the conscience the Wahhabi Ulema thought he ought to possess.

Residents of the Hejaz had to suffer this reformation in silence. It was a different matter with pilgrims from overseas. Possibly ibn Saud, and certainly the Ikhwan, would have liked to reform them too; but he himself was prepared to admit that the holy cities belonged in a spiritual sense to the whole of Islam, whoever ruled them and collected the pilgrims' gold. Accordingly, he did his best to separate the Wahhabis from the pilgrims of every other sect, and to try to persuade his Ikhwan to overlook the foreigners' shortcomings and treat them as their guests. There was only one serious clash. For a very long time, the Egyptian Government had provided each year a new black carpet to cover the Kaba, the central shrine of Mecca, and brought gifts of money and food for the poor of the city, and these gifts had been escorted from Jidda by Egyptian troops with a military band. Ibn Saud did not want to offend the Egyptians by putting an end to this custom, but he could not tolerate the band. The Egyptians came without it, but the Ikhwan watched them with suspicion; and when, from the Egyptian camp within the holy district a military bugle call was heard, the Ikhwan rushed the camp demanding that the impious music should cease. Alarmed Egyptian soldiers opened fire, a number of Ikhwan and pilgrims were shot and a panic began. Luckily Faisal, the second son of ibn Saud, heard the shooting and galloped through the mob and stopped the fighting; but Egypt broke off diplomatic relations with ibn Saud for the next ten years, and the annual carpet had to be woven in Mecca by Indian craftsmen. Nevertheless, in other Moslem countries, news had spread that the pilgrimage was safe, and that swindling in the holy places had been brought within bounds; and in 1926, the first year after Jidda had fallen, over a hundred thousand devoted Moslems came to Mecca, a greater number than had ever been seen before. The dues they paid brought ibn Saud the largest sum of money he had ever had.

In the same year, ibn Saud convened an Islamic Congress, of leaders from other parts of the Moslem world, to discuss the future government of the holy land. When he had sent his circular letter to them before his attack began, he had said he proposed to oust the Sherif in the name of the whole of Islam, and since then he had often said he would submit to any form of government the Moslem world approved, provided it could keep the land in peace. In a letter to Ali before Jidda fell, he had even written: "Await the decision of the Moslem world. If it chooses you or anyone else, we will accept its decision with the utmost joy." But this profession of democracy was never put to the test. The Islamic Congress agreed in criticising him, especially for having accepted the title of King, but it never began to agree on any kind of government which could replace him. It dissolved without any decisions and left him to rule alone.

He also made a point of meeting the foreign consuls in Jidda, and each of them after his session in the majlis emerged with admiration. The Dutch consul wrote in his memoirs: "His smile made his face radiate kindness. In repose his face was grim and forbidding, but when he smiled it was completely transformed and he became extraordinarily attractive ... I had to admit to being most impressed." The British consul wrote that "his most remarkable quality was his political wisdom," while a member of a British diplomatic mission referred to his boldness and sagacity and his calm and balanced mind, and believed that his re-establishment of Moslem ethics and Arab traditions was "probably the most profound, and may yet prove the most beneficial, change in Arabia since the preaching of Islam."

The admiration he always inspired in people of Christian nations had another side; the qualities of balance and wisdom which appealed to them were the last to appeal to the strictest of his followers. Political wisdom lies in compromise, and compromise was merely a sinful weakness in the eyes of the Ikhwan and most of the Ulema. His seizure of the Hejaz had in fact brought the schism he may have foreseen. The kingdom had become a dual kingdom: on one hand, the isolated desert and the backward towns which simple theocracy could rule, and on the other the holy land with its window on the world where subtlety was needed. To keep the loyalty of the desert towns, he had to maintain the Wahhabi faith; to win the loyalty of the holy cities, he had to relax it; to attract the pilgrims, he had to deal in friendly fashion with the infidels and heretics his followers abhorred. To accomplish this dexterous feat of government, he began as soon as he could to disband his Ikhwan soldiery and send them back to the desert where they belonged. When most of them were out of the way, he began to temper Wahhabi severity to the people of the Hejaz: for example, when the tobacco merchants complained that his ban had ruined them and left them with stocks on their hands worth a hundred thousand pounds, he gave them permission to sell the stocks provided they did it discreetly, and when the stocks were gone, he forgot to renew the ban. And finally, in case the loyalty of either half of his kingdom wavered, he began to invest in infidel inventions: arms and motor cars and radio.

In this he was somewhat aided by Philby, who appeared in Jidda again as soon as it fell, not now as a diplomat or explorer, but as the managing director of an import company he had founded and as agent for Ford cars and Marconi radio. Ibn Saud had ridden in cars when he went to Basra, and probably been introduced to radio. Since then, he had perceived the power these things might give him in desert war; and now he had an opportunity to buy them. He had to persuade the Ulema that although the Prophet had not sanctioned these inventions, they were not necessarily sinful and did not of themselves "involve disbelief."

He is said to have won their approval of radio by letting them hear a relay of a reading of the Koran, which forced them to agree that no machine which repeated the word of God could be wholly evil; but this story, often told, has the air of being invented in the west. At all events, they succumbed. Philby was ready to sell almost anything to anyone – he did not deal in weapons, but he imported coal and tents and introduced prams to the Jidda ladies – and he equipped ibn Saud with radio installations for Riyadh, Mecca and Jidda, and with mobile transmitters he could carry with him in the desert. His salesmanship was less successful with cars, because the Ford company was discontinuing production of the famous Model T and could not promise delivery of the Model A which followed it; but ibn Saud bought some Chevrolets from other dealers, and inherited those the Sherif had left behind.

In all the delicate process of governing his newly-won dominion, he spent two years in Mecca, neglecting the central desert. It proved to be too long.

CHAPTER FIFTEEN

REVOLT OF THE BROTHERHOOD

All history may equally be inevitable, but the causes of some events can be plainly seen while the causes of others are obscure; and some events have such obvious causes that one can hardly believe that nobody foresaw what was going to happen. Such an event was the revolt of the Ikhwan. From the moment when this Brotherhood was founded, a wise observer could have predicted its disastrous end: yet even when the disaster was imminent, ibn Saud and his family and his advisers seemed to be unaware of any threat.

The inherent defect of the Ikhwan movement was simply that there was no way of stopping it : once it was started, it was as certain to crash as a train or a car without brakes. The brethren's urge to kill or convert the unfaithful could never be satisfied: there were always more unfaithful to be conquered. In breeding this desire among the Bedouin, ibn Saud had created a blood-thirsty kind of army which might in another age have swept on and on to conquest after conquest, like Tamerlain's or Genghis Khan's, until its own zeal had burned itself out and it came to a halt through the loss of its own momentum. But the Ikhwan in the twentieth century could never have reached that point. Ibn Saud had given them the will to fight, but it was beyond his power to give them the means to fight, except against other people as primitive as themselves. They proudly relied on their camels and their muskets, but they lived in an age of aircraft and machine-guns. Even in the isolation of the desert, some of their leaders must have known they were centuries out of date; but if they knew it, they never lost their faith. They had never been beaten, except in the expedition to Transjordan which they preferred to forget, and they believed they never would be. It was true, they might have argued, that some infidels had machinery for war, but machinery had certainly not been sanctioned by the Prophet, and therefore, with the help of God, the faithful would defeat it. They expect a miracle.

Ibn Saud's own faith was strong, but not so blind. He must have known that sooner or later the Ikhwan's lust for conquest would bring them face to face with a mechanised army, and he had enough common sense to know that when that happened, there would not be a miracle: the mechanised army would win. But he never seemed to foresee the choice which he himself would have to make when it happened: the choice of leading the Ikhwan and sharing their defeat, or of refusing to lead them and turning their wrath against himself.

The moment for this choice arrived with the final capitulation in the Hejaz. After that, there was nobody left for the Ikhwan to fight without encountering British arms, because every other neighbour of the kingdom was protected by treaty with Britain. All the small sheikdoms on the periphery of Arabia, from Aden to Kuwait, had ancient agreements with the British; and in the north, Transjordan and Iraq had British forces stationed to protect them, or control them, under the League of Nations Mandates. It was certain that Britain would not allow any of these countries to be conquered, even in the name of the Prophet; and therefore it was also certain that the spreading of Wahhabism by the sword had reached its limit.

Probably ibn Saud's own personal ambition was satisfied by then. The kingdom he had was all that he could manage, and he may have been ready to turn from conquest to government. But he did not seem to understand that the Ikhwan's ambition had not been satisfied and never could be, or that they were not sharing with him the fruits of conquest or the solaces of power. The Ikhwan had seemed to him to be merely a nuisance in the Hejaz, once they had conquered it, and so he had simply sent them home to their tribal areas and left them there with nothing more to do. While he remained in Mecca, absorbed in the problems of sophisticated government, the Ikhwan were back in the desert where they had started, and their frustration and resentment, as he should have foreseen, grew like a pressure of steam until something had to explode.

The explosion happened on the frontier of Iraq, the imaginary line which Cox and ibn Saud had drawn together, and it threw into prominence two of the leaders of the Ikhwan; Feisal al Duwish and Sultan ibn Humaid. Both of these men had fought for ibn Saud for the past decade. Al Duwish had played a part in the capture of Buraida and Hail, and captained the siege of Medina; he had also sometimes talked treason with the Turks, but that had been forgiven. Ibn Humaid had been the Ikhwan commander in the massacre of Taif and the peaceful entry into Mecca. Each of them was not only a fighting leader in a cause he thought was holy, but also a sheik of a powerful tribe and the chief of an Ikhwan settlement, a prince of the desert in his own right. Al Duwish was Sheik of the Mutair, a notoriously warlike tribe from the north-east of the kingdom near the border of Kuwait, and his settlement was the original of them all, Artawiya. Ibn Humaid was a sheik of the Ateiba, whose grazing was in the west between Riyadh and Mecca, and his settlement had the ugly guttural name of Ghat-ghat, and an equally ugly reputation for extreme intolerance. He never met a European – if he had, he would certainly have wanted to cut his throat – and since Arabs are bad at describing each other, not even a verbal portrait of him can be given. But al Duwish met a number of Englishmen, mostly towards the end of his life when he was a beaten man and could not avoid or kill them; and they remembered him as dour and silent, thick-set, limping from battle wounds, perhaps a hunchback. One remarked on his very large nose and head, another on his long brown beard, projecting teeth and cunning little eyes – "the very face of the wicked ogre in a fairy story." But these men were describing an enemy they had striven against for years. They had often seen the results of his cruelty, and so they may have expected to find him an ogre in appearance. To do him justice they would also have had to admit that tens of thousands of desert Arabs had followed him with devotion, and that he only surrendered to an overwhelming force, and that he never recanted the creed he had been taught. Indeed, the Mutair, whom he ruled, were one of the proudest tribes of Arabia, and one of the few which gave its sheik an absolute right to execute any man of the tribe without question. Their pride had an emblem which was unique: a herd of three hundred black camels called al Shuruī, the Honoured Ones. For centuries, this herd had been kept apart, carefully guarded, inbred, and looked upon with reverence. In war, it was the rallying point of the tribe. In adversity, it was defended at any cost, and in attack it led the tribal army, not ridden but advancing alone in a compact trained phalanx which sheltered the fighters behind it. It was the boast of the Mutair that the herd had never been molested by an enemy, and al Duwish was the guardian of this tradition.

Five years had passed between the conference at Oqair, when Cox drew the frontier line of Iraq, and the fall of Jidda. Most of that time, the frontier had been a trouble-spot, even although al Duwish and most of the militant Ikhwan were away in the Hejaz. The fixed frontier had upset the balance of banditry. Before this innovation, when raiders stole a man's camels he never despaired: he organised a raid himself and stole somebody else's. In raiding seasons, the camels were always in circulation, and nobody who could ride and shoot was ever very rich or very poor. But once governments started to intervene, the sport was spoiled, as children's games are sometimes spoiled when grown-ups try to join them and cannot understand the accepted rules.

In earlier days, when the Rashids ruled at Hail and ibn Saud at Riyadh and Iraq was occupied by the Turks, there

144

had always been an area south-west of the River Euphrates which none of the three controlled, and any tribe which grazed there had to look after itself. Cox drew his frontier through the middle of this unclaimed desert, roughly parallel to the river and 150 miles away from it. No doubt he intended to keep ibn Saud's wild tribesmen well away from the towns and gardens on the river bank, and in that he succeeded. But in doing it, he gave a strip of desert to Iraq; and the Government of Iraq, a country which was settled, agricultural and even urban in its outlook, did not really want a desert and was poorly equipped to rule it.

Parts of this desert were grazed by nomad shepherds who spent the summer on the river bank. They were humble people, not Bedouin. They used donkeys, not camels, for transport, and in the old days it would have been thought undignified to raid them. But since ibn Saud had forbidden his tribes to raid each other, these shepherds, now citizens of Iraq, became a tempting quarry for the national pastime; and since they were not Wahhabis, raiding them was not only amusing but holy. The poor shepherds could not retaliate when their flocks were stolen. Under the old kind of rule, they would have appealed to somebody they recognised as lord, and he would have raided in revenge without delay. Under the new kind, they appealed to the Government in Baghdad, which in due course, through the British, lodged diplomatic protests with ibn Saud in Jidda; a process which did not return the missing sheep.

In another way, also, the frontier changed the rules of the game. It provided a sanctuary. A considerable number of the Ikhwan raided across it, and then heard that ibn Saud intended to punish them for doing so. For fear of him, they appealed to the Government of Iraq for asylum, which was granted, and then from Iraq they began to raid across the frontier in the opposite direction. Similarly, quantities of fugitives from Iraq were welcomed by ibn Saud and his sheiks and governors.

This situation did not upset the Iraqi Government very much, and might not have upset the British had it not been that on the edge of the Iraqi desert they had a man of the same type as William Shakespear. This was John Glubb, then a young army captain, and later in his life a famous man as Glubb Pasha of the Arab Legion of Transjordan. He had a curious appointment in the desert. The British, as mandatory power, had the novel idea of policing Iraq by air, and the Royal Air Force had a number of stations there for the purpose. It was a practical plan in that era of aviation, when military aircraft were slow and could land almost anywhere. But the plan required intelligence officers posted here and

145

there throughout the country to learn what was going on; and Glubb, who spoke Arabic well, was one of them. On Christmas day, 1924, a ghastly event occurred in the desert, and Glubb was there and saw it; and his emotional reaction to what he saw tipped the balance of power in Arabia for the next five years.

He had heard rumours at his headquarters that another raid was being planned, and he decided to hire a camel and three or four companions and ride out into the desert to warn the shepherds who were camping there. Officially, the shepherds' safety was no concern of his, but he knew the shepherd tribes and liked them, and wanted to keep them out of trouble. Sixty miles out in the desert, he met thousands upon thousands of sheep and donkeys moving northwards, and their owners running frantically behind them, driving them on. He was shot at, but he managed after a while to ride in among them, and he found the shepherds and their women overwhelmed in panic, only able to shout as they passed him "The Ikhwan! Oh, God help us! Hurry on!" Seizing one or two men, he heard a confused story of unsparing massacre, but nobody would stop to speak, the human and animal river flowed on around him, a chaos of dust and incoherent cries. Before he had time to consider what to do, a long line of camelmen came over a ridge, shooting the nearest shepherds and rounding up the flocks. The shepherds under attack abandoned all they had and ran, but while they were running away they were still shot down by the raiders.

Glubb sent one of his men to ride to the nearest telegraph station, sixty miles away, with a request for aircraft to counter-attack the raiders, and then he joined the fleeing people and rode among them. Women and girls, some clasping their babies, were driving the donkeys, constantly glancing over their shoulders and moaning their anguished prayers. There was nothing he could do. He had four men, the raiders probably thousands, and the only weapon he had was a revolver which he had borrowed from one of them in the heat of the moment. Yet he felt ashamed to ride on ahead and leave the fugitives. So he stayed with them till nightfall, when he thought the survivors would escape in the darkness; and then he rode away, and reached the telegraph station before the morning.

This was no ordinary Bedouin raid. The old chivalry was gone. The raiders had not been out to capture camels and enjoy themselves, they had been out to murder. In the next few days, the whole story began to be told as the women and a few surviving men reached the safety of the railway line which ran along the river. The raiders had followed like wolves, rounding up and isolating herds and shepherds, and
146

from those they had caught they had taken everything, sheep, donkeys, tents, food, clothes and money; and they had killed every man and boy and left the women and girls lamenting over the corpses in the empty desert. They had seized the smallest babies from their mothers and looked to see if they were boys or girls, and thrust the girls back to their mothers, and cut the boy babies' throats and thrown the bodies in the sand. Feisal al Duwish had led the raid in person. Farther west along the frontier, two other exactly similar raids had been made by his followers, and altogether many hundreds of shepherds had been killed – nobody ever counted them – and thousands left destitute.

Because it was Christmas, the Air Force was slow to react, but two days after the massacre Glubb flew with three aircraft across the battlefield and saw the bodies of men and sheep and donkeys scattered for mile on mile across the sands, and he found the retreating raiders driving their stolen flocks towards the frontier and dropped some bombs on them. It was not much more than a gesture. The bombs of those days did very little harm to camel riders scattered in the desert. It was more important that Glubb made a personal vow that Christmas Day to use all his energy and every opportunity to stop the Ikhwan's madness and protect the shepherds; and he did this for no other reason than the protective love of helpless people which, as one must admit, inspired the best of British empire-builders. After a while, he resigned his British army commission and took service with the Government of Iraq; and so it happened that the first effective opposition to the Ikhwan came not from the British Government but from one solitary conscientious Englishman.

For more than a year after the Ikhwan's raid there was peace. This was not the result of anything Glubb had done. It had two causes: ibn Saud forbade the Ikhwan to raid Iraq again, and al Duwish was busy in the Hejaz. But it was a pause which gave Glubb enough time to organise a defence, so far as he could in a desert the size of England where nothing had ever been organised before. He moved out himself to camp in the desert, with a radio set for communication with the R.A.F., and he persuaded the Iraqi Army to send out a company to man an old ruined fort. His friends in the Air Force began to patrol the desert and learn their way about it and practise landing on it. The shepherd tribes, whose flocks were certain to starve without the desert grazing, began to recover from their fright and move out again, and Glubb began to build up a primitive kind of intelligence system among them with a dual object: to tell him where the groups of shepherds were, and to give him warning of raids which were being planned beyond the border.

147

But it was also during this period of peace that the rift between ibn Saud and the Ikhwan grew serious. He had forbidden them to raid Iraq not only because he knew the British would oppose them there, but probably also because he was afraid the British would oppose him in the Hejaz. This was certainly hard on the Ikhwan. For years they had been told to slaughter infidels and heretics as a righteous act and a short cut to Paradise. The Iraqis were certainly heretics within their definition, and now they were told to stop. It seemed to them that Paradise was wantonly being denied them, and that their supreme leader was abandoning his religion and selling himself to Britain.

The explosion only needed a spark, and the spark was provided indirectly by Glubb himself. After the first of the raids, he had proposed that the Iraqis should put a police post well out in the desert to control the tribes, and he had recommended a group of wells called Busaiya as a site for it. After eighteen months of prevarication, the government suddenly agreed, and sent a dozen workmen and half a dozen police to Busaiya to begin to build a fort.

Ibn Saud sent a diplomatic protest as soon as he heard of the project, and he had some right on his side. His agreement with Cox at Oqair had provided that neither country should fortify the border line, or use the wells in its vicinity for military purposes. The Iraqis and British argued that the post they were building was meant for the police, not the army, and was eighty miles from the border. But this seemed to ibn Saud to be splitting hairs; nobody in his kingdom knew the difference between police and military, and nobody could measure the distance on a map. The argument might have been settled by negotiation, but the Ikhwan lost patience with ibn Saud and gave their own answer. One day in November, 1927, a solitary policeman from Busaiya made his way to the river, wounded, to report that al Duwish had descended at dawn on the half-completed fort and killed all the workmen and all the police except him – and he had only escaped by shamming dead.

This was a signal for war: a typical desert war of confusion and shifting loyalties, in which there were not merely two sides, but five or six. The Ikhwan made war on the shepherds, and the Iraqi Government and the British tried to protect them. The Sheik of Kuwait was dragged in, while ibn Saud, for a little while, tried to face both ways, sometimes supporting the Ikhwan by sending protests to the British against the provocations of Iraq, and sometimes opposing the Ikhwan so far as he dared. A month after the attack on Busaiya, he sent messages to Cox and the Sheik of Kuwait, which contained a desperate confession: very serious trouble had broken out in his kingdom, and forces of Ikhwan were marching north against his orders. On the same day that the message arrived in Kuwait, al Duwish entered Iraq again and began again to massacre the shepherds, and a few days later other contingents of his tribe of Mutair invaded the desert of Kuwait, intent on plunder.

It was a very exciting and yet frustrating war for the score or so of young British airmen who took part in it, and for Glubb, who often flew with them and often rode alone among the shepherds he had sworn he would protect. That winter, he never succeeded in spotting the raiders in time. The first news of each raid came from men who had escaped the slaughter by a stroke of luck, or from women who had seen their sons and husbands killed and all their possessions seized. Then the delicate, cumbrous, single-engined aeroplanes took off and scoured the line of retreat of the raiders, flying low, and almost always the pilots found them and took revenge with their bombs and machine-guns; but whatever damage they did was not enough to deter the Ikhwan from coming again, and nothing they did could retrieve the stolen herds. These battles from the air were not only one-sided. It was dangerous merely to fly the aircraft of that era over a hostile desert. Several of them crashed, or made forced landings, or were shot down by the rifle fire of the Ikhwan. Several pilots were killed, but whenever one was brought down another landed beside the wreckage to rescue him if he was still alive, and none of them suffered the horrible fate of being captured.

Aircraft were not enough; only a surface force which was nobile enough to catch the raiders could hope to defeat them. But as it happened, it was the people of Kuwait and not the British who had the first success in a battle on the ground. Probably the Ikhwan did not know, or did not care, where the boundary lay between Kuwait and Iraq, but on one of their raids, in January, 1928, they ventured dangerously near the town, and within range of another novel weapon: the Model T Ford. There were about twenty-five cars in Kuwait by then, and most of them were Fords; and the Sheik commandeered every one of them that could be made to go, and crammed into them as many troops and volunteers as possible, and sent them to drive break-neck across the desert to intercept the raiders. Ten broke down, but the rest succeeded, fought a running battle with the Ikhwan and recaptured a good proportion of the loot. One of the grandsons of old Sheik Mubarrak was delayed by engine trouble and missed the fight, and was so disappointed that he drove on and attacked the Ikhwan alone, one car-load of men against an army of several hundreds. He and his three or four passengers fought till they ran out of ammunition, and then they

149

surrendered and were put to death. A new element entered the archaic art of desert war that day; the end of the thousands of years of camel-mounted armies was coming near.

The plunder and glory won by al Duwish attracted Sultan ibn Humaid, and he marched out during the early spring with a huge army from his country west of Riyadh. He is said to have raised twelve thousand men, and to have proposed to al Duwish that they should join forces and declare a holy war against Iraq; and if they had, nothing could have stopped them short of the Euphrates. Through March, Glubb and the Air Force intensified patrols and preparations, expecting each dawn to find an irresistible host descending on them from the southern desert. But the month passed, the horizons were still empty, and by April the rainwater pools in the desert dried and the watering of such an army on the march became impossible. Perhaps ibn Humaid knew he had left his attack too late, or perhaps Glubb's preparations had deterred him; or perhaps ibn Saud had persuaded him to halt. Whatever the reason, he turned back, and the desert fell into its scorching summer peace.

Part of the summer was spent in a fruitless conference. Iraqi and British representatives travelled to Jidda, by way of Cairo and the Red Sea, and they met ibn Saud and spent a month discussing the right of Iraq to build police posts. It was really a trivial question. Ibn Saud had lost the power to control his raiders, and Iraq needed the posts to protect the unoffending victims, and there ought to have been no argument about it. But the Ikhwan regarded the harmless fort at Busaiya as a symbol of ibn Saud's subservience to foreign infidels. He knew that if he could not persuade the Iraqis and British to abandon their police posts, the Ikhwan would attack them, and whether they won or lost the battle, he would have lost another degree, perhaps the last, of his authority. In the conference, he took refuge in a mulish naïvety: his friend Cox, he said, had promised the border would never be fortified, and as a simple Bedouin he had trusted Britain's word. It was certainly not the first time a shrewd but backward ruler had tried to embarrass Britain with this over-simplified argument, but the British could be as mulish as anyone. The conference adjourned, and the forts remained.

So the winter of 1928 began with all the contestants determined not to yield and well prepared for a decisive clash of arms and wills. In the religious fervour of the Ikhwan's leaders, a naked wish for power could now be seen. Al Duwish and ibn Humaid had been joined by a third important sheik: Dhaidan ibn Hithlain, chief of the Ajman tribe of the Hasa district. It is likely that these three, in secret, had al-
150

ready agreed to divide the kingdom between them when ibn Saud was overthrown, as they were confident he would be. Meanwhile all of them intended to raid Iraq in spite of his orders.

Glubb was determined to stop them, and he started the winter with a victory. He had succeeded in sending spies across the border, and one evening in December, when he was camped far out in the desert with the shepherds, one of the spies came riding in to tell him al Duwish's tribe was on the warpath. It was not al Duwish himself, only a minor sheik with a force of a hundred men; and Glubb and his Bedouin were able to deduce which wells he was certain to visit. Glubb flew to the wells next day, and found some shepherds camped there. He landed, and persuaded them to wait where they were until nightfall, and then light their camp fires and leave them burning and run for their lives. He believed the raiders' spies would see the fires, and the raiders would attack the camp-site in the morning.

The next day at dawn, he took off again with three aircraft, and he found a hundred camels in the place where the shepherds had been. There were no men in sight, and he flew round and round, hardly hoping that his ruse had worked so well. He could see it was not a herd of grazing camels, because there were no young ones. It might possibly have been a merchant's caravan. He signalled his pilot to fly lower, and lower still. At five hundred feet, he saw that every camel had a riding saddle, not a pack saddle – the certain sign of raiders. He wrote on a slip of paper "Shoot", and passed it to the pilot.

When the first bomb fell, the scene was instantly transformed. Men had been crouching motionless and invisible, wrapped in their cloaks; now they sprang up and mounted, and in a moment there was a man on every camel, all riding full speed in different directions. The three aircraft pursued them with bombs and guns, and Glubb watched their panic flight with intense excitement, undisturbed by pity or remorse. It seemed a just punishment and a healthy warning.

But the next encounter was a failure. Dhaidan ibn Hithlain entered Kuwait territory and attacked an Iraqi tribe which was grazing there, and stole its flocks and killed its men. By an extraordinary mischance, he also killed an American, although Americans in the desert were as rare as ostriches in those days. Charles R. Crane, a millionaire and ex-ambassador, was motoring from Basra to Kuwait with a missionary whose name was Henry Bilkert. They were seen by a party of raiders who shot at their car. Bilkert was killed, but Crane escaped – a fortunate escape, because Crane played a beneficial part, a few years later, in the affairs of ibn Saud. After the raid,

151

ibn Hithlain passed close to the border between Kuwait and Iraq, driving the stolen flocks. On the other side of the border, like a hunting dog on a leash with the quarry in sight, was Glubb. He had his camelmen with him, and several trucks in which he had fitted machine-guns, and a detachment of Air Force armoured cars – and he was not allowed to cross. It was a ludicrous situation, and there was something very British about it. The British had created the border line; nobody else wanted it, nobody else was taking the slightest notice of it, probably nobody else in the desert but Glubb knew or cared exactly where it was: yet the British had forbidden their own forces and Iraq's to violate it. They were perfectly correct, but such a high standard of international etiquette was as much out of place in the desert as the border line itself. A less punctilious people, with such a target on the other side, would have crossed first to recapture the stolen herds and made excuses afterwards; but Glubb applied for permission to cross. The application was forwarded to London, and no doubt referred to the ruler of Kuwait. Three days later permission was granted. Glubb dashed across and followed the raiders' tracks to the southern frontier, but he was too late. Ibn Hithlain had crossed a few hours earlier into the Hasa, and Glubb had not had permission to follow him there.

Nevertheless, his tactics began to have some effect. He revived an ancient defensive trick of desert war. The trick was simply to pitch tents close together in two parallel lines and hobble the livestock between them. The criss-crossing guy-ropes made a barrier which raiders could not possibly ride across on camels or horses; to get at the herds, they had to halt and dismount, and so they lost the advantages of momentum and surprise. This defensive position could only be held for a day or two, because the herds had to graze and be watered, but Glubb taught the shepherd tribes to concentrate quickly when his spies brought him warning of a raid. The first time he tried the plan, it succeeded far better than he or the shepherds had expected. Warning was brought that al Duwish himself was approaching. The tribes formed their lines of tents, and Glubb put himself and his machine-guns in the middle. They waited in trepidation for the dawn – and nothing happened. Al Duwish also had his spies, and they had warned him of the new defensive tactics. Never before had the shepherd tribes done anything but run away in panic at the sound of the name of al Duwish; now, hearing of their determined attitude, and believing perhaps that there was more behind it than one Englishman and a couple of machine-guns, he abandoned his expedition and turned back without attacking.

On the same day, farther west along the frontier, the second of the Ikhwan leaders, ibn Humaid, was also hesitating to enter Glubb's defensive zone. He had marched up again from his country west of Riyadh with three thousand men, intending to invade Iraq. Just short of the border, he captured a minor sheik from an Iraqi Bedouin tribe, and asked him, no doubt with the threat of a knife at his throat, where the border was, and whether it was patrolled by cars or aircraft, and where the shepherd tribes were grazing. Not even this local sheik knew the exact position of the border, but he knew who was in the district: some Iraqi shepherds were camped by an ancient cistern, and farther south, well short of the border, there were several camps of one of the Bedouin tribes of ibn Saud, and a large party of merchants from the Hasa, taking herds of camels to Egypt for sale.

Ibn Humaid then divided his force into three, and laid waste to the district. He led an attack on the camping ground at the cistern, only to find that the shepherds had fled into Iraq: Glubb had heard he was coming and warned them. He could have caught them, but instead of crossing the border he turned on ibn Saud's tribe and the merchants. For a day, that part of the desert was a scene of brutal ecstasy, and on the other hand of suffering and grief; the Ikhwan ranged from well to well on horseback, slaughtering men and boys and plundering camps, and leaving the women and little girls among the debris and the corpses to lament.

That single day changed everything, and settled the Ikhwan's doom. The victims of it were not Iraqis or heretics, they were Wahhabis and subjects of ibn Saud. Nobody could pretend that this was a holy war: it was naked anarchy and revolution. So far, ibn Saud had had to temporize; probably, while the Ikhwan merely raided Iraq, he could not have raised enough men to challenge them in battle; most of his people did not disapprove of the raids. But ibn Humaid's one day of horror caused a revulsion of feeling in the desert and the towns. The massacre of Bedouin roused the desert and the massacre of merchants roused the towns, and suddenly hosts of men who had been waiting to see which side was likelier to win were demanding that ibn Saud should take revenge and pledging their support. Sure of himself, he assembled an army again and marched from Riyadh.

The armies met on 24th March, 1929, at wells called Sibilla, not far from al Duwish's settlement of Artawiya, and they camped four miles apart: ibn Saud on one side, in command of a large but motley force, and on the other al Duwish and ibn Humaid, each with his own mad warriors behind him. On both sides, men were itching for battle, but all three commanders hesitated. Ibn Saud had brought with him three of

153

the most learned and faithful jurists of the Ulema to decide whatever subtle arguments the rebels might put forward, and al Duwish sent his son Azaiyiz across the no-man's-land to negotiate; and for a short time this young man, riding alone with the eyes of both armies on him, held the future of Arabia in his hands.

It may be true that al Duwish was an ogre, but what little is remembered of his son is attractive. Azaiyiz was only twenty-five, but he must have had the qualities of a desert prince, because men followed him faithfully to death; and he must also have had some common sense and finesse, because his father often used him as an emissary. He is said to have been fair-haired, which suggests a northern slave-girl in his ancestry; and his name suggests that people held him in affection, because Azaiyiz, as everybody called him, is a nickname, a diminutive of Abdul Aziz. For all the blood-thirsty hatred of his time, nobody seems to have hated Azaiyiz, except perhaps ibn Humaid. In him one may therefore see, or imagine one sees, the chivalrous, religious knighthood of the desert which the Ikhwan might have been, and which ibn Saud in his youth intended it should be. The loyalty of Azaiyiz was divided when the armies met. Like any Arab, he put his own father first, but three months earlier he had been sent to Riyadh by his father to negotiate with ibn Saud, and had been so overwhelmed by his formidable charm that he had sworn allegiance to him. It certainly distressed him that his father and the King could not be reconciled.

Most of the argument at Sibilla was on old insoluble problems which had often been discussed before. The Ikhwan leaders still demanded that the forts in Iraq should be attacked and demolished, and they demanded that ibn Saud should renounce and destroy the inventions of infidels he had adopted, motor cars and telephones and radio. To this he gave the obvious reply: he was perfectly willing to do without these things if the Ikhwan would renounce and destroy their rifles and ammunition, which were equally the products of infidels. But there was something more than stubborn ignorance in the Ikhwan's mistrust of these innovations. Perhaps they could not have expressed their true objection, even to themselves, but they must have been afraid that the only kind of life they understood would be brought to an end by such inventions, and that they themselves could never master them but would be in the power of any man who could.

The discussions Azaiyiz took part in led to no agreement, but from ibn Saud's point of view they did some good: they led to disagreement, between al Duwish and ibn Humaid. Azaiyiz persuaded his father to speak to ibn Saud, but ibn Humaid refused to meet him except with a sword in his hand.

154

A tent was pitched at an honourable distance in front of ibn Saud's army. Ibn Saud and al Duwish both rode out to it and met in it alone, and they stayed there alone together all night.

It is said that during the night, ibn Humaid went to Azaiyiz and told him his father had been kidnapped by ibn Saud, and proposed an immediate attack to kill ibn Saud and rescue al Duwish. Azaiyiz refused to believe him, or to fall in with his plan. If he had been a little less strong-minded, the whole of the subsequent history of Arabia would have been changed, because a surprise attack on the tent in the darkness could hardly have failed, and if ibn Saud had been killed at that moment the kingdom would have fallen into ruins.

In fact, ibn Saud and al Duwish were simply talking. It was not the only time that ibn Saud sat up all night to try to win back a rebel, and when he had the opportunity, and took the trouble, he never failed. Neither he nor al Duwish ever revealed what arguments, appeals or flatteries he used; but in the morning, when al Duwish left the tent, he had promised to live in peace under ibn Saud, and to try to persuade his fellow-rebel ibn Humaid to do the same; and he had also promised that if ibn Humaid refused, he would leave him and go back home to Artawiya. Presumably, ibn Saud in return had promised him his life and his position as Sheik of the Mutair.

But ibn Humaid was adamant. He would not have anything to do with ibn Saud except in battle. One can only guess the reason for this foolish determination, for ibn Humaid can only have been a very primitive and bestial man. Al Duwish, living in the Hasa, had met the Turks and seen the town of Kuwait, the sea, the River Euphrates, and possibly even Basra. Compared with ibn Humaid's experience, this was sophistication. Ibn Humaid's tribal district was in the very centre of Arabia, and not a breath of civilising influence had ever reached it except at second hand. Probably he had never seen any horizon but sand and stone, until he entered Mecca as its conqueror. So he must have been the ultimate, inevitable product of the Ikhwan teaching: a human being totally ignorant of anything but desert lore, guided by animal instincts, inflamed to madness by a sectarian outlook a thousand years out of date – and absolutely satisfied that he was the finest flower of humanity. It is not much use to look for logic in such a man's decisions. Perhaps he reasoned that what he had done was unforgivable, and that ibn Saud would break any promise he made and put him to death. Perhaps he simply believed that ibn Saud was in league with the devil. Whatever he thought, al Duwish sent back a reply to ibn Saud: ibn Humaid would not compromise, and he himself

155

had decided not to leave him, and not to go back to Arta-wiya. This was a challenge to battle. Ibn Saud consulted the Ulema, and then, with their approval, gave the order to unfurl the flags of war – reluctantly and sadly and yet, no doubt, with the tingle of anticipation which old soldiers feel.

The Battle of Sibilla, on 29th March, 1929, was the last time ibn Saud ordered an army to charge. It was also the last great Bedouin battle ever fought, the last in the series which had continued since the time of Abraham, the last before mechanism finally entered desert wars. It was perfectly typical, except that each side perhaps had more unmounted men than usual; beside the true Bedouin, ibn Saud had his levies from the towns, and the Ikhwan their farmers from the settlements, who had reached the battlefield riding tandem on the camels of other men. Ibn Saud advanced with his men on foot in the centre, his horsemen on either flank, his camelmen skirmishing beyond and behind the army, his banners carried with the pride which has always been induced in men by martial episodes. The rebels, seeing their enemies approaching, scorned to wait in prepared positions, from which they could have shot down the advancing infantry; pride and tradition made them also advance, and the armies charged each other. Once more there were the clouds of dust, the thud of hooves, the boastful war-cries; once more, when the armies clashed together, the rifles were brandished like swords, and the swords drawn when the rifles were empty. It was a splendid, absurd anachronism.

It may be doubted if anyone knew what the battle was about. To the townsmen, it may have been revenge, to the Ikhwan the work of God, to the tribesmen a sporting event. To al Duwish, it may have seemed to be a judgment on him, to ibn Humaid a final bid for power, to Azaiyiz a disaster whoever lost; and even ibn Saud could not have given a single reason for it. He was fighting to preserve his worldly power, and also to vindicate his creed against a variation of it he considered false, and also to prevent the Ikhwan bringing down the wrath of Britain on themselves and him. Those were immediate reasons, but in the long term he also had to fight because he perceived that desert Arabia had lived in the past too long, and that the Ikhwan's refusal to progress beyond the time of Mahomed would weaken the Arabs so much, in relation to other more liberal people, that in the end they would lose any independent existence. What had to be decided at Sibilla was whether Arabia should move backwards or forwards in the general process of civilisation.

The battle lasted a quarter of an hour. That also was typical; a Bedouin battle had to stop, or at least to pause, as soon as everyone was out of ammunition or out of breath. The first clash at Sibilla decided the outcome. The Ikhwan were better organised but they were far outnumbered, and they broke and ran. Ibn Humaid escaped, al Duwish was shot in the stomach and carried away, and their armies scattered throughout the desert, each man hoping to avoid the retribution of ibn Saud. But he called off the chase; the Ulema told him the fighting had gone far enough. The next day, al Duwish offered his surrender by the time-honoured method of sending veiled women to ask for sanctuary in the winner's tent. Ibn Saud consulted the Ulema again, and asked them what terms he should impose; in so far as the rebellion was religious, his repression of it had to be within religious law. They advised him that killing should end, and that al Duwish and his tribe should surrender their loot, and their horses and rifles and riding camels. Azaiyiz should surrender in person, but his life should be guaranteed. Al Duwish should give himself up without conditions.

Accordingly, al Duwish was carried on a stretcher to the camp of ibn Saud. He seemed to be dying, and in an emotional and dramatic scene ibn Saud forgave him and sent him home with his wives to die in peace.

Bedouin battles, like battles anywhere, were often re-fought in gossip and camp-fire stories, and in the gossip about Sibilla people sometimes said that ibn Saud had cheated, that al Duwish had expected another meeting and been taken by surprise. To the last, the Arab warriors remained like schoolboys and their wars like playground games; they usually played with good humour, but sometimes somebody lost his temper and the game grew out of hand, and it was typical then that the loser should protest "It wasn't fair. I wasn't ready."

There was also a more sophisticated piece of gossip about Sibilla. Ibn Saud, it was said, had forgiven al Duwish after the battle, firstly because he was sure he was dying and could not do any more harm, and secondly because he hoped ibn Humaid would hear of his generosity and give himself up. If this was a ruse, one half of it succeeded. Ibn Saud sent his brother Abdullah to Ghat-ghat, the notorious settlement of ibn Humaid, and ibn Humaid surrendered to him without fighting. Thereupon Ghat-ghat was razed to the ground and its people scattered, and ibn Humaid was imprisoned in the fortress of Riyadh. Later, when there were rumours of a plot to rescue him, he was moved to an especially ghastly underground dungeon the Turks had built at Hofuf, and he never came out again. But the other half of ibn Saud's plan, if it was a plan, was a failure – for al Duwish did not die. On the contrary, he only waited for his wound to heal before

157

he began to raid again, and while he was out of action, he sent Azaiyiz raiding.

Azaiyiz embarked, in the summer of 1929, on a raid which less brave or more prudent leaders would never have undertaken. In the scarcely bearable climate of August, he rode with six hundred men for five hundred miles, north of Hail and up to the borders of Transjordan, seizing camels and terrorising local tribes. By the end of the month, his men were driving vast herds of captured animals back towards their own country. These herds were not of much practical value – the proud tribe of Mutair already had all the camels it could possibly have needed – but they were a symbol of success, much like the useless territory which European conquerors acquired, and it would have been a youthful triumph for Azaiyiz to have brought them home. But to go so far afield in summer was reckless. He could only return by routes which his enemies could predict, for he had to find water at the permanent wells. While he was far in the north, ibn Saud's governor set out from the town of Hail and picketed the wells with riflemen in prepared defences which were easily made impregnable.

At one well after another, Azaiyiz and his men and animals were turned away by overwhelming rifle fire, until at last, on an August afternoon when the temperature in the shade may have risen to 120 degrees – and there was no shade – he approached a well where he knew he must drink or die, for the last of his waterskins had been empty the day before: and the well was defended, as all the others had been. He called his men to prayer, and they formed the customary line facing Mecca while the defenders watched them in silence; and then he launched them in an attack which was only less hopeless than marching on.

There is no more desperate spur than thirst, and Azaiyiz came nearer success than he could have expected. He was helped by the heat of the day; the mirage gave a kind of cover in the open desert, and made the defenders' aim inaccurate, and a hand-to-hand fight of utter ruthlessness developed round the well-head. Azaiyiz led five hundred men into battle: thirty-eight survived. They slaughtered hundreds of the defenders, but they did not reach the water. When all was lost and those who were still alive were scattered, Azaiyiz himself was led away by a few of his bodyguard, and two months later his desiccated body was found in the desert, on the track towards his home, where hope and strength had failed him.

Sibilla should have ended the revolution, and victory over Azaiyiz should have confirmed that ibn Saud was in control again, although it was not a victory he would have claimed
158

with any pride. But in the same summer, an episode in the Hasa roused the Ikhwan's anger again to a pitch as high as ever, and shook the confidence of a great many other people in ibn Saud. It concerned Dhaidan ibn Hithlain, the third of the rebel leaders, and Fahad ibn Jiluwi, who was the eldest son of the Governor of Hofuf. Dhaidan had not been present at Sibilla, and Fahad was sent out by his father with an army on behalf of ibn Saud to meet him and persuade or force him to renew his allegiance. When the armies were close, Fahad sent Dhaidan an invitation to come and see him; some people, afterwards, said he also sent a letter which promised Dhaidan safety. Dhaidan accepted it, and rode to the rival camp with a dozen attendants, and was received according to custom and given coffee. To drink coffee with an Arab in his tent had always been an absolute pledge of mutual confidence, but when Dhaidan stood up to take his leave, he was seized by Fahad's men and put in chains. One of his followers saw what was happening and leaped on his horse and escaped to rouse the tribe; and that night, fifteen hundred of Dhaidan's men charged into the camp and overran it, searching for their sheik. Another scene of merciless fighting began, and Fahad, seeing it going against him, committed the worst of all crimes against Bedouin chivalry: he ordered his father's negro executioner, who was in attendance on him, to cut Dhaidan's throat, and the executioner did so. Then, seeing that he was beaten, Fahad mounted his mare to escape, but his own body-servant, shocked at such treachery, shot him dead.

The story of this scandalous affair swept through the kingdom. It was nobody's fault but Fahad's, but he had been acting for ibn Saud and was the son of ibn Saud's cousin and most trusted and oldest friend, and so ibn Saud had to share the blame and disgrace of it. Memory was as short and friendship as fickle as ever; sympathy for the rebels' cause flared up again. Dhaidan's tribe, the Ajman, rose in revolt. Al Duwish, recovering from his wound, had been deeply distressed at the death of his son and was furious at the murder. He brought out five thousand men and ten thousand camels to join the Ajman, and at once the whole of the north-east of the country was up in arms again, the Ikhwan were riding and humble people were reduced again to terror.

By then, however, the rebels were surrounded by inexorable forces. In Iraq, Glubb was prepared with Vickers and Lewis guns in trucks, to pursue them wherever they crossed the frontier. In Kuwait, the Sheik had no love for ibn Saud and had been known to sell the rebels arms in spite of their raids on his people, but the British, at ibn Saud's request, had warned him not to support them and not to offer them asylum.

The Royal Air Force had begun to take a positive interest in the desert war; instead of merely sending a few sporting pilots when Glubb requested them, it had moved a whole composite unit of aircraft and armoured cars into the desert under a senior officer.

So there was no retreat for the rebels to the north; and from the south and west, ibn Saud again assembled all his power against them. The governors of Hail and Hofuf were both in the field; and most important of all, ibn Saud himself, who was in Mecca, was preparing finally to discard his respect for tradition. He had learned the lesson of the Sheik of Kuwait's successful foray in his Fords, and of Glubb's tactics in motorised patrols, and he had assembled all the cars and trucks he could in Mecca and Jidda, those which the Sherif had left behind and those he had bought himself. As the winter approached, he set off in a convoy of Fords and Chevrolets to drive across Arabia, from Mecca to Riyadh and thence to the rebel territory in the Hasa and the shore of the Persian Gulf.

This expedition almost deserves to be compared for incongruity with Hannibal's crossing of the Alps. It was a journey of seven hundred miles on camel tracks or no tracks at all, and the motor cars of the 1920s were not much better suited to sand and heat than Hannibal's elephants to ice and cold. In the previous year or two, a few cars had made the journey as far as Riyadh, but nothing on wheels had ever travelled beyond, not even a cart. It would be pleasant to give ibn Saud the credit for generalship which has always been given to Hannibal; but Hannibal's feat is unjustly praised, because he only attempted it through ignorance, and ibn Saud was equally ignorant of the technical problems his drivers would have to solve. Motor cars, he knew, could travel from Jidda to Mecca, or even Taif, much faster than camels; why not, then, take them to the Hasa and use them in war? A western commander would have encumbered the expedition with spare parts and service depots and well-calculated logistical support, but ibn Saud had never heard that cars needed service. His drivers were mostly Indians he had imported with the cars, and if they protested, nobody listened. So, with the virtue of total ignorance, he not only embarked, but arrived at his destination.

These few jalopies, which he alone possessed, were the final key to power. By the time they reached the Hasa, most of them were wrecks, some tied together with leather thongs and some without springs and riding on their axles, but they would still go, and he could still pile his riflemen into them and outpace and surprise the rebels whenever he wished. They caused the same consternation in the central desert as the elephants in northern Italy. After their advent, desert strategy was never the same agin, and there was never another revolution.

Indeed, the rebels never fought another battle which was more than half-hearted. Suddenly, they seemed to understand that they were beaten, the spirit that had possessed them seemed to die, the terrible pride of al Duwish seemed to crumple. He had been a master of desert strategy; now, with the carelessness of despair, he left his camp unguarded and neglected the elementary rules by which a desert prince survived. In a final gesture of defiance, he rode into the desert of Kuwait with a few attendants and asked to see the Sheik and the British Political Agent. Both refused to see him and ordered him to leave, but he sent the Agent a letter. If he moved south, he asked, to battle with ibn Saud, and left his women and herds on the frontier, would the British promise not to bomb them, and would they let them enter Kuwait if anyone else attacked them? The Agent would have liked to make the promise, but the British Government told him to give "a rather vague negative answer." With that, al Duwish went back to his people and began to advise them to leave him and make their own peace, if they could, with ibn Saud.

The cars and machine-guns which surrounded him had proved to him he could not hope to win, but in hopeless situations in the past the Ikhwan had flung themselves into suicidal action, positively seeking death and Paradise. Al Duwish's sudden collapse could not have been caused by fear of defeat or death. It may more have been caused by a revelation that there was nothing left to die for. The Arabs who looked for an explanation of the sudden change in him believed he was broken-hearted at the death of Azaiyiz; but broken-heartedness has seldom if ever been more than a figure of speech. Perhaps the slow, useless, horrible death of his son, and the knowledge that there was no sanctuary left for his wives and younger children, brought him to look afresh at the cause he had fought for, and to see at last some semblance of the truth: that ibn Saud had founded the Ikhwan movement with sincerity and used it so far as it could go, but abandoned it when he saw that to use it further would only destroy what it had already won. Perhaps he even saw that this was not betrayal, but the course of wisdom, and that the movement was not the ultimate expression of God's will, but a weapon to be discarded when it was blunted.

That is only surmise; the curious fact is that in his despair he turned for advice and relief not to any fellow-Arab or fellow-Moslem, but to the arch-infidels, the British; for by then the British representatives in the desert, standing a little aloof from the passions the rebellion had aroused, were the only people left that all of the contending Arabs could hope to trust, the only custodians of the chivalry which had been the Arabs' pride. One of these representatives was Glubb, the other was the Political Agent in Kuwait. For the post which had been held by Knox and Shakespear, the British had managed to find yet another man with a genuine love of desert Arabs. His name was H. R. P. Dickson. Unlike Glubb, he had a purely peaceful interest in the desert, and unlike Lawrence he sympathised less with princes than with the poorest, simplest Bedouin. Whenever he could leave Kuwait, and the neighbouring desert was not at war, he camped with his wife and two children among the local tribes, and lived with them in an intimate family concord which no other European had achieved, or indeed attempted. He explained his affinity by recollecting that he had been born in Syria and suckled by a Bedouin wet-nurse: whatever the cause of it, it was invaluable in the last phases of the revolution. Glubb's defence of the shepherds had been the first rock which broke the wave of Ikhwan power: Dickson's sympathy restored the desert people to calm and peace.

A year before, al Duwish had marched out of Artawiya with his banners of war, swearing he would not come back without capturing Glubb, alive or dead; now he asked first for Glubb's protection in Iraq. Glubb could not promise it; the British and Iraqi Governments had both already promised ibn Saud they would not give the rebels asylum. Some lesser leaders marched into Iraq with their followers, refused to go back and surrendered their arms to Glubb, and so forced him to look after them for the moment. Others tried to escape to the south and run the gauntlet of ibn Saud's advancing army, but all who tried that were caught and put to death. Al Duwish himself and his dwindling army stayed hesitantly on the border. There, a sheik much less distinguished in battle attacked his unguarded camp, and seized thousands of his camels. For the first time in the long history of the Mutair, the sacred black herd which had been the symbol of their pride was scattered. Finally, in January, 1930, al Duwish and his remaining men and their women and children and herds rushed suddenly in a panic flight across the border into Kuwait: they had heard that ibn Saud with the whole of his army was upon them. Glubb followed them with some Air Force armoured cars. He found them humiliated and aimless. None of them knew where they were going, their only thought was to flee to the north, away from ibn Saud; their route was marked by dying exhausted animals, and the sacred herd was neglected. He remembered the shepherd tribes they had pitilessly driven to exactly the same extreme, but now he
162

could only feel pity for the beaten raiders, and only feared he might be ordered to shoot at them or to drive them back to be slaughtered by ibn Saud.

Dickson also came out from the town of Kuwait to follow them, dressed as a Bedouin, and he was equally shocked at the scene of abject desperation. He found al Duwish among the mob of his army, and begged him to surrender to the British Air Force. Like Glubb, he could not promise him protection, because he was bound by the same undertakings; but he could not leave the rebels at large in Kuwait, for fear that ibn Saud would invade and destroy them there. Surrender to the British offered at least a chance of delay and mediation. Al Duwish refused, but Dickson turned his power of persuasion on the lesser leaders, and one by one they agreed. At last, after days of hesitation, al Duwish took horse with Dickson, and the two men rode together unattended to the Air Force camp; and there the wild old warrior handed his sword hilt first to an Air Vice-Marshal. He was taken away to Basra. Before he went, he told Dickson he was leaving his women under his personal protection.

This was the best way the revolution could have ended: perhaps the only way, except by extermination. With al Duwish in their hands, the British bent all their energy to saving his life and making peace for him. Dickson's wife took all al Duwish's women into her care – his principal wife, his sisters and daughters and other unspecified relations, thirty-seven in all; she found them starving and ragged, and fed them and clothed them as her guests. Dickson flew with two senior officers to plead with ibn Saud, and found him willing to show himself merciful. He insisted that all the rebels should be returned to him, with all their property and loot, but he promised to spare their lives and to temper his punishment with kindness. He also agreed to compensate the tribes of Iraq and Kuwait for what had been stolen from them, and even to pay ten thousand pounds at once in advance of their claims.

Accordingly, Dickson put al Duwish himself in an aircraft, with two of the other leaders, and flew them to ibn Saud's war camp. He handed them over in the majlis, and observed that tears poured down ibn Saud's cheeks as he allowed the prisoners to kiss him. Ibn Saud's own people seemed to expect him to cut off al Duwish's head in spite of his promise, but he did not. He imprisoned him in Riyadh, which was probably the least he could do to reassert his own authority, and he confiscated the rebels' riding camels and horses and mares. As a sign of the overthrow of the pride of the Mutair, he seized the sacred herd of camels. It still exists to-day among the royal herds of the House of Saud.

A year later, al Duwish, who had cut so many throats, died in prison of a natural haemorrhage of the throat which was probably caused by cancer. When he knew he was dying, he sent a message to ibn Saud, not asking for ibn Saud's forgiveness, but offering his forgiveness to ibn Saud.

CHAPTER SIXTEEN

THE AMERICAN CONCESSION

It has sometimes been said that if ibn Saud had been a lesser man he would have given up the endless struggle to make a nation from such unpromising material as the Bedouin and the desert. It is true that there was never a period more than a few months long when he had nothing to struggle against. But nobody except the kings and queens of stable monarchies possesses power without contention, and the will to contend may more be a sign of hungriness for power or of pleasure in contention than of greatness. Ibn Saud loved power, revelled in battle, was happy in his desert wars, and even enjoyed the intrigues of desert politics. Not much credit could therefore be given to him for those kinds of contention, which merely indulged his taste; and when he was beset by other kinds which he did not enjoy, he pretended as long as he could that they did not exist. The measure of his greatness was not in his willingness to struggle, but in his success, and in being so little corrupted by success.

The revolt of the Ikhwan ended in 1930, and the dust had hardly settled before a trouble started which he did not understand or enjoy at all: he ran out of money again. The world economic depression of the early thirties reached the desert. In the old days, nothing that happened in the outside world had any effect in the centre of Arabia, but when he absorbed the Hejaz he linked his own prosperity to the rises and falls of prosperity in the rest of the world. The dues he levied on pilgrims became the main source of his income, and the pilgrimage was a sensitive meter of world trade. To come to Mecca from the far ends of the Moslem world cost any pilgrim quite a large sum of money, except the very poorest who walked and begged, and in times of depression they simply could not come. From 1926 onwards, when the scare of the Wahhabi invasion had subsided, Mecca had had some prosperous busy years; in one of them, 130 thousand pilgrims came from overseas and spent their money. But in 1930 and 1931, the number who came was disastrously small. In the rich years, ibn Saud had spent freely, especially on the infidels' inventions by which he was to govern and control the desert – £35,000 on arms from Poland, £30,000 on radio equipment from Britain, many more thousands here and there on American cars, and roads built by Indian contractors, and even some obsolete British aircraft. Then, when his income fell, he was left with debts he could not or would not pay.

Of all the aspects of government, finance concerned him least. At the age of fifty, his only interests in money were still to buy weapons and indulge his royal generosity – to give a jewelled sword to a visiting ambassador or a golden necklace to a pretty girl, or to throw silver coins in handfuls to beggars beside the road. To hoard it or count it, or worry where it came from or where it went, seemed to him intolerably sordid. Accordingly, he delegated all the financial affairs of the kingdom to his treasurer al Sulaiman, and was only resentful or bored if al Sulaiman had to bring them to his notice.

As the kingdom grew in size and its administration began to grow a little in complexity, al Sulaiman became a powerful man: some people said the most powerful in the country. Luckily, he was retiring by disposition, and honest and efficient by Arab standards. But the kingdom was still organised as a vast family estate. All the gold that came in was the King's personal property, all that was paid out was his personal bounty. The first charge on the nation's resources was still the King's personal needs. So long as these were met, the King was satisfied, and al Sulaiman's mission as a loyal servant was to keep him satisfied. When what was left was not enough to satisfy other creditors, al Sulaiman spread it among them as best he could, and felt he had succeeded if he avoided having to upset his master by telling him what had happened.

The foreign debts were not desperately serious. Al Sulaiman promised payments by instalments. Although the sums which were owed were large for Arabia, they were not very large for the international firms which had to wait, and on the whole the King's reputation and credit survived. The internal debts were more insidious. The pay of minor officials began to fall into arrears, and to make both ends meet they began to swindle the public and the King.

In the Hejaz, this was simply a return to the old days: the Sherif had not paid his officials at all, on the assumption that they were swindlers anyway and did not need to be paid. The Turks had not been much better, if any better at all, and indeed corruption in officials was an age-old eastern custom: but it was a sad relapse from the high if narrow ideals of the Wahhabis. Ibn Saud was too ignorant of money, and al Sulaiman with his primitive book-keeping was too innocent for Mecca, because Mecca had been a centre of trade for centuries and its citizens were commercial brigands as practised as any in the world. In the prosperous years, fear of ibn Saud had kept corruption underground: in the lean years which followed, it blossomed openly again and ibn Saud, if he knew it existed, did very little to stop it. This was the beginning of the tragic failure which marred his achievements in

166

old age. Perhaps when nobody had much money, corruption did not seem to matter much, but a tradition of graft was founded in the kingdom then which grew to a monstrous conspiracy of swindling when ibn Saud became a multi-millionaire.

In this period, Philby finally attached himself to the court of ibn Saud by becoming a Moslem. He had been in Jidda on and off for the past five years, selling his coal and prams and Ford cars and radio apparatus to ibn Saud and anyone else who would buy them, and making many friends and many enemies, as he always had, and collecting baboons: one could always depend on him for an eccentricity nobody else had thought of. Not even his friends were very sympathetic about his conversion, and he never gave any convincing reason for it. The effect of it was that he could escape from Jidda, where every non-Moslem was penned, and travel more or less freely to Mecca and through the country, and the least charitable explanation was that he knew he could sell more goods that way. But he was more interested in exploration than in money, and it is rather more likely that he embraced Islam to give himself freedom to explore the desert, and especially to fulfil his dearest ambition to be the first to cross the Rub al Khali, the Empty Quarter of southern Arabia – an ambition in which he was beaten in the end by the British explorer Bertram Thomas. More likely still, his motives were muddled, as most men's are in love – for he had fallen madly in love with Arabia. The only motive which nobody ever suggested, not even himself, was religious conviction, and the immediate cause of his decision, by his own account, was a fainting fit in the summer heat of Jidda which made him feel he could not bear the coastal climate any longer. Whatever the reason, it was an important event in the history of ibn Saud's Arabia; for he was welcomed to Mecca and given the name of Abdullah Philby by ibn Saud himself, and he haunted the court in Mecca and Riyadh for the next quarter of a century.

Sometimes, Philby's self-righteousness drove ibn Saud to fury, as it had driven many lesser men, but he was always forgiven, and he was certainly very useful. Whatever his faults, he was honest in money matters, and sincerely had the interests of ibn Saud at heart; and whatever his eccentricities, he brought to the King's council a stubborn independence of opinion and some experience of life outside the desert. Night after night, he took his part in the tedious conversations which were the only intellectual pastime ibn Saud had ever known; day after day he drove out to the picnics and to the motorised slaughters which had taken the place of the hunting with hawks and salukis – the expeditions when ibn Saud with his relays of rifles would urge his driver to chase gazelle across the open desert to the destruction of his cars, and bring down hundreds of animals in a day at point-blank range. It was on the way home from one of these sorties that ibn Saud made an epochal admission which Philby often quoted. He was bemoaning his poverty. Philby, provocative as usual, told him there was no need for despair if he would only help himself instead of waiting for God to help him; the country must be full of buried riches which he could not exploit himself and would not let anyone else exploit for him. "I tell you, Philby," ibn Saud is said to have replied, "that if anyone were to offer me a million pounds he would be welcome to all the concessions he wanted in my country." Philby told him he knew somebody who would help. The man he had in mind was Charles R. Crane, the American the Ikhwan had shot at and missed in Kuwait.

Crane was the millionaire son of the celebrated manufacturer of sanitary fittings, and it was from this incongruous source that modernity first began to come to ibn Saud's domain. Years before, in 1919, he had been chosen by President Wilson to serve on the commission of inquiry which led to the establishment of the mandates in Syria, Palestine and Iraq. He was a worthy person of a type less common now than it used to be, a travelling philanthropist, and one form of his philanthropy was helping middle eastern potentates. He had just been providing the Yemen with a harbour and roads and bridges, and he willingly came to Jidda. His first meeting with ibn Saud, in February, 1931, was not propitious: ibn Saud presented two Arab stallions to him, and he presented in return a box of dates. The dates had a special significance for Crane, because they came from a private oasis he had created in California, but the gift must be reckoned as one of the least appropriate ever offered to a head of state; since dates were the staple food of the poorest Arabs, it was rather like presenting a parcel of fish and chips of dubious foreign origin to the Queen of England. When Crane had gone, ibn Saud asked Philby, who was present, if he liked dates, and gave them to him. What Crane did with the stallions is not recorded. (One must add that this is one of Philby's stories, and some of his best may be taken with a grain of salt; he was angry with Crane, who he said "did not even send him a postcard" to thank him for the introduction.) But the rest of the visit was successful. Ibn Saud gave a banquet and so did the leading citizens of Jidda, who seemed to believe that Crane should provide their town with a water supply there and then; and Crane offered to lend ibn Saud a mining engineer he employed, whose name was Karl S. Twitchell.

So, step by step, ibn Saud began an approach to the western commercial world: first Philby, then Crane, then Twitchell. It was inevitable. He had ruled as long as he could, and perhaps as long as he wished, by the rifle and the sword, and had glimpsed enough money to be tempted by what seemed a much less arduous source of power. The path he took was dangerous for a puritan, but so far he had no idea of its dangers or its end. Since Major Holmes's fiasco in the Hasa ten years before, he had hardly given a thought to oil or other minerals. He knew what Philby was thinking of, but what he wanted first, like the people of Jidda, was water. The Bedouin paradise had always had running brooks in it, and water was the gift of God the desert people valued most; and so, when Philby spoke of buried riches, his own first thoughts were simply of water underground. He had heard of artesian wells, and had visions of flowing springs which would irrigate the desert and make it flower like heaven, and that was what he hoped that Twitchell would discover.

Accordingly, in April, 1931, Twitchell travelled through the Hejaz, and observed its geology, looking for water resources. In contrast to Philby's amateurish optimism, he brought to the country the bleak and reasonable caution of an engineer. There was no water in the Hejaz, or hardly any, and he said so; there was no hope whatever of agriculture there. Ibn Saud and al Sulaiman absorbed this disappointment, and only then asked Twitchell frankly whether he could think of any other way of making money. In fact, he had seen some seepages of oil along the Red Sea coast, and had looked with interest at some ancient gold mines, but he was too strict a professional man to arouse their hopes. He only answered that there might be some minerals worth working in the country, and explained as well as he could the task of surveying which would have to be undertaken before they were found.

At this stage, the whole project of modernisation was nearly abandoned. Ibn Saud was willing to engage a corps of engineers and geologists, and even advanced £700 for their travelling expenses, but when he understood how much a survey was likely to cost, he admitted he could not afford it. Crane himself was hit by the depression and had to put a limit of time on Twitchells explorations. Within the few months he was given, Twitchell installed a windmill which pumped a little more water into the conduits of Jidda, and investigated several of the long-abandoned gold mines, including one which was said to have been King Solomon's and still seemed workable. But for one man to explore the resources of all the arid wilderness would have been a lifetime's work, and when Twitchell went back to America and tried to interest mining companies, all of them turned him down.

However, things were happening outside the kingdom, unknown to ibn Saud, which were turning the thoughts of oil men again towards the desert. Ibn Saud himself was never interested in the history of oil development in the middle east, and so this is no place to describe its complicated details. A struggle for concessions had begun before the first world war, and it still goes on to-day. But the permutations of alliance and rivalry among the oil companies were even more confusing than those among the Bedouin tribes; for the tribes at least maintained their own names and individuality, but the companies owned shares in each other, formed and abolished subsidiaries, changed their names and disguised themselves by pronounceable abbreviations – Socal 'for Standard Oil Company of California, for example, and Bapco for Bahrain Petroleum Company. Among the changes of ownership, the sales and assignments, failures and successes, the names which are seen on petrol pumps all over the world occasionally come to the surface of the turbid history, and so do the names of rich men like Paul Getty and Calouste Gulbenkian; but among the twenty-five companies which survive to operate the middle eastern fields to-day, and the scores more companies which own the operating companies, only a few are known outside the world of oil. Yet, through the first half of the sixty-year period since the first discovery of oil, one trend can be distinguished, and that is the gradual entry of Americans to the middle east. In 1920, the companies were mostly British and entirely European; by 1930, when Twitchell embarked on his one-man survey, four of the major American companies were involved in the neighbouring countries.

Among the picturesque and buccaneering pioneers of oil, Major Frank Holmes was still at large in the Persian Gulf, and had long since abandoned his interest in butterflies. His syndicate, Eastern and General, had lost their rights in the Hasa by failing to pay the rent, but they had had more success in the island of Bahrain just off the coast. In 1925, Holmes wrested a concession from the Sheik, and in 1927, after failing to interest any British company, the syndicate sold the concession to the Gulf Oil Corporation. Then, however, difficulties typical of the industry began. Gulf held an interest in the Iraq Petroleum Company – which was then called the Turkish Petroleum Company – and had agreed with its associates that none of them would act independently within a vast area which included the whole of Arabia, and Bahrain. The others were not interested in Bahrain, and Gulf was forced to assign its option to Standard Oil of California – Socal. At this, the British Government objected. In 1914, the Sheik of Bahrain had signed the form of treaty with the British which had preserved the existence of all the sheikdoms on the coast. The British had guaranteed his independence, and he had undertaken not to make this kind of deal without British approval; and the British now advised him not to renew the concession unless the company concerned was under British management and control. A device was needed to solve this problem, and it was found when Socal formed a new company under Canadian law, and called it the Bahrain Petroleum Company, and assigned its rights to that. In 1930, Socal, very thinly disguised as Bapco, began to survey the island.

Its surveyors found promises of oil, but Bahrain is a very small island, and they started to look with longing at the vast deserted coast of ibn Saud, which could be seen on clear days as a thin yellow line on the western horizon twenty-five miles away. But Socal made no approach to ibn Saud, for a curious reason: Major Holmes had persuaded them that he was an old friend of the King, and was more likely to succeed with him than they were. This was a very unlikely story: Holmes was an amiable fellow, but in the eyes of ibn Saud he still owed three years' rent for the Hasa, and if he had been an Arab, a debtor's dungeon in the fortress, rather than a royal welcome, would certainly have awaited him in Riyadh. But Socal, with the diffidence the rest of the world finds so disarming when Americans display it, believed what he said, and waited for nearly two years while Holmes postponed again and again his journey to see the King.

In one respect, the delay gave Socal an advantage. Ibn Saud heard what was happening in Bahrain, and in Kuwait: the two Sheiks, whom he had always looked down on, were being given money for concessions in their tiny territories while he was getting none. Of course, he began to be anxious to find a company which would do the same for him, and he consulted Twitchell; but Twitchell wisely advised him to wait and see what happened in Bahrain.

What happened changed everything: in June, 1932, Socal struck oil in Bahrain, and at once the chance of finding oil in the Hasa, just across the narrow shallow sea, became a likelihood. Ibn Saud at last had something of value to sell, and a few months later Socal abandoned Holmes as a go-between and sent a telegram to Philby in Jidda to ask him to act on their behalf. They only offered to search the Hasa and negotiate a concession afterwards if conditions were promising, but ibn Saud was well-advised again and insisted on a concession agreement before the search began. So, early in 1933, big business came to Jidda.

Socal sent one of their senior men, Lloyd N. Hamilton, with Twitchell as adviser. The Iraq Petroleum Company, which was owned jointly by British, Dutch, French and American groups and had said, five years before, that it had no interest in Arabia, sent a British expert, Stephen Longrigg. Holmes turned up to bid for his syndicate, but was reminded that the King thought he owed him £6,000 and left the next day on the ship he had come by; and Philby, who had a genius for putting himself in positions which were perfectly honest but seemed to be otherwise, was retained by Socal to put their case to the King while he still remained one of the King's most close advisers. Hamilton and Longrigg both had interviews with ibn Saud, and ibn Saud told Hamilton that he would prefer the American company, and Longrigg, equally politely, that he would prefer the British. But in Philby, the Americans had an asset. As adviser to Socal, he was able to tell them from day to day how the thoughts of the King and al Sulaiman were moving, and as adviser to the King he was able to express or imply his own mistrust of his own country-men's imperial instincts. The outcome of the battle depended largely on gold. The Americans, guided again by Philby, of-fered payment in golden sovereigns, which the King and al Sulaiman understood; the Iraq company would only offer In-dian rupees. In the middle of the negotiations, President Roosevelt, who had recently been elected, closed all the banks in the United States, and a little later the United States put an embargo on gold exports and went off the gold standard, and Socal began to wonder whether it could find the cash it was promising: but it persevered, and won.

In May, ibn Saud assembled his council to hear al Sulaiman read the draft agreement, and once again Philby was witness of the occasion. Socal was to have a sixty-year concession for the Hasa, and preferential treatment in other vast areas of the Kingdom. It was to pay a minimum of five thousand sovereigns a year, and make an immediate loan of thirty thousand, recoverable from future royalties, another loan of twenty thousand eighteen months later, and two more loans of fifty thousand each if oil was found in commercial quantities. It was to pay a royalty of four shillings gold per ton of oil.

It was a hot afternoon, and al Sulaiman's voice droned on: exemption from tax and customs duties, unwanted lands to be released, a small refinery to be erected. The King fell asleep. In the sudden silence when the reading ended, he woke with a start. "Ah, must have been dozing," he said. "Well, what do you all think of it?"

His questions were usually accepted as rhetorical, and an-swered by a murmur of assent. So it was. He turned to al Sulaiman. "Very well," he said. "Put your trust in God, and sign."

Three weeks later, on another hot summer's day in Jidda, thirty-five thousand golden sovereigns were laboriously coun-ted one by one and passed across a table to al Sulaiman.

172

PART FOUR

THE MILLIONAIRE

CHAPTER SEVENTEEN

THE OIL STRIKE

It would not have been surprising if the British had been disgruntled at the Americans' victory. For a hundred years, the British had kept the peace, or what peace there was, in Arabia, by subsidies and scholarship and lifetimes of service. They had never had any reward, and to do them justice they had never looked for any, except in war. They had sometimes made mistakes, and sometimes judged wrongly, but there was not one ruler in Arabia, not even ibn Saud, who could say he would have been where he was without British help and protection and advice. The peace in the desert which made a search for oil a possibility was firstly due to ibn Saud's endeavours, but secondly to Britain's. The Americans, arriving at the last minute, were the beneficiaries of the work of Colonel Pelly, Cox and Knox, Shakespear, Dickson, Glubb, and all the other instruments of British power, and they reaped the first and only profit from it.

But it may have been just as well, at least in the early stages, that Americans won the concession; the American invasion of the Wahhabi desert may have been less painful than a British invasion would have been. It was not that the British would have had imperial designs on ibn Saud; the time was past for colonising or wanting to colonise. Philby had been ahead of the times in disliking his own country's imperialism as early as he did, at the end of the first world war, but by 1933 he was behind the times in mistrusting it. He was out of touch with Britain, and had not understood the unique revulsion of feeling which had begun to spread through Britain in the meantime; the revulsion through which the British wished and began to renounce imperial power even before the second world war had made them too poor to keep it. And yet, if British geologists and engineers and administrators had flooded into the desert among the Wahhabis, their outlook would have been coloured, more or less, by the deeds their countrymen had done there in the past, and by the contradictory blends of courage and greed, of kindliness and powerlust, of self-aggrandisement and selfless service, which had been building the British Empire for generations; and they would have been the victims of suspicion, because suspicion of British imperialism lasted long after the motive forces of imperialism had disappeared from the British national character. To use a trite illustration, a British geologist on a camel might have seen himself as a Lawrence, a Philby or a Glubb; an American geologist on a camel was merely comic, and knew he was, and that was a healthier attitude.

The winning of oil from the desert was a saga which showed American industry at its best and most enlightened; but ibn Saud never even tried to understand the elementary facts of oil technology, so the story of the industrial struggle is not really a part of the story of his life. However, the early stages of it deserve more interest than he gave them, because they had the elements of drama: a nearer approach to total failure than anyone had foreseen, and a final success much greater than anyone had hoped.

Socal assigned its concession to a subsidiary it had formed, the Californian Arabian Standard Oil Company – Casoc for short – and some years later Casoc changed its name to Arabian American Oil Company. Ever since, the shortened form of the latter name, Aramco, has been the most common word in Saudi Arabia's history.

The American vanguard entered the country at the end of the summer of 1933, as soon as the desert was tolerably cool There were eight geologists and surveyors, and they came across from the island of Bahrain in dhows; and the first thing they inspected was a hill they had already seen on clear days from Bahrain. It proved, as they hoped, to be the kind of dome-shaped hill which is the likeliest sign of oil underground. They asked if it had a name, and were told it was Jebel Dhahran. Greatly encouraged by it, they divided into pairs and began to scour the desert, believing their work was going to be a cinch.

Most westerners would have thought of this as a great adventure, but oil prospectors spend their lives in outlandish places and become phlegmatic about it. All the American pioneers had searched for oil in other countries, and their sense of adventure was specialised. They were not much excited by the desert as a part of the world few westerners had ever seen, or as the home of a unique kind of people; but they were very much excited by it as a possible source of oil which no prospector had ever effectively tested – an enormous new oyster, one of them called it, which was theirs to open. From the beginning, their explorations were efficient, not romantic. They travelled in cars and trucks, and never used camels except for transporting goods or to have their photographs taken to send to the folks at home, and they lived entirely on canned American food, except when they hunted. They called on ibn Jiluwi as governor of the Hasa, but otherwise there was not much need for them to meet the Arabs.

Segregation was easy to achieve: the desert was empty enough and big enough for the Americans to disappear in it. This was what they wanted; they were there to find oil, and for no other reason, and the Arabs could not help them. It was also what ibn Saud wanted; he had admitted the Americans to his country, but he still hoped to avoid exposing his people to their alien influence. To protect the Americans and keep them apart, he provided each pair with a guide and an escort of a dozen soldiers; and somewhat encumbered by this following, each pair made a journey of four or five months, in which they were only connected to their base by radio which often did not work. It was a hard life, full of irritations, and afterwards some of the pairs confessed that most of the time they had not been on speaking terms.

But nobody molested them. In the very parts of the desert where desperate battles had been fought four years before, they travelled unconcerned, and their chance encounters with Bedouin were on the level of chewing gum and candy bars. One of them described the desert Arabs as "a human, likeable lot, with a well-developed sense of humor"; and so they were, except when they were engaged in being exactly the opposite. The Bedouin, on the whole, were equally unmoved by the Americans. The Ulema and the Ikhwan had bitterly opposed all western inventions in theory, but like most primitive people, and like children, the ordinary Bedouin were not in the least impressed by mechanical gadgets when they saw them; they accepted aircraft and motor cars and radio as gifts of an all-knowing God, no more mysterious than His other gifts of rain and sun. The Americans' reception would have been less friendly in the towns and villages, where Wahhabism had always been stronger and more extreme, but their guides steered them clear of those. When they camped near them, they were sometimes aware of dour faces and had an uncomfortable feeling of displeasure. Some of the Ikhwan and Ulema, in fact, resented the coming of the infidels very deeply, but their resentment was mainly directed against ibn Saud for letting them come, and less against the Americans for coming. The Ikhwan were docile by then, but their characters and beliefs had not changed very much.

As it happens, the clearest impression which still remains of those early years of surveying comes not from the Americans' reports, which were strictly technical, or from their recollections, which were diffident, but from the story of one of their guides, which was written down and translated literally, by another Arab, some years afterwards. His name was Mohammad ibn Khursan, and he worked for the Amir of the village where the Americans landed. The Amir appointed him to escort an American named Barger, and in the course

177

of time his expeditions took on the airs and decorations of a Bedouin camp-fire story:

"The Amir sent for me and said; 'These men want to explore in the kingdom. They are dear to us. Now, this man who is called Tom Barger is dear to the Government, and we want to send along with him a man of ability. We know that none but you here will do the right thing. We want you to serve them well and to tell them the truth.'

"I said: 'All right, it will be a blessed hour when I am able to be of service to one and all.'

"So, I went along with him, that is with Tom Barger, who was accompanied by his assistant Berg, and we began to explore. He started to survey with a rod, a thing that has numbers, and a telescope. We explored caves everywhere. There was one detestable long cavity which was so deep that we could not find an end to it. We went right down, Tom Barger and I, with a pressure lamp. We went into it with the lamp, crawling and creeping on our bellies for four hours without reaching its far end. He picked up rocks and shells, sea shells, something like oyster shells. We did the same thing in many caves. In every cave he found, Tom Barger did the same, and I went with him.

"Then the King, His Majesty King Abdul-Aziz, came from Riyadh and encamped to the west of us. My boss Tom Barger said to me: 'Mohammad, we would like to pay a visit to King Abdul-Aziz and invite him to coffee, but I do not know Arabic.' At that time he did not have an interpreter.

"I said: 'That's not a bad idea, but after greeting him and sipping his coffee, you should speak all the Arabic you can the minute the coffee boy leaves.' (He knew one out of ten words of Arabic.) 'Then I, Mohammad, will speak to the King all the good words you desire.'

"Then we went by car to the King – I, Tom Barger, and also Berg. We reached him and by God we found him sitting there. We greeted him, and he ordered us to approach. He bade us sit down. As we sat down, coffee was brought, and the King ordered coffee to be served to us, which we drank. When we finished, Tom Barger said: 'We wish to make you some coffee' – using the English word coffee.

"The King replied: 'What are you saying? What is he saying?'

"I said: 'Yes, your Majesty, may God prolong your life. This boss of mine Tom Barger wishes to invite you to coffee at the time you choose, any hour you like.'

"The King said to me, for Tom Barger spoke no more: 'It is a blessed hour. This night you'll have dinner at my
178

place, you and all your companions. The day after to-morrow, Monday (I think it was Monday), in the morning, we shall be with you, God willing.'

"And the King said to me: 'This companion of yours will not be here more than a couple of years more before becoming a real boss, because he is a first-rate man. It is evident that he is one of those excellent men who undertake to do things properly.'

"I said: 'By God's glory, may God prolong your life, I have never been the companion of the likes of this American, whether Arab or any other, who is better than he or a better acquaintance. All are on good terms with him.'

"When evening came, we were served two large trays with four sheep on each. Tom Bargar and I dined with the King. The King spoke to Tom Barger, saying; 'We would like to dig here a well of sweet water, if you can find it.' Tom Barger replied: 'It is a blessed hour. Whatever you wish, I'll arrange to do.'

"After dinner, we went back to our companions and our camp. Then Tom Barger and I took shotguns and went hunting in the hollows. We hunted birds, bustard and sand-grouse. We brought these back with us, and they were prepared for the King's breakfast. The King came as he had promised. The King and Tom Barger spoke through an interpreter about many things which I cannot recall. The King thanked Tom Barger and said of him: 'Well, here is a good man indeed.'

"The King then asked me: 'What are they searching for here? What is their work? What places seem to interest them most?'

"I said: 'By God, may God prolong your life, the thing they mostly pick up, the thing they look for most, is anything that shows the mark of the sea. There is a mountain beyond Khuff, that is to the west of Khuff, which they dearly love. They like to come to it often, and they take from it rock samples. This mountain is Huqayl, it is called Huqayl, to the west of Khuff; this is most frequented by them. I, by God, do not know the reason for that or their aim at all. Some of what they know I have no knowledge of'."

In telling this story, Mohammad may have been anxious to please, because by the time it was told Tom Barger was the President of the oil company; but it was certainly a fact that ibn Saud sized men up quickly, and judged them by their faces, and that from the beginning he liked the faces of most of the Americans he saw. The last sentence of the story reflected neatly the attitude of ibn Saud and nearly all his people to technical knowledge: they did not know about it, and did not want to know; the results of it were all that concerned them.

For a very long time, however, there were no results. The search went on for several successive winters. The first produced nothing. The second revealed that existing maps were wrong and the company's concession area was several thousand square miles bigger than it had bargained for; but that was cold comfort, because the dome of Jebel Dhahran, which the pioneers had seen in the first few days, was proved to be the only one in the country.

Through experience, the Americans' technique of desert travel improved. They brought in aircraft for reconnaissance, and sand tyres for their cars and trucks. Sand tyres had been developed by the British for military use in Egypt; they are large and soft and spreading, like a camel's hoof. They opened the desert to larger and heavier vehicles, and ultimately to comfortable air-conditioned caravans, with attendant radio and generator trucks, water tankers, kitchen and refrigerator trucks and field laboratories, which even drove in and out of the Empty Quarter where earlier explorers had been certain nothing on wheels would ever penetrate. To Philby, it seemed that the Americans were everywhere, and it is said that another explorer of the old school, struggling on his camel with his retinue of Bedouin across what he thought was virgin territory, suffered the shock which explorers anywhere in the world to-day must dread: riding over the crest of a dune, he found himself looking down on a camp with vehicles parked in rows, and generators throbbing, and radio antennae overhead, and blazing electric lights in the desert dusk. There was not much mystery left in Arabia, except the mystery of whether there was oil.

Oil prospecting has always had an element of chance. An oil-bearing stratum is always buried and hidden. If it were exposed, its oil would all have evaporated in the course of aeons and left nothing but a pool of bitumen. Prospecting is therefore seldom a matter of looking for the oil-bearing stratum itself, but for the other necessities of a workable oilfield. These are an impervious cap-rock, which confines the oil beneath it, and a folding of strata which concentrates the oil in its domes and upward curves. In the desert, the objects of the search were signs of folding, and of the cap-rock which was known to exist in Bahrain; but the search was difficult because almost the whole of the area was covered by more recent unfolded strata, and by sand. Folding was a probability; the principal doubt was whether the cap-rock extended under the Hasa. The general dip of the strata suggested that if it did, it ought to outcrop somewhere near Riyadh; but Riyadh was outside the concession area, and the surveyors had no right to search there. To find the cap-rock became the main criterion of whether the search was worth continuing.

At the end of the second fruitless winter, the surveyors' attention began to return to the dome of Jebel Dhahran. That at least seemed to them to be a "sure shot", and during the spring and summer of 1935 drilling equipment was landed and the first well was begun. It was very laborious. Every nut and bolt and piece of wood was brought from America and landed from barges on the shallow sandy shore; the nearest safe drinking water was a spring under the sea eleven miles away, and the shade temperature rose in summer to over 120. All the effort only proved that there is no such thing as a "sure shot" in oil. One thousand nine hundred feet down, there was a showing of oil, but after hopes had risen it petered out. In the main Bahrain zone, which was deeper, there was only some gas and a little oil and water. After ten months' work, at a depth of 3,200 feet, the well was abandoned.

At the end of the fourth year, in 1937, nothing had moved any further. Six more wells had been drilled at Jebel Dhahran without success, and nothing had been found to justify a trial well anywhere else. There were about fifty Americans in the country by then, and a few of them had their wives and children in a camp of huts at Jebel Dhahran; but all of them were sunk in gloom at their failure and expected every day to be told to pack up and go home.

Not much of this gloom was communicated to ibn Saud. He remained vaguely interested in what they were doing, but his main interest was still in water. The Americans had drilled a good many artesian wells for him – a very much smaller operation than an oil well – and at last he invited them to Riyadh to drill some there; and while they were looking for water, not oil, near Riyadh, something happened which entirely changed their prospects. Two of them went on an offday to look at the water-hole called Ain Hit, where ibn Saud with his forty men had watered his camels on the night of his capture of Riyadh in 1902. Ain Hit is a natural hole, formed by the collapse of the roof of a water-worn cave some hundreds of feet underground; such cavities are not uncommon in Arabia. At the bottom, a hundred and fifty feet down, there is a deep dark pool of water, and on one of the sides of the hole, which is not quite so steep as the others, there is a zigzag track that travellers have used for centuries, going down to fill their waterskins. The two surveyors clambered down the track, with an interest more historical than scientific; and near the bottom, they found the Bahrain cap-rock.

It was absurdly romantic that this chance discovery was made in the very place where the history of the kingdom of
181

ibn Saud might be said to have started. Nevertheless, it revived all the hopes that had dwindled through four years'
disappointments. Since the same impervious stratum existed
in Bahrain and Riyadh, there was every chance that it extended under the area in between, and it was almost impossible to believe that worth-while oil deposits had not been
trapped under it somewhere. The whole enterprise was given
a new lease of life, and the whole staff a new enthusiasm. As
a fresh start, they deepened the seventh of the abortive wells
at Jebel Dhahran; and in March, 1938, after four and a half
years of thwarting, unproductive labour, nearly a mile below
the surface of the hill, they struck oil.

All this activity had made surprisingly little impact on ibn
Saud and his people. Probably everyone in the country knew
the foreigners were there, and had heard some garbled account of what they were doing; but nobody really understood
it, and only a very small proportion of the people had seen
an American in the flesh. The beliefs and traditions and ways
of life of the desert and the desert towns continued much
the same as they had for thirteen centuries. The only difference – and this was not the fault of the Americans – was
that tribal feuds and raids had been forbidden: a deprivation
which made some of the Bedouin complain that life was unbearably dull. Ibn Saud, with his cars and trucks and radio,
and his personal reputation, had once and for all established
his power in the kingdom, and although some people still
resented it, it was far beyond the challenge of any upstart
sheik.

He himself had not changed his habits in the least – the
harem, the majlis, the picnics and hunting, the camps in the
desert which had once been a necessity of war and now were
continued as a pleasure. Philby remarked that without any
battles to fight he became more "uxorious" than ever, and
people who had marvelled at his prowess as a lover in his
youth were delighted to find he could do even better when
he was nearly sixty. The oil company's rent and loans went
into al Sulaiman's coffers; but all Sulaiman had never told
his master what was in the coffers unless they were almost
empty. Ibn Saud may have noticed that when he gave outrageously generous presents to his visitors or his girls, al Sulaiman's face was not quite so glum as it had often been in
the past, but that was still the limit of his interest in finance.
Nobody dreamed of doubting that the money the company
paid was his personal property.

Of course, he hoped the Americans would succeed, and
find enough oil to let him rule and live without the money
trouble which had dogged him all his life. But he still had
not begun to understand the scale of the gamble he had taken,

or to imagine that too much money might be more trouble-some than too little. If he had asked the Americans, before the discovery at Ain Hit and the strike at Jebel Dhahran, they could only have honestly told him that the £50,000 he had already had from them was likely to be all he would ever have. If he had asked afterwards, he might have been given some idea of the fate which was waiting for him. Some of the senior executives of the company went to see him in Riyadh, and were photographed there, self-conscious in the Arab robes he still expected everyone to wear, and still con-triving to look like business executives in spite of their dis-guise; and they tried to explain what they hoped to do. But it was difficult to translate industrial hopes into Arabic dia-lect, and ibn Saud was too far from their world to grasp what was happening: that the first well was flowing, that he had been promised a pound in gold for every five tons it flowed, and that America's industrial genius was inexorably poised to turn the first flow to a flood.

In the summer of 1938, success seemed to be round the corner. The two discoveries made the company pour equip-ment into the country. The camp of huts, with its name shortened to Dhahran, grew to a curiously suburban settle-ment with a hundred family houses, apartments for bachelors, a club, shady gardens, clipped lawns with sprinklers on them, a swimming pool, a dining hall, a hospital and clinic. A separ-ate industrial area contained a power station, laundry, garage, shops and a central air-conditioning plant – enough to make some British Arabists of the older generation sourly call it Little America.

At the same time, the hill of Dhahran and the desert round it sprouted wells and pipelines and storage tanks. The com-pany surveyed the Persian Gulf, with the help of the British Admiralty, to find a channel for tankers, and built a loading berth on a long spit of sand called Ras Tanura; and while that was being done it shipped its first oil in barges to the refinery in Bahrain. The number of Americans in the Hasa rose to three hundred. They brought in some thousands of foreign labourers, most Italians, Indians and Sudanese; and slowly, the local Arabs were drawn into their orbit. At first, these were mostly men from the villages near the coast, who were not too proud, as the Bedouin were, to work with their hands for wages. There were not very many at that stage – perhaps a thousand; but the effect the Americans had on them was profound, and typical of the effect on the whole of the country later. Materially, it was all to the good. The pay was good and reliable, the food was good, the medical service was excellent and generously given. Morally, it was the most unsettling thing that had ever happened in Arabia.

The Americans in general were tactful and sympathetic; their wives, though bare-faced, dressed discreetly, by company orders. Everyone was friendly. But Little American showed the local Arabs that people who neither made pilgrimage nor seemed to pray, nor gave any other visible service to God, could be infinitely more prosperous than the faithful themselves. The American presence created desires for things which more money could buy, and created doubts of the things of the spirit which Arabs in their poverty had always valued.

In May, 1939, the first tanker called to load oil at Ras Tanura, and to celebrate that occasion the company invited ibn Saud to inspect their installations. This he did, with great festivity and little or no comprehension. It seemed that the company, and therefore the King, were on the threshold of fortune. But four months later, the second world war began, the markets for oil all over the world were disrupted, and no American tankers could be spared for the long and dangerous voyage to the Persian Gulf. The whole enterprise came slowly to a halt.

CHAPTER EIGHTEEN

ROOSEVELT AND CHURCHILL

In his history of the second world war, Sir Winston Churchill wrote of ibn Saud: "My admiration for him was deep, because of his unfailing loyalty to us." It is presumptuous to disagree with Churchill, but on reading this one must reflect that political habits of thought may cause the greatest of politicians to deceive himself. Churchill might well have admired ibn Saud as an old war-horse, as a man of principle, as a human leader, or even as a statesman. But ibn Saud was loyal to himself and his creed and people, and had never been influenced in his policies by any motive so nebulous as loyalty to Britain; and even the least critical of his admirers could not have found anything glorious in his conduct in Hitler's war. He simply did nothing.

Of course, there was no real reason why he should have done anything. The moral issues of the war against Hitler were even more remote from his kingdom's interests than those of the war against the Kaiser. He always said he hoped Britain, and later America would win, and he had sentimental and practical reasons for this hope: he still remembered men like Cox and Shakespear with a kind of affection, and he liked what he had seen of Americans, and he knew his financial future depended on America's victory. But the only practical help he gave their victory was to disagree with some of his advisers who were openly pro-German.

Another good reason for him to want Britain and America to win was that he was bankrupt again and living on subsidies. The war threw him into the worst of all his financial disasters. The prospect of gold from oil, which had seemed so near and certain, was snatched away. The pilgrimage stopped because the seas were not safe to cross; the merchants of Mecca and Jidda lost their trade, and al Sulaiman soon reported the coffers empty. Not only the kingdom's income disappeared: in the winter of 1939, there was drought, the desert pastures failed, herds died and the Bedouin went hungry.

Drought and hunger were nothing new; bad years had come to the Bedouin from time to time since history began, and when they came the people tightened their belts and put their trust in God, and in the generosity of anyone who had a little food. At the point of starvation, they expected their sheik to help them, and in the past they had never asked
185

for help from ibn Saud and not received it. But by 1940, he had no food to give them, and no money to buy it with.

Since Britain had helped him so often before, he turned to Britain again. That was exactly the moment when the British were left alone in the war against Nazism, and were only avoiding starvation at home by the virtues of fair dealing and organisation which the Arabs so notably lacked; but they sent him cargoes of wheat and flour from Egypt and Canada, rice from India, and Saudi coins and British sovereigns from the Royal Mint. His fleet of trucks was almost out of action through lack of spares and service, and his camels were scarce through drought; and so he asked Aramco to lend its transport to take the food from the coast to the central desert. Later in the war, when American Lend-Lease began, the American Government took over most of Britain's burden of keeping him solvent.

It would be pleasant to think the British and Americans were purely altruistic. In Arabia, the British sometimes had been in the past, and the Americans sometimes were in the future, but the altruism of governments and industry is very seldom pure. Both governments knew ibn Saud would never repay what they gave him, and they did not even trouble to ask him; but they both hoped they would win goodwill from the Moslem world if they kept its Holy Land from starving. The American oil men still in the country were moved to compassion by such poverty and hunger as they had never seen before; but their company knew its future profits depended on peace and contentment in the desert. Through these mixtures of motives, the two countries kept ibn Saud in power, and kept his people alive and his kingdom quiet throughout the war.

Unfortunately, they also kept the kingdom's unworthiest people in self-indulgence. Diverting public funds to private use was a wide-spread occupation by then, especially in the Hejaz, and on some of the money the hard-pressed British had sent to feed the poor, a few ingenious Arabs lived in a luxury the richest of Britons could hardly have remembered, and invested what they could not spend in gems and gold. A British envoy protested once, but ibn Saud only smiled his winning smile, and said he was sorry and it was all his fault, and nothing was done to stop it.

A more idealistic kind of help was also given by Aramco and the American Government. Fifty miles south of Riyadh, near the village of Dilam where ibn Saud had fought his first battle against ibn Rashid, there are two huge water-holes like Ain Hit, and a wide area of potentially fertile desert called Al Kharj. Some years before, under British guidance, pumps had been installed to raise the water for irrigation, and Aramco took this project in hand as a form of loan against future royalties from oil. They put in bigger pumps and dug a canal eleven miles long. Agricultural experts from the southern deserts of the United States came over, and made three thousand acres of the desert blossom with date palms, corn, alfalfa, melons, grapes, oranges and vegetables, and dairy and poultry farms. This was a splendid example of what could be done in the desert by raising underground water to the surface, and the Americans hoped Arab farmers would learn from it and copy it in other suitable places. Ibn Saud was charmed with it: so was al Sulaiman, who had always hoped that home-grown crops would make the country self-supporting. But it needed more skill and foresight than Arab farmers could master, and more patience than Arab capitalists possessed. Al Kharj is still flourishing; but in the course of time it became nothing more than a kitchen garden for the royal palaces, and nobody ever successfully copied it anywhere else. Arabs were difficult people to help.

During the war, ibn Saud began rather suddenly and pathetically to grow old. His body was covered with battle scars, and soon after he was sixty he began to suffer from arthritis. Within a year or two, he could only walk with difficulty, and could not lift his feet far enough to go up stairs. All his life, he had lived frugally, except for his sexual indulgence, and physical prowess on the march or in battle or in bed had been his pride: when the physical failing of age began, he lost hope and succumbed to it very quickly, turning abruptly from active to sedentary habits. In a last sad act of vanity, he dyed his hair.

News of the war displaced religion and women as the principal topic in his evening conversations. Secretaries wrote down the Arabic broadcasts from Germany and Italy and Britain and read them to him every day, and he discussed them endlessly. At the beginning, German propagandists led the field with a flamboyant and persuasive Iraqi speaker in Berlin. Nobody took much notice of what the Italians said; they were despised as fighters and disliked since their attack on Abyssinia. The British, starting late as usual, were too factual and sober in their Arabic broadcasts to please a race which valued the art of story-telling; but time proved, even to the Bedouin, which of these voices in the air most often turned out to be right. Like any supporter of Britain anywhere outside Britain in 1940, ibn Saud had a hard time persuading himself that the British were not beaten. When the German battleship *Bismarck* sank the British battle-cruiser *Hood*, most of ibn Saud's attendants were openly jubilant, but when the *Bismarck* was sunk a few days later, he ordered them all to clap. But none of these men, with their recollections of
187

desert battles, had any clear mental picture of a naval battle in the north Atlantic; and news of the war in general was equally remote, a mere serial story told by the voices in the radio apparatus, unconnected with the reality of daily life in Riyadh.

Not even Philby was there, during most of the war, to carry on his self-appointed task of explaining the world to ibn Saud; but if he had been, his interpretation of events would have been more personal than ever. He had become a pacifist, and was quite out of touch and out of sympathy with the mood of reluctant heroism which was animating Britain. Just before the war began, he had gone to England to look after ibn Saud's son Faisal, who was attending a conference on Palestine; and while he was there, he decided it was his duty to help to persuade the country not to involve itself in war against Nazism. He offered himself as a parliamentary candidate to the Labour party and was assigned to Epping – not a popular constituency for Labour candidates, because it was Mr. Churchill's – but the local selection committee turned him down. He wrote dozens of pacifist letters to national newspapers, and in July, 1939, he fought a by-election as a member of a forgotten political group called the British People's Party. The only plank in his platform was the avoidance of war, and he lost his deposit; and six weeks later, when war was declared in spite of his advice, he hurried back to Riyadh, believing yet again that he was right and everyone else was wrong.

Philby had all the makings of an impossible person, yet at his most impossible there is always some fact to be found which seems to redeem him. One of these facts is that he had a British wife and three children, who continued to love and admire him although he left them in England for years at a stretch while he revelled in the reflected glory of his attachment to ibn Saud. When France fell, and Britain, he believed, was likely to fall, he found himself cut off from his family, and whatever domestic conscience he possessed was awoken. He decided to go to America for a lecture tour, and hoped his family would be able to join him there. But the British Home Office suspected his lectures would be defeatist and harmful, for America had not yet entered the war; and when he landed in India on his way to New York he was arrested, to his surprise and disgust – he used the word kidnapped – and shipped to Britain and interned there. After a few months, he was let out as harmless but he was not allowed to leave the country until the war was over; and ibn Saud was deprived of his constant stream of talk.

There was only one occasion during the war when ibn Saud was brought out of his seclusion in Riyadh and appeared on the surface of world events, but that occasion was certainly notable. In February, 1945, when the war against Germany was almost over, he went to Egypt to meet President Roosevelt and subsequently Mr. Churchill, who were on their way back from the conference with Stalin at Yalta. He had not been out of his own country since his short trip to Basra during the previous war, nearly thirty years before, and in some ways the journey was the most bizarre event of his career.

It was Roosevelt who proposed the meeting. His apparent reason for it was to try to win ibn Saud's approval of the settlement in Palestine of Jewish refugees from Germany after the war was ended, though in this he was setting himself a hopeless task – so evidently hopeless that it is tempting to look for other reasons, and to guess that he also may have wanted to make a friendly impression on ibn Saud for the sake of the American oil industry.

The invitation was conveyed to ibn Saud by the American Minister in Jidda, Colonel William A. Eddy, and the idea was pursued with such secrecy that nobody in Saudi Arabia knew anything about it, except Eddy and his wife and his coding clerk, and ibn Saud and his closest advisers. The Dutch Minister, whose name was van der Meulen, came nearest to guessing that something unusual was in the wind. He was on his way from Jidda to Riyadh to see the King. It had been raining, and when he was nine days out from Jidda he was still eighty miles short of Riyadh, stuck in the mud and surrounded by flooded desert. Sheltering in a ruined fort, he saw a cavalcade of motor vehicles trying in vain to go in the opposite direction, and he counted two hundred of them. This could not have been anyone's caravan but the King's, and van der Meulen watched the pitching of an enormous camp.

Ibn Saud's habits on the march had not changed very much since the days of his desert wars. The resemblances to his old war camps could still be seen – the majlis tent in the centre, the herds of sheep and heaps of firewood, and the cooking pots for which the sheep were destined; but the camp also had differences – a telescopic radio mast, four red trucks with mounted machine-guns, and the cars which had ousted the camels. A separate camp was pitched for seventy women, for the caravan had already been delayed for a week by rain, and ibn Saud had sent for the ladies of the harems that he and his court had left behind. Van der Meulen met him in the majlis, and was embarrassed to hear him make an oration to the company of sheiks and Ikhwan, describing the Jews as arch-enemies of the Arabs. To recover from that embarrassment, he went for a walk alone up a neighbouring hill, and hearing a furious outcry behind him he found he had committed the ultimate solecism: he had climbed to a point where he could see into the women's camp.

If Roosevelt had known of the speech which van der Meulen heard, or if ibn Saud had known what Roosevelt wanted to talk about, the journey might as well have been abandoned there and then. But ibn Saud reached Jidda, still without letting his people suspect he was going to leave the country, and the fantasy began. The American destroyer *Murphy* had been sent to pick him up. He had never been to sea before, except for a trip on a British sloop off Kuwait in 1930; and the reasons why the journey was bizarre were that he remained unchangeably a desert Arab whatever the American Navy did, while the American Navy remained unchangeably American, whatever he and his followers did.

As the *Murphy* was a small ship, the American Government had asked, through Colonel Eddy, that not more than four advisers and eight servants should accompany the King. But the King, or his advisers, found it hard to imagine travelling with less than two hundred people in attendance, and Eddy had the greatest difficulty in persuading the advisers that a harem would be an inconvenience on board a destroyer. A compromise was made. When the royal party arrived, it had forty-eight people in it, including the King's brother Abdullah, three of his Ministers and two of his sons, his private physician, his chamberlain, and his coffee-servers, cooks and seven-foot Nubian slaves with swords. There was no cabin fit for a king on the *Murphy*, but the Arabs provided bolts of canvas which were used to build a tent over the whole of the foredeck, and they brought carpets to spread on the deck, and a throne. There was a minor crisis over water, for the destroyer could only supply distilled sea-water to drink, and the King, for many years, had insisted that he could only drink from two wells, one at Mecca and the other at Riyadh. But this problem was solved by taking on board a supply of water from the Mecca well; and the problem of getting the King on board – since he was too lame by then to climb a gangway – was solved by hoisting the ship's launch with him inside it. At the last moment before he arrived, a dhow came alongside the *Murphy* to deliver eighty-six live sheep: the King was so used to feeding everybody that he assumed he would feed the crew. The captain refused to embark the sheep, and explained that his lockers were stocked with frozen meat, and his crew were fed on a carefully balanced diet; but the Arabs could not contemplate eating old meat killed months before by alien non-Moslem hands. Eastern and western habits of thought confronted each other. At last the Arabs agreed to take only enough sheep for them-
190

selves, and the captain agreed to have ten of them coralled on the after deck and slaughtered there day by day; but the King's sense of hospitality was a little offended, and so was the captain's sense of naval decorum.

The *Murphy* sailed, leaving Jidda full of inevitable rumours – that the King had been kidnapped by the Americans, or that he had abdicated like the Sherif twenty years before – but the journey went well. Ibn Saud was entertained by demonstrations of gunnery, and he entertained ship's officers at an Arab feast in the tent on the foredeck: some of his followers had to leave it to be sea-sick, but he remained jovial. He was shown a movie in which the heroine was an aircraft carrier, while the crew, in another part of the ship, was shown one with a human heroine who behaved very naughtily in a men's dormitory; and his sons and most of his entourage contrived to see the latter. Five times a day, the Arabs prayed together, after checking their own estimate of the direction of Mecca with the navigating officer. There were the stories which might have been expected of Arabs lighting charcoal fires to boil their coffee in the ammunition magazines. The captain presented a pair of binoculars and two sub-machine-guns to ibn Saud, and ibn Saud gave each seaman in the crew $40, each officer $60, and each officer an Arab costume and a watch, with gold daggers for the commodore and captain. Throughout it all, the Americans were much more surprised and impressed by the Arabs than the Arabs by the Americans, or at least they showed their wonder more frankly. The manners and outlook of the Arabs made them accept, or seem to accept, the destroyer and its works as gifts of God, just as they had accepted every other mechanical invention they had seen.

Roosevelt was waiting in a cruiser in the Great Bitter Lake. The meeting was cordial, and if its object was only to impress ibn Saud with the friendliness of Americans, it had a passing success. The heads of state, searching for something in common to talk about, discovered they were almost the same age, and told each other they were both farmers at heart. Also, they compared their lameness, and this at least was a bond. Roosevelt gave ibn Saud his spare wheel-chair, and it was taken across to the *Murphy* there and then. It was much too small for the King and he never used it, but he kept it as a souvenir in Riyadh, and had a larger and stronger replica made to carry his weight.

On Palestine, Roosevelt made no impression at all. He told ibn Saud of the horrors the central European Jews had suffered from the Germans, and asked him how he would suggest the survivors should be rehabilitated; and ibn Saud, with Bedouin directness, proposed that the Jews should be

191

given the choicest parts of Germany. When Roosevelt ventured to mention Palestine, ibn Saud was adamant. Amends for a crime, he said, should be made by the criminal, not by the innocent bystanders; the Arabs had never injured the European Jews; it was the Germans who had taken their homes and lives, and it was the Germans who should pay. Roosevelt returned again and again to the point, until ibn Saud grew impatient and said he was only an ignorant Bedouin who could not understand the President's solicitude for Germans. Bedouin were kinder to their friends than their enemies. Palestine, he added, was one of the smallest of the countries on the Allied side, and one of the poorest in land, and already had more than its share of refugees.

Ibn Saud refused to give an inch; but on the other hand, he did not ask for anything from the President except his friendship. The use of that word between politicians is often a sickening travesty, but ibn Saud may have used it in the sense of an alliance between tribal sheiks, which was one degree less offensive. Roosevelt replied not only with professions of friendship but with two promises, which he confirmed a few weeks later in a letter. He promised that he as President would never do anything which might prove hostile to the Arabs, and that the Government of the United States would not make any basic change in its policy for Palestine without consulting both Arabs and Jews beforehand.

These promises were a mistake. Ibn Saud knew too little of democratic government to see any distinction between a personal promise made by the President and a promise made by the Government. If he had made such promises himself, they would both have been equally binding and permanent, because he was the Government and the State. Receiving them, he could only believe that American policy in Palestine would never be hostile to the Arabs. The President, for all his wisdom, had stumbled into the same trap that the British had laid for themselves in the previous war: the trap of making promises to Arabs during war which conflicted with other promises and could not be redeemed in peace. Within two months of the meeting, he died; within four months, the war in Europe ended; within the year, Mr. Truman summoned his Ministers in the Arab countries to Washington, and annulled both promises with the words "I'm sorry, gentlemen, but I have to answer to hundreds of thousands of people who are anxious for the success of Zionism; I do not have hundreds of thousands of Arabs among my constituents." For a while, the Saudis' opinion of American trustworthiness sank as low as their opinion of the British twenty-five years before; but hard feelings were forgotten in the end in a common interest in oil.

Roosevelt had not told Churchill, until the last day of the Yalta conference, that he meant to meet ibn Saud and other middle eastern potentates. Colonel Eddy, writing about it afterwards, implied that the British were not to be trusted with such a secret, and said that Churchill was "thoroughly nettled" and "burned up the wires to all his diplomats" demanding to see the same rulers as Roosevelt. This looks like nonsense: Eddy wrote sourly of the British with less reason than many of their critics. It is much more likely that Roosevelt forgot to tell Churchill, or never had an opportunity; both of them had far more important things to talk about and far more important secrets to keep. At all events, Churchill did not hurry back from Yalta. He paused to inspect the ancient battlefield of Balaclava, and then to make a rousing speech in Athens, and he arrived in Egypt to meet ibn Saud three days after the President.

It is said that ibn Saud liked Roosevelt better than Churchill, and if this is true, it is not at all surprising. Churchill made no promises. He had been concerned in the problem of Palestine, on and off, ever since it began, and he knew only too well there was no solution both Jews and Arabs would willingly accept. He probably only wanted to meet ibn Saud through curiosity, as a statesman and warrior with a career which was almost as long as his own, and in his brief report of the meeting he did not mention any political discussion at all. His own account showed him in one of his naughtiest moods. Roosevelt had been courtesy itself; he was a chain-smoker, but he had not smoked at all in the presence of the Wahhabi King, and had had to hide in an elevator on his cruiser to light a cigarette before dinner. Churchill, however, "said to the interpreter that if it was the religion of His Majesty to deprive himself of smoking and alcohol I must point out that my rule of life prescribed as an absolutely sacred rite smoking cigars and also the drinking of alcohol before, after, and if need be during all meals and in the intervals between them. The King graciously accepted the position."

Nothing much was therefore exchanged at the meeting except expensive gifts. Churchill presented a case of perfumes which had cost £100; ibn Saud responded with jewelled swords, and a portmanteau of robes and perfumes, pearl necklaces and diamonds worth many thousands. These must have been purchased with the money the British and Americans had sent to keep the country solvent, and so they rather resembled the birthday presents small children, suitably subsidised, buy for their fathers. Churchill, however, feeling he was outclassed, and knowing perhaps that Roosevelt had promised a gift of an aeroplane, told ibn Saud the case of perfumes was only a token: the British Government had decided to present him with "the finest motor car in the world, with every comfort for peace and every security against hostile action." It would be interesting to know how this paragon of motor cars was produced at that stage of the war and delivered to Arabia, but Churchill only reported that the swords and portmanteau were handed over to the Treasury, which almost paid for the car with them. Now, the transaction is buried too deep in the Treasury's archives to be exhumed, and the Rolls-Royce company, which would certainly have been insulted if any-one else's product had been described as the finest in the world, has no record of supplying the car. Nor can it be iden-tified for certain among the few old Rolls-Royces which trundle round Riyadh* to-day.

Ibn Saud came back to Jidda and Riyadh in scenes of re-joicing at his return from the perils of the outside world. Until he was disillusioned, he was deeply grateful for Roose-velt's promises, and exceptionally well-disposed towards Americans. This was just as well, for in the unpredictable tides of war – and perhaps with an eye to the peace – the American decision to halt the production of middle eastern oil had been reversed, and the stagnation in the Hasa had suddenly turned to a hectic activity. The American Govern-ment, indeed, had proposed to acquire an interest in Aram-co, and to build a large refinery at Ras Tanura and a pipe-line from the Persian Gulf to the Mediterranean. This idea was strongly opposed by American industry, as being "incom-patible with traditional American concepts", and it was aban-doned; but instead of it, materials were released from war-time control for Aramco to build the refinery from its own resources, and to lay a submarine pipe-line to the existing re-finery in Bahrain. When the war ended, both these outlets for Saudi oil were ready.

* Since this was written, the small mystery has been solved. The Ministry of Supply, by a stroke of luck, found that a firm of coachbuilders had had a new Rolls on their hands since the beginning of the war. The British Lega-tion in Jidda was asked to advise on structural refinements and coachwork to suit ibn Saud's tastes. The car was sent to Jidda and delivered to Riyadh by a member of the Legation staff. Ibn Saud exclaimed in admiration when he saw it; but then he noticed that it had a right hand drive. Nobody had told the Legation that ibn Saud sometimes sat in the front of his cars, especially when he was hunting, and he could only do that in the British Rolls by sitting on the left of his chauffeur – an intolerable humiliation by oriental convention. Before the man from the Legation left the majlis, he heard ibn Saud tell his brother Abdullah he could have the car.

CHAPTER NINETEEN

MONEY AND DISHONOUR

In that summer of 1945, when most of the human race was earnestly thankful for peace, the country of ibn Saud, which had been at peace throughout the war, was standing on the verge of chaos: chaos both spiritual and material. Nobody foresaw it, and perhaps if anybody had foreseen it, nobody would have been able to stop it, because its causes were all inherent in what was happening then and what had happened in the forty-three years that ibn Saud had ruled. Before one plunges into the turbulent and often shameful history of the next decade, one should look at these causes again.

By over-simplifying, one might narrow them down to two. The first was the ignorance and innocence of ibn Saud and almost all his people, and the second was money from oil – far too much money. But if this had been all, the worst of the chaos might possibly have been avoided. There were other more subtle influences.

The country and people were still as simple and primitive as ever, and as closely wrapped up in their own unique intolerance. Ibn Saud himself, for all his shrewdness, was still a blend of Bedouin and desert townsman in material outlook, and a Wahhabi in belief. He had gone beyond the limits of Wahhabi teaching in accepting some western inventions, but only because they were useful; he had never accepted a word of western philosophy or morals or social standards, or even the technical knowledge on which the inventions were based. His kingdom was still his personal estate, his rule was patriarchal, his God was all-knowing, and his law was the seventh-century law of the Prophet; and the study of the Koran and Sunna was still the only teaching or learning he approved.

He had never anticipated that the kind of society which had existed in Arabia since the dawn of history would ever have to change; much less that he represented its final generation. So he never thought of giving his forty-two sons any education, except the kind of education he had been given himself, a kind which fitted them only to live in the desert and carry on the autocracy he had founded. Saud, the eldest surviving son and his heir-apparent, had learned the Koran by heart when he was twelve, but after that he was not taught anything more academic than desert lore and strategy and horsemanship, and he was not allowed to go abroad until he was middle-aged. Faisal, the second, had mastered the Koran a little younger, because he was a more intelligent person; he had travelled quite extensively since his first official mission to England when he was a boy, and through his native common sense he had profited from his journeys and acquired a good idea of how the Christian democracies worked, and how people behaved in them. But he was the only one; the rest of the brothers, who ranged in age from Saud at forty-four to infants in arms, had not the slightest training to enter the twentieth-century world, or to lead any life except the customary life of Arab princes: the harem, the mosque, the majlis, the picnics and the hunting field.

Ibn Saud was not only simple, he was also tired and lame and in pain with arthritis, and although he was only sixty-five his mind and speech were not so incisive as they had been. People who had known him before the war and met him again were shocked and saddened by the change: sometimes, his old wit and fire and charm flashed out, and sometimes he was still terrible in anger, but often he seemed to be sunk in his own thoughts and to lose his interest in conversation. For many years, he had encouraged his doctors to dose him for any ailment he imagined he had, and perhaps their miscellaneous medicines sometimes deprived him of his power of concentration. He had begun to neglect the less glamorous duties of kingship; but he had never authorised anyone else to do them. Saud was his viceroy in Riyadh, and Faisal in the more sophisticated Hejaz, but neither had any independence. Even the least of decisions was still the King's; but sometimes he could hardly bring himself to make decisions. Nevertheless, in spite of these signs of age, his reputation and his people's respect for him held the kingdom together. Arabia had never before been so stable and peaceful, or on the whole so contented.

No social system, no ruler and no people, could have been much less fitted for the deluge of wealth that the western world suddenly thrust upon them, poured over them and drowned them in: wealth beyond all need, beyond all dreams, and beyond all reason. In the first year of oil production after the war, five million pounds or so were handed to ibn Saud, but that was nothing. Five years after the war ended, by 1950, he had been given over £80 million, and that was before the big money started. By the end of his life, he was receiving well over a million pounds a week, and every week the payment was growing bigger.

All this money went into al Sulaiman's coffers, and all of it for many years was paid in British sovereigns. It did not belong to the State, it was ibn Saud's personal property, as all the income of the country always had been. The coffers, the actual boxes which had been so often empty, were instantly full to bursting point, but the country possessed no banking system of its own, no means of investing or even safeguarding money, except by setting carpenters and smiths to work to make more boxes. That was easy enough: what was impossible was suddenly to expand and adapt the country's social system to make any reasonable use of so much money.

Ibn Saud had no idea what could be done with it. He did not want it for himself – or at least, a hundredth part of it would have been enough for him. He had all he had ever wanted in life: power, women, and the knowledge of his own integrity. He was too old to develop new expensive tastes; and besides, he was still, as he always had been, a man of high principle, who believed the austerity imposed by the desert was a virtue. The only thought he had in the first few years was to indulge his old Arab instinct of generosity and give the money away; and this he began to do, in quantities far too big to be wise, first to his sons and then to his brothers and cousins and nephews – there were roughly two thousand princes of the royal blood – and then to his close attendants and the multitude of people who had always lived on his bounty.

Unfortunately, his sons' first taste of riches coincided with their first glimpse of western luxuries. Just before the end of the war, the American Government had persuaded ibn Saud to declare war on Germany. He did it reluctantly, perhaps because he saw that as a warlike act it was ridiculous when British and American armies were already well across the Rhine. But its object was not strategic, it was simply to make his country eligible as a founder member of the United Nations. It entitled him to send a bevy of princes, led by Faisal, to the San Francisco Conference in 1945. Two months in America opened the eyes of the younger princes. Life in a mud-walled city in the desert never seemed the same to them again, and rumours of things they had seen which money could buy were spread among the other members of the family. According to Philby, one of them said the thing that impressed him most in the western world was an underwater restaurant where he had been able, through a glass wall, to watch girls swimming while he ate; and that was a fair enough measure of the taste and comprehension of a good many of them.

Back in Riyadh, they had to find something to spend their money on, and among their thoughts were palaces. Ibn Saud himself set them an example by beginning to build a new palace outside the walls of the town. He built it in the traditional desert style, a sprawling set of mud-brick houses
197

connected by bridges and arcades, and surrounded by a mud-brick wall with square defensive towers on it. It was larger but not much more pretentious than the teeming insanitary warren he had lived in since 1902. This was the only kind of palace that desert craftsmen could build, and the only novelty in it was an arrangement of mud-brick ramps up which, in view of his lameness, he could be driven in his car to the bedroom floors above. The princes had much more up-to-date ideas, but neither they nor anyone else in the country had the knowledge to put them into practice. Saud embarked on a concrete edifice decorated in pink and gold, set in walled gardens equipped with swimming pools and fountains (supplied from artesian wells Americans had drilled), and with singing birds in cages, mosaic terraces, thousands of electric lights among the shrubs, and flood-lit minarets with loud-speakers on top for the call to prayer. It was said to have cost £4 million, and after a few years he grew tired of it and bull-dozed it down and built another on the same site which, by same rumour, cost £11 million, and was even more garish and tasteless than the first.

His garden, of course, was precisely the desert Arabs' vision of Paradise, and it may be unfair to blame a man for creating a semblance of heaven on earth if he can afford it; but to create it in the middle of the desert needed contractors, designers and craftsmen the desert could not provide. For this project, and many others the same but rather less expensive, experts both genuine and bogus flocked into the country; and since Moslems and speakers of Arabic were favoured, most of them came from other parts of the middle east where swindling had always been endemic. To protect themselves against their contractors, the princes and ibn Saud himself engaged advisers; but they did not have the worldly knowledge to distinguish good advice from bad, and soon they also needed protection against some of their advisers, who often awarded contracts to the men who offered the highest bribes. Most of these foreign experts and tradesmen shared a single urgent wish: to extract as much money as possible and take it home as quickly as they could. Thus, as soon as the news had spread that Riyadh was a goldmine, the artful rogues and impostors of the middle east, of whom there were plenty, descended on the city and ensnared the Saudi family in such a web of fraud and trickery as history has never recorded before. The Saudi people themselves, although some of them did their best, were left far behind in the rush of more expert thieves, and a large part of the money America was pouring into the country leaked out again in huge and secret fortunes.

The crazy spending spree might not have mattered much

if the money had stayed in the country. Then some of it would have filtered down to the poor, and the general standard of living of the people might have risen. But on the contrary, it was prices that started to rise, and while the rich grew richer, most of those who were poor or stupid or scrupulous grew poorer. This economic process was beyond the understanding of ibn Saud, or of his advisers. At one point on the spiral of inflation, they demanded that Aramco should double the wages of all its Saudi employees, of whom there were thousands by then, in the naïve belief that this would increase the country's prosperity. The company tried to explain what would really happen, but it complied; and consequently, prices rose again, the employees were no better off than they had been, and everyone not in the company's pay was poorer. It was not only the incoming rogues who were guilty of taking their plunder abroad; alarmed by the inflation at home, most of the shrewder Saudi Arabs who had been given money or succeeded in stealing it, or even earning it, also did their best to salt some down in Switzerland or invest it in apartment houses and villas in Lebanon or Egypt; and ibn Saud himself, so far as can be known, was the only rich man in the country who never possessed any property outside it.

Everything that happened, indeed, was exactly parallel to what might happen if somebody rashly threw handfuls of five-pound notes to a crowd of hungry uneducated children: the mad scramble to pick up as many as possible, and more than anyone else; the discovery that anything in any toyshop or sweetshop could be had for the asking; the conflicting advice from honest and dishonest adults, only leading to confusion and the disregard of everyone's advice; the shopkeepers putting their prices up and restocking with shoddier goods; the robbers and people with specious arguments taking the children's money away by threats of force or guile; and finally, the children left, still hungry, with nothing but broken discarded toys and indigestion. Only in the last particular was the parallel not exact, for the same benefactor, in Saudi Arabia, continued an unending shower of notes, and the process went on and on.

Beside the spirals of inflation and corruption, the family of ibn Saud was caught up in a spiral of scandal. Some of the princes gave it its initial impulse by irresponsible and gullible behaviour, but once it was started it grew of its own accord. Foolish extravagances and expensive vices always make good stories. The princes certainly provided such stories liberally, some printable which the western and middle eastern press enjoyed, and many unprintable which circulated verbally. But they won such a reputation for rich stupidity that stories about

199

them were invented, and nobody now can be certain which of the stories were strictly true, and which were fiction, and which were half-truths or misunderstandings. All one can do with a clear conscience is disentangle some threads which ran through them all.

Of these, misunderstanding is the most important. Most of the princes entirely misunderstood the west; they saw and craved its luxury, but never saw its foundation of morality and taste. To some degree, the west misunderstood the princes; it saw a brood of playboys, but never saw the sternly moral world they came from. They gave the impression they had had no moral training, but in fact the extreme restriction and propriety of their upbringing was one of the causes which made them fall so far. The Wahhabi standard was hard enough to live up to in the desert towns where temptations were few: in the Hollywood world they suddenly discovered, such a standard simply did not fit and seemed ridiculously strict and out of date. So they abandoned it wholly, although they might have clung to a system of morality which was a little more forgiving and elastic; and they had nothing to put in its place. At home in poverty, they had had a certain elegance; abroad with money, they were vulgar. The contrast was visible in the robes they wore at home, and the spiv suits and winkle-picker shoes the worst of them wore abroad.

It was their upbringing which made them think at first that far more western women could be bought than was the case in fact; coming straight from Wahhabi Arabia, it took them some time to learn that women in low-cut evening dresses or bikinis might be as jealously guarded as women in veils. But that was only one example. As with women, so with every other western commodity, they could not tell good from bad. If one of them bought a beautiful Wedgwood dinner service of a thousand pieces, it was seldom because it was beautiful or because he could distinguish it from earthenware, but more often because the person who sold it to him could make more profit by selling him something expensive. They were push-overs for salesmanship, the perfect suckers, and the wives they left in Riyadh were a prime example of keeping up with the Joneses. There is probably not a word of truth in the famous stories of golden Cadillacs, but any salesman could easily have persuaded them that all the best people had their cars gold plated, or even – if there were any such thing as a dishonest Cadillac salesman – have told them the plating was solid gold and charged them accordingly.

This country-cousin gullibility increased the west's misunderstanding. Few critics saw the difference between buying absurdly expensive useless things and being sold them; too much blame was given to the princes, and too little to callous

200

salesmanship. But whenever the princes emerged from Arabia, for orgies in the Lebanon or shopping trips in Europe or America, vultures gathered. In Beirut, every kind of trader, pimp and confidence trickster was openly gleeful when the ignorant young millionaires from the desert came to town, and they all competed to think of novel attractions to separate them from their money. It would be a hopeless task to whitewash the Saudi princes in general – too many of them were only too eager to be tempted; but when the experts of a middle eastern city set themselves to provide the most ingenious temptations their long experience could devise, then better men might have fallen sometimes. In the west, the exploitation was more subdued, but it certainly existed. When they told a hôtelier, for example, that they wanted to give a little dinner for fifty people, that was often the only order they gave; brought up on rice and mutton, they lacked the savoir-faire to order a western dinner in detail. The hôtelier, knowing their reputation, perhaps could hardly be blamed for flying caviare from the Caspian and strawberries from any part of the world where they were in season, and basking in the resulting publicity and profit; and the princes could hardly be blamed for enjoying the astonishment of their guests. But the princes seldom if ever chose the fantastic repasts they ate. Few of them would have known the distinction, or cared very much, if they had been served a square meal of fish and chips; and when they handed out hundred-dollar bills to bell-hops and waiters and porters, they did it for just the reasons which make other people tip too much when they feel unsure of themselves in surroundings too grand for them. Some people can find no excuse for the princes' behaviour, but to people who know where they came from there seems something pitiable in their plunge into wickedness, and their lack of any understanding of the facts of western life. It was unconsciously revealed by one of them who looked out at New York from the window of his top-floor suite in one of the most exclusive hotels in the world, and is said to have been heard to say: "I sometimes wish I was just an ordinary American. I'd live right here in the Waldorf Astoria...."

The way they spent money on their travels made people think they lived in luxury at home, but that was not so. They could pay for luxurious living in Europe or America, where the finest hotels reserved whole floors for them, but not even the vastest fortune, in their hands, ever made Riyadh a comfortable place to live. They tried, but they failed for two good reasons – apart from the inherent discomfort of a town in the middle of a desert. One reason was that they never learned to make proper use of the luxuries they bought and took home with them. It may not be true that one of them drove his new Cadillac until the petrol tank was empty, and then abandoned it as broken and bought another, but that was not far from typical. Machinery fell to pieces in their hands, and their mechanics and chauffeurs had to be either Saudis who knew very little more than they did, or foreigners who were swindlers. The fairy-lights in Saud's palace garden fused by hundreds, and nobody mended them; maladjusted refrigerators froze and broke the bottles in them and were discarded; air-conditioning ducts became the home of rats and circulated smells. At the other end of the gamut of misuse, Chanel Number 5 lost its aura of luxury when it was bought in litre bottles and used like bath-water. Nor could all their wealth procure good service. Money could not turn a Saudi cook into a Parisian chef, or a Sudanese slave into a polished waiter, and foreign servants tempted by fabulous wages despised their masters and never lasted long.

The other reason for the Saudi family's lack of luxury at home was, again, the conspiracy of swindling. Most of the goods they ordered there cost five or ten or twenty times their value. When they told an official to order something, he passed on the order to a friend and invited another friend to arrange the transport, and everybody in a chain of middlemen took his hundred per cent. The family knew this happened, but the only thing they did to try to stop it – and this at a later stage – was simply to refuse to pay at all. A contractor for a palace which ought to have cost a hundred thousand pounds, would add on a profit margin of another hundred thousand, and then multiply the result by five and make a tender of a million, in the expectation that his client would not pay. Years after the work was finished, an official appointed by the client would offer a first and final payment of four shillings in the pound, and the contractor, glad of his hundred per cent, would accept it – although he might be sure the client had authorised ten shillings, and the other three hundred thousand pounds had stayed in the official's pocket. This remarkable way of doing business became so well understood that it seldom broke down; but sometimes reputable firms which were not in the know made genuine tenders and were badly bitten. Sometimes also, the client's refusal of payment came too soon, or contractors, since cement was very expensive and sand was free, mixed concrete so economically that buildings began to fall down before they were finished. For both these reasons, many palaces can be seen in Riyadh to-day, half-built and already falling into ruins; and when it is said that Saud's palace cost eleven millions, this gives a totally false impression of quality and comfort. It was nothing in fact but a hollow, silly, pathetic caricature of grandeur.

The kingdom ibn Saud had built had been old-fashioned, simple, poor and sometimes cruel, yet it had valued chivalry and honour, and been true to its own morality. What happened to it was undeniably wrong. It was wrong that so much money – enough perhaps to have solved the whole of the world's refugee problem – should have been given to people totally untrained to use it; and it was also wrong to expose these people to temptations which were sure to undermine their strong religious faith. Yet there was nobody who merited all the blame: there was no single villain of the piece. In the last analysis, one can only whole-heartedly blame the convention by which a sovereign state, or its ruler, can absolutely own the natural resources of the part of the world it happens to have inherited or conquered. Ibn Saud and his people, left to themselves, would never have discovered the oil beneath the Hasa, and never used it. His grandfather had owned the Hasa, his father had lost it, and his own right to it was only based on one night's fight with sword and musket against the Turks in the fortress of Hofuf in 1914, and the primeval tribal battles which had kept it quiet since then. In an ideal world, a product of nature which all the world needs, like oil, probably ought to belong to all the world. But the world being what it is, the right of ibn Saud to possess the oil was unquestionable; he had a perfect right to sell it, and Aramco had a perfect right to buy it.

It was also wrong that the money was given to ibn Saud with hardly a word of reliable advice on the spending of it. Aramco could not be blamed for that; it was only an oil company, and its only reason for being in Arabia, or existing, was frankly to make a profit. It made such a handsome profit that it could afford to take a very liberal view of its responsibilities towards Arabia, and its senior men, who became quite friendly with the King, gave him excellent personal advice when he asked for it. But an oil company could hardly have been expected to act like a mandatory power, and that was what was needed. Advice was a job for a government. The British Government could not have interfered in what had become a purely American development, but one cannot avoid the conclusion that the American Government should have done more than it did. It might not have been easy to advise ibn Saud, and after the rot had started, and he had learned to mistrust advice, and almost everyone in the country had something to hide, it might have been impossible; but in the past he had taken advice from people like Cox and Shakespear, and he still took it sometimes from individual oil men whose faces he liked; and if the American Government had been a little more alive to the situation America had created, and a little more tactful and insistent in offering him financial advisers at the very beginning, the worst of the tragedy might never have begun. Perhaps they were rather too afraid, just after the end of the war, of being accused of colonialism, or perhaps even this degree of help for the Arabs would have offended Mr. Truman's Zionists.

This was exactly what the British, being less inhibited, did in Kuwait, and the results in the long run were happier. The Sheik of Kuwait, the descendant of old Mubarrak, had sold his concession to a company which was half British and half American. There was even more oil in his territory than in ibn Saud's, and even more money, and he certainly had no more idea than ibn Saud of how to use it; but the British Government, which had had its Political Agents there ever since Knox was appointed forty years before, stayed on to give him honest and expert advice. The problem was simpler, because the country was so much smaller and more amenable to government, and nobody would have claimed the solution was perfect; but while the Saudi money was still being squandered or poured down the drain of corruption, the Sheik was not only living, to say the least, without stinting himself, but was also building schools and hospitals for his people and becoming, it was said, the largest individual investor on the London Stock Exchange.

Some of the blame, of course, must rest with ibn Saud, if it is right to blame a man for his limitations, and if one can bear to blame an old man who sees what he has striven for all his life destroyed by a thing he cannot understand. While his kingdom was dissolving in an anarchy of money-grabbing, he sat in his majlis in his new mud-palace, always insisting the money was his to spend or give away as he alone decided, always ready to drive a hard bargain for more when he had a chance, and always believing, or seeming to believe, that al Sulaiman's money methods were perfectly able to cope with it. The American Minister, Colonel Eddy, once ventured to ask him whether he was not afraid of being swindled; he only replied that he had already given al Sulaiman enough to make sure he would never be tempted. Yet anyone inclined to blame him for what he did, or what he failed to do, should also ask himself what he would do with a sudden fortune of tens or hundreds of thousands of pounds a day. Even an educated person in a civilised country with all the facilities of an established financial system would find it a problem, and ibn Saud had no education in that respect, and no system. People in England who merely win a football pool find it hard enough to use their winnings wisely, and what happened to ibn Saud was like a major win on every pool, every day, year in and year out.

In the face of these problems which seemed to him insoluble, he became more morose. It was not only, as Philby said, that his failure to make his wives pregnant was weighing on his mind: his moroseness was also caused by his fear for the future. Even while he was handing out fortunes to his sons, he was afraid that money might corrupt them. In fatherly lectures, he begged them to use wealth wisely and expounded his simple philosophy. They were to be proud of their family's history, and follow the example of their illustrious forebears. Fair and open dealing would lead to happiness, but trickery would lead to misery. What God willed would always come, but men should do their best; to be able to say "I have done my best" would lead to the highest satisfaction.

Of course, he was deceiving himself; perhaps like some other fathers with similar problems on less dramatic scales he did not really want to know the truth. It is impossible to say how much of it he did know. Certainly there was a tacit conspiracy to hide things from him, and it would have been a brave man who tried to tell him how far some of his sons had sunk; but a few of the scandals could not possibly be hidden. One of his sons was invited by a British consul to a party in Jidda, and was asked to leave because his host did not like his behaviour, and then came back and shot the consul dead through a window. Another prince, one of the Rashidi children, gave a party with women present, and some of the guests died of drinking a poisonous brew which they thought in their ignorance was whisky. On both these occasions, ibn Saud was furious; on one, he is said to have fainted at the shock. He sentenced both princes to death, but both were reprieved through other people's intercession, imprisoned for a while and then released. These incidents led him to ban the import of alcohol, and even to forbid the Americans in Aramco to bring it in for their own use. He suspected the Americans had been too free with it; he never knew his own sons were importing it to Riyadh by the truck-load, or that they went on doing so, by paying a higher price, long after he made it illegal. Yet any American could have told him one cannot stop a drunkard drinking simply by forbidding him to drink, and some of his sons by then were chronic drunkards.

Such incidents, and his stern reaction to them, also increased the conspiracy to keep him in the dark and to undermine the strict impartial justice he had founded the kingdom on. When his sons were brought before him for misdemeanours, he still had the authority and the strength of arm to seize his camel-stick and beat them almost insensible, in public in his majlis. But in giving them money, he gave them the power to avoid his own retribution: caught in crime, they bribed his officials to keep them quiet, and so established that even in Wahhabi Arabia there could be one law for the poor, and another, or none, for the rich. Swindling officials did the same. Amputation was still the penalty for theft, and it was still applied as harshly as ever to ordinary thieves. But it could not be applied for embezzling public funds, on the curious ground that any citizen was already a part-owner of such funds; and so men who stole a sheep were mutilated, while those who stole hundreds of thousands of pounds went free.

In this declining period of his life, ibn Saud only twice emerged from the perplexity and seclusion to which old age and wealth had driven him and entered again the international scene: once to inspect the Aramco installations in the Hasa, and once – his third and last expedition outside his country – to pay a state visit to Egypt.

It was a sign of the times that he arrived in the Hasa with his immediate entourage of a hundred men, not in a caravan of camels as he had in 1930, or of cars as he had in 1938, but in a fleet of aircraft. But otherwise it was only Aramco that had grown and changed; the King, who once again, for the moment, was in his most genial mood, remained himself, enfeebled but still displaying the force of personality which had won his kingdom. The company showed him the flourishing American town of Dhahran and the vast apparatus of oil production and refining, and presented its hundreds of senior employees and, on a separate occasion, their wives and children. It had spent $300,000 in preparing to entertain him, but its dinner parties, excellent though they were, seemed snacks beside the banquets given by the King himself and by the Governor of the Hasa, the son of Abdullah ibn Jiluwi. At the King's, a table cloth ten feet wide and 225 feet long was covered all over by food. At the Governor's, in the neighbouring town of Dammam, American guests were confronted by a whole cooked camel, legs, head and all, 280 whole cooked sheep on the customary mounds of rice, two thousand chickens and six thousand eggs, and roughly ten thousand side dishes of fruit and vegetables and puddings. When the first sitting of five hundred guests had made what impression they could, servants and soldiers had their fill, five hundred at a time, and finally, early the following morning, the citizens of the town were let in to eat what was left and wrap what they could not eat in their skirts and take it away. Observers of this final mêlée saw men who made for the doors with legs of mutton raised above their heads, but were left holding nothing but the bones as the incoming crowd tore the meat off, and they noticed that soldiers posted at the doors made each departing guest unload his skirtful of stew on the ground, and stirred it with their bayonets to retrieve the cutlery the Governor had provided for his foreign visitors, before they allowed the guests to scrape it up again.

The scene astonished Americans, but on all the American technical marvels he was shown, the King only made a single comment. "A great enterprise," he was heard to murmur, as he was driven through a stabilising plant. "May God help you in handling it."

The visit to Egypt, in 1946, was an even more grandiose occasion, but it did not seem to be so happy. There was banquet after banquet, and the crowds of Cairo and Alexandria turned out to line the streets and cheer the legendary old warrior, who perhaps represented to them the wild romantic Bedouin which the most urban of Arabs sometimes likes to imagine he is at heart. But Philby, who went with ibn Saud, observed that he was hesitant and ill at ease, and made no visible response to the enthusiasm round him. In the whole of the tour, he never made a speech or gave an interview to journalists, and he seemed not to know what to do when bands played his own National Anthem, which he had never heard before. One evening there was a passing flicker of the man he once had been. "There are some nice girls in this country," he said to his companions. "I wouldn't mind picking a bunch of them to take back to Arabia, say a hundred thousand pounds' worth of the beauties." But it was said nostalgically.

He may have been confused at his first experience of modern cities, but his silence may more have been due to the political undertones of the state occasion. Cairo at that moment was the centre of the simmering pot of Arab politics, as it has often been; the pot was not far from boiling over, and almost anything ibn Saud had said would have made him an enemy somewhere. The Egyptian monarchy was almost finished; opposition to it was strong and vocal, and his host, King Faruq, was so unpopular that his overthrow, which happened six years later, could already have been foreseen. Behind and apart from the hollow ceremonial stood the Arab League, an association of Arab states which ibn Saud himself had joined, together with Egypt, the Yemen, Syria, Lebanon, and his old Sherifian rivals of Transjordan and Iraq. The League had been formed with British support as an attempt to bring about co-operation in the Arab world; but inevitably, its policies were anti-British, because the only wish which all the Arabs shared was to throw the Jews out of Palestine as soon as the British mandate ended. Ibn Saud was one of its least co-operative members. He had always been adamant about the Arabs' rights to Palestine, and had always been liable to rages when Palestine was discussed; nevertheless, he still looked on it as a problem beyond his own frontiers, and was not prepared to do anything very active to solve it. The League proposed to fight the Jews, and he acquiesced, but he believed the British and Americans would never allow them to be defeated; and when the time came in 1948 for the mandate to end and the League to declare a War of Liberation, he was less surprised than most of the Arab leaders to see the Arab campaign end in fiasco through inefficiency and lack of liaison between the separate national armies. Meanwhile, at the time of the visit to Egypt, he did not want to offend the British, for whom he still had some friendly feelings, or the Americans, on whom he depended for his money. He accepted the British Ambassador's invitation to a party; but the Ambassador declined an invitation from the League to a reception it gave for the two Kings, on the apparently rather slender ground that he had to present the speech-day prizes at a girls' school in Alexandria. According to Philby, ibn Saud was glad to go home; but as a token of appreciation for his fortnight's visit, he promised King Faruq an allowance of £200,000 a year in gold.

The visit had one long-lasting effect on ibn Saud: he came home with a passionate desire to build a railway. He is said to have ridden in a railway train when he went to Basra in 1916, but that may have been an unimpressive military train, and if it made him want one of his own the wish was too far-fetched to be worth considering then. However, his royal progress by train from Cairo to Alexandria woke all his stubborn determination. Saud had wanted a heavenly garden, and other sons had wanted splendid cars and concrete palaces: what he wanted was a railway – specifically, a railway from the Persian Gulf to Riyadh, and then an extension right across Arabia to Jidda. All the advisers he consulted opposed him, so far as they dared. His idea was widely regarded as an old man's folly, based only on a belief that all the best countries and all the best rulers had railways. American experts on transportation tried to tell him railways were out of date, and a first-class road and a fleet of trucks would be cheaper and more efficient. But he would not change his mind. One of his arguments against a road was that the truck drivers would be tribesmen and would always be stopping or turning off into the desert to visit their friends, whereas a railway engine driver, once he started, would have no option but to go on till he came to the other end. Perhaps he thought, with some reason, that trucks on a road were too obviously a mere development of the old camel caravans, and might revive the Bedouin tradition of robbery: it was harder to imagine Bedouin robbing a train. At all events, he wanted a railway, and he was the King; and so Aramco built it for him, with a seven-mile deep-water pier at Dammam, and equipped it with rolling stock from the New York, New Haven and Hartford Railroad, and set off the cost, which was $70 million, against his oil royalties. It was completed in 1951, and ibn Saud, in-augurating the Riyadh railway station, remarked that it stood on the very spot where he and his forty men had left their camels on the night of the raid almost fifty years before. Oddly enough, the enterprise was successful, and to that ex-tent, the old man was proved right. It is still quite an efficient railway, and it enabled Riyadh to grow – outwardly, at least – into a major modern city. But when a paved road from Riyadh to the coast was finally built in 1962, the railway lost its traffic, and the extension to Jidda has never been begun, and undoubtedly never will be.

It seems extraordinary to any western critic that with the exception of the railway, and a good many water wells, ibn Saud spent hardly any money on anything that might be clas-sified as public works. During his lifetime, plans were made for a hospital in Riyadh and another in Taif and a pier in Jidda, and al Sulaiman raised loans for them in the United States; but as Taif, the scene of the massacre which began the capture of the Hejaz, had become the summer capital, one may suspect the hospitals were more intended for the royal family and court than for the public, while the pier was certainly intended for the pilgrims. It seemed never to occur to ibn Saud that his overflowing wealth laid any duty on him to give his people the amenities they lacked: a medical service, schools, sanitation, roads and public transport, or any kind of insurance less whimsical than his personal bounty. This was the saddest of his failures; but knowing the history of his life, one can go some way towards seeing these things as he saw them.

The blessings of a welfare state, of course, are valued more highly by people who have them than by people who have scarcely heard of them. The Arabs had a welfare state of a sort, in so far as they could always go to ibn Saud and sit in his majlis and ask him for help when they needed it. They valued the right to ask for help from the King, but had never heard of a right to demand help from a government; nor had they learned to expect any kind of help which God or the King could not give. In the matter of medicine, a few people in the eastern part of the country, and some of the royal family, had been treated by American medical mission-aries from Bahrain for many years, and the King himself had a qualified Syrian doctor. But the vast majority of the people still looked after themselves, and submitted to what they believed was the will of God, and their medical know-ledge had not progressed beyond camel's urine for internal complaints and cauterisation for anything visible.

To ibn Saud, if he ever considered it, a public medical service would have seemed a formidable undertaking, full of dangers. There was nobody in the country who could run it;

all its staff, from a Minister of Health to the doctors, dentists, nurses, dispensers and orderlies, would have had to be brought from abroad and spread through the towns and villages, bringing not only medicine but unpredictable sins and heresies. The foreign influence of the oil men was confined to the Hasa; the influence of the pilgrims had always been confined to Jidda and the holy cities; but the influence of foreign doctors would have spread through the heart of the country, and certainly undermined the Wahhabi faith.

These considerations were more acute in the matter of schools. There were no native teachers except the Wahhabi learned men themselves. If the young men of the country were educated by foreigners, its religion would be diluted and its social system inevitably changed; and ibn Saud was too old and too pure a product of the old régime to believe it would change for the better.

To some degree, he was right to hesitate. To start to educate a backward race is always a delicate process, and not always entirely beneficial. If Bedouin boys were taken away from the life they were born to and taught in schools, they might grow up to be almost anything, except contented Bedouin. If the boys of the towns were taught to read and write, the towns would have to evolve to provide them with work to satisfy their learning. Nobody, in either case, could be certain that learning would make the boys happier adults, and in the case of the Bedouin ibn Saud and the Bedouin themselves would certainly have insisted it would not; for the Bedouin still believed their way of life was nobler than any other people's.

So the social system remained, swaddled in ibn Saud's conservatism – conservatism short-sighted but not entirely blind, for there was much that was good in the old ways and much that was bad in the new. Yet change had to come. At one end of the social scale, princes were importing the callow desirable gadgets of western life and defying the holy law; at the other, the Bedouin and poor people of the eastern villages were watching what seemed to them the high life of the American oil camps; and between the two a wider and wider gulf was opening in a society which had hitherto been free of class-consciousness. In neighbouring Arab countries where western influence had penetrated deeper, revolt was brewing: in Egypt, Lebanon, Syria and Iraq. In poverty, Saudi Arabia might have remained a backwater, as Muscat and the Yemen did for many years; but with wealth, and with the glimpse of foreign living standards the Americans provided, demands were sure to grow for everything that other countries had. The tragedy was that ibn Saud and his family could have anticipated these demands, but instead they waited until they were forced to concede them one by one; they could have led the country through its evolution, but they shut their eyes to any social change.

Aramco, however, worked on an assumption opposite to ibn Saud's. With wordly wisdom, it assumed the country would change, and change quickly, from the archaic to the modern, suffering an industrial revolution, a social revolution and a religious reformation all at once. Some of the philosophical members of its staff may have wondered whether the American way of life was entirely superior to the Bedouin way of life, but even they knew the change, for better or worse, was coming. The company on the whole, as even those who mistrust big business must admit, did all a company could to help the kingdom in the crisis it had made. Good relations with the King and the people were good commercial policy, but in pursuing them it sometimes seemed to take a step beyond the self-interest of an oil company. It gave work to a growing number of Saudi Arabs – up to a peak of nearly fifteen thousand in 1952 – and provided them all not only with wages which made them envied throughout the land, but with services worth more than the wages themselves: superb hospitals, loans to build themselves houses, water and power supplies, community facilities from mosques to launderettes, roads and public transport and, above all, training. Practically all the Saudis started work without any education at all, but the company proved to its own satisfaction that they equalled Americans in their inherent aptitude; and as their industrial training and company-sponsored education took effect, they were moved up into higher grades of work, displacing Americans and other foreigners, until by 1959 not only all the unskilled jobs but two-thirds of the semi-skilled and higher grades were filled by Saudis. Likewise, the company trained its American employees, before it sent them to the country, in elementary Arabic and in Arab manners, customs and beliefs and constantly preached to them that they were the Arabs' guests, and that friendly relations with Arabs were as important as any other responsibilities of their jobs.

Simply by being a good employer, Aramco hastened the process of change. If the Americans had behaved badly, as the strict Wahhabis had expected of infidels, Wahhabi beliefs and the whole ancient social system might possibly have been strengthened; the Americans might have been blamed for anything that went wrong. But the opposite happened. There were a few Americans, especially in the early days, who spoke of the Saudis as damn' niggers and tried to kick them around, but they were weeded out, and the great majority were patient, generous and friendly. Thousands of Arabs

211

and their families therefore returned to their tribes and villages after a spell of work with the company, and spoke well of the new breed of infidel and boasted of the luxuries they had enjoyed. Probably very few of them had lost their Moslem faith entirely, but they had certainly learned to neglect its observances, especially its prayers, and were quite out of sympathy with the extreme restrictions of Wahhabism. To these influences, neither ibn Saud nor the Ulema had any positive reply; commonly, a restrictive creed has nothing more to offer once its restrictions are rejected. There were futile attempts to forbid the Arabs to watch the American movie shows, or to play soccer – the latter on the ground that shorts were indecent – but this creation of new sins defeated its own purpose and only showed that Wahhabism was in retreat.

So ibn Saud was assailed in his old age by conflicts on three sides: the immorality, extravagance and stupidity of many of his sons, the shameless robbery of many of his officials, and the slow awakening of many of his humble people. By 1950, it could be seen that none of these conflicts would be resolved while he was still alive. He could not condone such lapses from his moral standards, or contend with them; he did no more than ineffectively deplore them, retreating more deeply into an old man's petulant isolation.

It was an intensely sad end for a warrior of religion. For several years before he died, his body failed him and he knew the physical exploits he had delighted in were over: the horsemanship, the camel journeys in the desert night, the charges into battle, the amorous adventures – all the old ecstasies were done. Old men expect such deprivations; but he was also denied the satisfaction old men deserve, of seeing his life's work finished and fulfilled. It was true he had finished it: he had created the stable, sternly moral kingdom he had dreamed of. But its fulfilment had been taken away from him. He had lived too long – long enough to see his moral standards scorned, his most profound beliefs denied, and his kingdom undermined by the most sordid of all lusts, the lust for money.

Nobody recollects that he ever expressed remorse, although it might have been said he had sold his own creation; he never seemed to regret that he told al Sulaiman, in 1933, to put his trust in God and sign the oil agreement. Perhaps nobody after a lifetime as a king could still be so self-critical; or perhaps, if the thought ever came to him, he reminded himself that nobody had foreseen what a vast amount of oil would be found, or persuaded himself anew that if he had not sold his mineral rights, some powerful nation would have come and stolen them. Perhaps he was able to argue, in his own mind, that money was not evil in itself, but only in the uses people made of it.

Everybody, on the other hand, who was close to him in the final years remembers him as a deeply unhappy man, and many of those who were closest confess he was bewildered. Peering out at his world from his mud-palace in Riyadh or his summer home in Taif, he saw wickedness and confusion, and could not think which way to turn to put a stop to them; and if he suspected nine-tenths of the wickedness was being deliberately hidden from him, he could not bring himself to insist on being told. Beyond his own world also, it seemed to him that honour was dying and God was being defied. The power of Britain on which he had so often leaned had faded, and the cold war showed an attitude of mind he could not grasp. Philby was still among the few of his followers who were perfectly faithful to him, and still the only westerner who regularly talked to him; and Philby recalled that he detested communism, not merely on the grounds one might expect from an autocrat and a leader of religion, but largely because he had been told and believed that communists habitually slept with their mothers and sisters – a mark of shame which characteristically impressed him. He thought the Americans stupid not to use the atom bomb on such people while they had it and the communists had not. That might be Armageddon, but sometimes he wished that Armageddon would come, to put an end to the trouble in the world.

A hush fell on his palaces long before his death. The throngs of visitors and courtiers and servants, which his personality had always animated, dwindled and lost their urgent air. An air of stealthy secrecy replaced it, because there were so many things that had to be hidded from him, and because he was tired and ill, and because nobody else could make decisions while he was still alive. It could be seen that an ultimate end was coming: not only the end of a life, and not only the end of a reign of fifty years, but the end of a form of human society which had changed so little and lasted so long that it had seemed unchangeable.

Cox had once said, years before when ibn Saud's triumphant rise was at its height, that he had never known him to make a mistake. In his old age, he was still the simple honest man that Cox had known, but the simple world in which his touch was sure had disappeared. He died of a heart attack in his sleep, at Taif on November 9th, 1953, and his body was taken at once to Riyadh and buried without ceremony, according to Wahhabi practice, in an unmarked grave. Few people now in Riyadh remember where it is, and nobody visits it.

SOURCES AND
ACKNOWLEDGMENTS

SOURCES AND ACKNOWLEDGEMENTS

This book has three sources: conversation, unpublished and published documents. Material from all three is closely mixed together in the text.

Conversation

Many people, Arab, American and British, have told me their personal recollections of ibn Saud, his country and his times, and given me expert interpretations of Arabian problems. I am very grateful to them all, and especially to those who have also read and criticised my manuscript. I shall not thank them all here by name, because I cannot hope they will all agree with every shade of opinion I have expressed. There are still political, moral and emotional divergencies of view about the history of Saudi Arabia, especially its recent history. Whenever I have been able to find a consensus of opinion, I have accepted it, but when I have not I have had to form a purely personal judgment. This is a process which cannot satisfy everyone. It does not entirely satisfy me. I am aware of writing as an outsider, a non-Moslem and a westerner, and of being to that extent one-sided; of course, a book on this subject written by an Arab for Arab readers would be quite different from mine. But even though each of my informants may disagree with some things I have written, I hope they will all accept my thanks and concede that I have tried to write with sympathy and without prejudice.

Unpublished Documents

I have made use of the archives of the British Foreign Office and India Office up to 1913, the last year available under the British Government's "fifty year rule," and I am grateful to the librarians of these offices for their patience in finding all the relevant papers for me. The Arabian Affairs Division of Aramco very kindly allowed me to see many documents of Arab and American origin in the Company's unique library at Dhahran.

Published Documents

There is a vast number of books and articles on every aspect of Arabia, and it would be a rash man who claimed to have read them all. I have found useful information in *Life, True, The Geographical Journal, The Economist, The Middle East Journal, The Muslim World, The Saudi Weekly Newsletter* and daily newspapers of London, New York and Cairo. I have also drawn in widely varying degrees on the following books, either for information on Arabia in general or on particular episodes.

George Antonius, *The Arab Awakening,* Hamish Hamilton, London, 1938

H. C. Armstrong, *Lord of Arabia,* Arthur Barker, London, 1934

Gertrude Bell, *Letters,* Bell, London, 1927

 The Arab War, Golden Cockerell Press, London

Sir Reader Bullard, *The Camels Must Go,* Faber, London, 1961

J. L. Burkhardt, *Travels in Arabia,* Colburn, London, 1829

Sir Richard Burton, *Pilgrimage to Al-Medinah and Meccah,* Longman, London, 1855

R. E. Cheesman, *In Unknown Arabia,* Macmillan, London, 1926

Sir Winston Churchill, *The Second World War* (vol. VI), Cassel, London, 1954

H. R. P. Dickson, *The Arab of the Desert,* Allen & Unwin, London, 1949

Kuwait and her Neighbours, Allen & Unwin, London, 1956

Charles M. Doughty, *Travels in Arabia Deserta,* C.U.P., 1888

William A. Eddy, *F.D.R. Meets ibn Saud,* Amer. Friends of the Middle East, 1954

Gerald de Gaury, *Arabia Phoenix,* Harrap, London, 1946

Arabian Journey, Harrap, London, 1950

Gibb and Kramer, *Shorter Encyclopaedia of Islam,* Luzac, London, 1953

H. A. R. Gibb, *Modern Trends in Islam,* Univ. of Chicago Press, 1947

Sir John Bagot Glubb, *Britain and the Arabs,* Hodder & Stoughton, London, 1959

War in the Desert, Hodder & Stoughton, London, 1960

Philip Graves, *Life of Sir Percy Cox,* Hutchinson, London, 1941

Paul W. Harrison, *The Arab at Home,* Crowell, N.Y., 1924

Philip K. Hitti, *The Near East in History,* Van Nostrand, Princeton N.J., 1961

D. G. Hogarth, *The Penetration of Arabia,* Lawrence & Bullen, London, 1904

T. E. Lawrence, *Seven Pillars of Wisdom,* Cape, London, 1935

Secret Dispatches, Golden Cockerell Press, London, 1940

Roy Lebkicher, George Rentz & Max Steineke, *Aramco Handbook,* Arabian American Oil Co., 1960

S. H. Longrigg, *Oil in the Middle East,* O.U.P., 1961

D. van der Meulen, *The Wells of ibn Saud,* Murray, London, 1957

R. C. Mowat, *Middle East Perspective,* Blandford, London, 1958

W. C. Palgrave, *Narrative of a Year's Journey through Central and Eastern Arabia,* Macmillan, London, 1865

H. St. John Philby, *The Heart of Arabia,* Constable, London, 1922

Arabia of the Wahhabis, Constable, London, 1928

Arabia, Benn, London, 1930

A Pilgrim in Arabia, Hale, London, 1946

Arabian Days, Hale, London, 1948

Arabian Jubilee, Hale, London, 1952

Forty Years in the Wilderness, Hale, London, 1957

Ameen Rihani, *Ibn Sa'oud of Arabia,* Constable, London, 1928

Around the Coasts of Arabia, Constable, London, 1928

Eldon Rutter, *The Holy Cities of Arabia,* Putnam, London, 1928

Richard H. Sanger, *The Arabian Peninsula,* Cornell U.P., N.Y., 1954

Sir Ronald Storrs, *Orientations,* Ivor Nicholson & Watson, London, 1939

Wilfred Thesiger, *Arabian Sands,* Longmans, London, 1959

Bertram Thomas, *Arabia Felix,* Cape, London, 1932

The Arabs, Thornton Butterworth, London, 1937

K. S. Twitchell, *Saudi Arabia,* Princeton U.P., 1958

Kenneth Williams, *Ibn Saud,* Cape, London, 1933

GERTRUDE BELL
H. V. F. Winstone

Gertrude Bell (1868–1926) – traveller, linguist, mountaineer, diplomat, historian and scholar – found the fullest expression of her exceptional talents in the Middle East. Her involvement in military intelligence during the First World War and her brilliance as custodian of the archaeological treasures of Babylon and Assyria made her the most famous contemporary English figure in Arabia.

'Mr Winstone, an excellent biographer . . . has written the definitive biography of The Lady'   Jan Morris *The Times*

'H. V. F. Winstone neither idealizes nor psychoanalyses her; he shows her fairly from all angles – she is both admirable and intriguing'   *Newsweek*

'Winstone really shines in his role as guide to the labyrinth of Middle Eastern politics . . . a maze in which almost every statesman who ventured into it got lost, and in which Gertrude Bell seemed unnervingly at home'

Jonathan Raban, *Sunday Times*

£3.95   illustrated

CAPTAIN SHAKESPEAR
H. V. F. Winstone

'He was one of those Englishmen Kipling delighted to
picture. Nothing daunted him; he lived for enterprise and
rejoiced in the handling of men; the more difficult and
dangerous the job, the better it pleased him. He bore an
English name not easy to add glory to, yet he succeeded'

The World, 23 February 1915

Captain William Henry Shakespear was one of the most
accomplished explorers that Britain produced in the heyday
of the British Empire, a fascinating figure who has suffered
undeserved obscurity for far too long and who died drama-
tically in battle against pro-Turkish forces during the First
World War.

'H. V. F. Winstone has found a rich vein to mine, and he
does it entertainingly and well'

Patrick Seale, *Observer*

£2.50   illustrated

FAR ARABIA
Peter Brent

The story of the founding of a legend, and the travellers in history, who, on their journeys through the deserts and domed cities of Islam have helped create it.

'For those looking for a history of the men who explored Arabia, and sometimes themselves, here is a rich diet indeed to feed the stuff of their dreams'

Margaret Forster, *Evening Standard*

£2.95   illustrated

THE DESTINY OF ISABELLE EBERHARDT
A Biography

Cecily Mackworth

'To be alone, to have no needs, to be unknown, a stranger and at home everywhere, and to march to the conquest of the world . . .' Isabelle Eberhardt's extraordinary life was based on this dream of freedom.

Born in 1877 and raised by a half-mad father, an ex-pope of the Russian Orthodox Church, Isabelle and her brother and sister were confined in an isolated villa on the outskirts of Geneva. Tragedy after tragedy marked her childhood until she escaped to Algeria and became a Muslim. Dressed as a man she lived the life of a nomad, her unconventional lifestyle giving rise to legends of sensational debauchery which are potent even today.

Her writings provide an unparalleled revelation of Muslim life which ranks among the best literature that has been inspired by Africa. She died at the age of twenty-seven in a flash flood in the Sahara.

£2.25

A SHORT HISTORY OF THE ARAB PEOPLES
John Bagot Glubb

'The rise of Christian Europe cannot be explained without some understanding of the accomplishments of Arab civilization, from which Western culture largely derived its knowledge and its early ways of thought. Thus some acquaintance with Arab history is necessary to the comprehension of our own beginnings'   John Bagot Glubb (Glubb Pasha)

John Bagot Glubb, author of many books about the Arab countries and people, including *The Story of the Arab Legion* and *War in the Desert*, traces their history from the seventh century to the mid-twentieth century in this interesting and invaluable volume.

£2.95

All our books and catalogues are available from our Trade Counter at 29 Goodge Street, London W1P 1FD. Tel: 01-636 3992.